RAYMOND CARVER
WILL NOT RAISE OUR CHILDREN

Writers Tribe Books

writers tribe books Copyright © 2012 by Dave Newman

All rights Reserved. No part of this book may be reproduced without written permission from the publisher.

This book is a work of fiction. Any resemblance to actual persons, living or dead, is entirely coincidental.

Book design by Amy Inouye
Cover art and cover design by Paulette Poullet

Published in the United States of America
ISBN 978-1-937746-03-2

Library of Congress PCN 2012934730

www.writerstribebooks.com

RAYMOND CARVER
WILL NOT RAISE OUR CHILDREN

DAVE NEWMAN

writers tribe books

Dedication

Jakiela!

The doctors of the law say this book shouldn't see the light:
the word *rainbow* can't be found anywhere in it,
much less the word *sorrow*
or *torquate*.
Sure there's a swarm of chairs and tables,
Coffins! Desk supplies!
All of which makes me burst with pride
because, as I see it, the sky is coming down in pieces.

—Nicanor Parra

PROLOGUE

One of my former students calls drunk at three in the morning to say he loves me and to offer me a gig. In between talk of books and writing, he weeps but not continually, and other times he laughs too loud. My former student, Bill, teaches Creative Writing at a bush league college in West Virginia and he says he can get me five hundred dollars to do a reading and talk about how novel writing is a sure ticket to the poor house and poets are mostly homosexual.

Bill is a homosexual and a poet and a novelist.

"Just kidding," he says. "Make it sound glamorous."

He taps the phone a couple times and says, "Is this thing on?"

I say, "How are you holding up?"

He says, "The students are stupid as stones, and there are a ton of inbreeds down here. I absolutely love it. You in?"

I say, "I'm in."

"Fucking A," he says. "I miss you."

"I miss you, too," I say, but I also need the money.

I assume he has the money or can get the money or at least someone in his department knows he is making me an offer but I also know Bill is an addict.

He smoked a lot of dope when he was my student and drank alcohol poorly and threw up on other students and once he cut a line of blow in my office and offered me some and I said, "You can't do that here, no matter how well you write," not because I was against cocaine but because I was against getting fired.

Someone else told me Bill is a crackhead and another person said, "No, it's meth."

Bill says, "Let's get this thing set up."

I say, "When do you need me?"

He says, "Seriously, don't condescend to these kids, man, because they're smart and they're tough. They'll kick your ass and mine when you leave."

Bill's addictions come through the phone in a series of slurs and runny-nose sounds and wet coughs. He drops the receiver and picks it up. I can hear him sweating.

He says, "Just don't read too long. These kids have no fucking attention span."

Bill's name is Li Xianoning but he calls himself Bill Xing and pronounces his last name Crossing. His parents were teachers who fled China during the Cultural Revolution. They crossed into Canada then into New York then into Pennsylvania where Bill was born. His grandparents are still in China, his grandfather locked up in some prison, doing time for writing a book about a mountain cat. Bill's parents don't talk to him because he's a drug addict and a homosexual. Sometimes his mother calls to say she won't be calling ever again.

I saw Bill four years ago. He stopped in my office the summer after he finished grad school. A book of poems had been accepted for publication and Bill was on a bender. He wore a clown hat and we did a shot of Jack Daniels from the bottle and he kissed me on the cheek and stumbled out into the city.

Since then, Bill has published a collection of short stories, another collection of poems, and a novel, the novel on a major press. Bill has tenure down in West Virginia.

When I think of that kind of success, so much more than my own, it's hard to consider Bill a fuck-up. Even if he is a fuck-up, I still need the money.

The next day, I tell my wife, "Bill got me a reading in West Virginia."

She says, "I'm just glad he's still alive."

I say, "Five hundred bucks."

She says, "Take that, electric bill," and karate-chops the air.

We need the money. We always need the money.

A week later, I kiss my wife and children.

I drive to East Pittsburgh, where Bobby Pajich lives.

Bobby Pajich is a professional gambler and a poet. He plays poker four nights a week in the backrooms of dive bars all around the city, winning money from casual gamblers and old men who like to lose and twenty-something hipsters who still get an allowance from their parents. Bobby's house is red brick, two stories, old but well-kept except for the back gutter which needs to be repaired and the beer cooler on the side porch, the beer inside growing hot all summer then freezing and exploding in winter. The neighbor's house is the same. The neighbor's neighbor's house is the same.

Bobby's house sits on a hill as steep as a ski slope. Once, during a bad winter, I saw two teenage boys trying to drag a quarter barrel of beer into a duplex where the parents were out of town. The roads were icy. The boys set the keg down to rest their hands and the keg slid like a hockey puck down the hill for a quarter mile, gaining speed, steering straight until it reached the bottom and crossed Route 30 and smashed into the front wheels of a city bus, knocking the bus into the fancy bakery that overpriced their breads and went out of business. No one was hurt. It made the national news.

Pittsburgh is seldom on the national news. It should be. For our teenagers and our kegs and our beautiful hills that you can skate on in winter. For the maple trees that line the streets and drop whirly-bird seeds then turn a brilliant red in fall. It rains here all the time, but there's always enough sun, sun to dive in the river, sun to fish on the shore, unless it's early December and then it's dark before dinner and everyone stays inside and drinks. Not far from here, Bobby's dad owns a dive bar, a blue-tiled dump with the family name on the sign and a drink special that never ends. The old man always shakes my hand and never remembers my name and floats me my first couple drinks and makes me take my tip off the bar at the end of the night.

Pittsburgh is a postcard that the rest of the country never sees because no one here has time to send it, because in Pittsburgh we work all the time. The teachers wait tables. The bartenders teach school. The nurses nurse and go home and raise families, and the rock 'n' rollers pack up their guitars and sell real estate until the next weekend when they come back and sing songs to salesmen and house painters and stay-at-home moms who want to get smashed and fall into the music for one night of relief. Firemen grind meat in the basements of burger joints. Taxi drivers sell hotdogs at stadiums. In Pittsburgh, our most famous poet is a retired cop, because here it is required that you must do to be.

Now I say to Bobby, "Why don't you write about your dad?"

Now Bobby says, "I plan to. How'd you get a reading in West Virginia, anyway?"

"An old student," I say

"An old student, christ," he says.

We climb into his Jeep and he turns the key and we drift down the hill until the engine catches with a chug and a lurch. The Jeep doesn't have reverse. The windshield is cracked.

Bobby says, "You ever think about leaving Pittsburgh?"

"All the time," I say, but I'm lying. I've lived my whole life within fifty miles of this city and never want to leave. Once, for a day, I moved to Horsehead, New York. I had a job there, managing a furniture store. I found an apartment and signed a lease in the morning. I ate a sandwich in the afternoon. Then I walked the streets and listened to the people, fine people, nice people, but no one sounded like Pittsburgh or moved like Pittsburgh, and they all dressed like people buying from the same catalog, sweaters and comfortable pants, and all the bars and stores were chains, and the buildings all appeared new and made of pink brick that looked like it would crumble if touched. The rest of the day I spent begging the landlord to let me out of the lease. It took hours. "Unbelievable," he said and kept my security deposit, but that night I was back in Pennsylvania, in my favorite bar, drinking with Bobby. The bartender said, "People in Pittsburgh are like homing pigeons. We leave and fly right back." Then he looked at me and said, "But a day? Are you fucking serious?" and laughed.

Now Bobby says, "If I could do anything, I'd smoke dope for a living and get a big house on the South Side Slopes and sit on the porch and that's it. Nothing else. I'd smoke dope for a living and look down on this city and maybe sometimes walk down the hill and swim in one of the green rivers. Then I'd pay someone to carry me up the hill."

We get on Route 376 and head east. You can see the TV tower for WTAE before it disappears behind the side of a mountain. All the mountains are the size of huge hills here in Pittsburgh, or the hills are the size of small mountains.

Bobby says, "What are you going to read? Novel? Poems?"

"I don't know," I say. "I'm doing it for the money."

"Will they have booze?"

"I hope so."

"You going to get laid?" he says.

"I'm married," I say, which means I don't talk about getting laid with other women in front of anyone, even my best friends.

Bobby says, "You have a good wife."

I say, "I have a great wife."

We head into the Squirrel Hill tunnel at a crawl, the morning traffic backing everything up. The lights inside are bright then dimmer. Some guy in a Beamer changes lanes illegally.

Bobby says, "I'm going to Vegas."

"For what?" I say.

"For what?" he says, laughing, incredulous. "To gamble! I need to make some money. I gambled six nights in a row last week and I barely made a grand."

"That's great money."

"That's not great money."

"It's way more than I make teaching."

"How much are you getting for this reading?" he says, digging for a cigarette in the front pocket of his flannel shirt.

"Five hundred bucks," I say.

"Literature is pathetic," he says.

In ten minutes, we're downtown at the bus station. The bus station is by the train station. I step outside. Bobby steps outside. I don't have any luggage. Bobby's shirt comes up so I can see his gut, a round growler of beer. From the bus station, you can walk a block and get a drink in half a dozen different bars. Walk another block and an old Polish woman will sweep you off her porch and an Italian store will pull you in with its sounds and the smell of tomato and meat then charge you six dollars for a hoagie the size of my arm.

Bobby says, "I'm going to miss Pittsburgh while I'm in Vegas."

"I'll take care of it for you," I say and hug Bobby, but I barely look at Pittsburgh anymore, such is my life with teaching and writing and kids and a wife who teaches and writes and all the other things we do to make money and still come up short. I pat Bobby on the back and say, "Thanks for the ride, you fucker."

"Not a problem, you jagoff," he says and climbs back in his Jeep and heads up Liberty Avenue towards the old Iron City plant where they used to make beer but don't anymore.

Inside the bus station, a man behind glass, smoking a pipe in front of a No Smoking sign, takes my ticket and says, "This fucking world," but at the TV across the room and not me.

I get on the bus and go to sleep and wake up in West Virginia. The bus station is more like a rest area. They sell homemade blankets and paintings from local artists. It's very folksy.

I look for Bill, the poet and novelist and story writer, but Bill is not here. Bill may never be here. I have a credit card but I do not know if it will fit another bus ticket before it falls over the limit. I buy an iced tea and a bag of pretzels. I wish someone back home would give me five hundred dollars to read from something I wrote.

I sit down near the front doors and wait. It's ten minutes. It's an hour. No one looks like Bill. Everyone wears sweatshirts and ballcaps, even the women, and none of them are Asian.

I eat the pretzels. I drink the iced tea.

A woman who dresses like a secretary comes through the front door and scans the place. She's maybe fifty, pretty, lots of curly black hair. She wears heels and a black skirt and a gray blouse. She stops by my table.

She says, "Dan?"

I say, "You're not Bill."

"No, but at least you're Dan."

She shakes my hand. Her hand is very sweaty.

I say, "Should we go?"

"I need a minute," she says and pulls the chair from underneath the table so the metal legs sound like a tiny train collapsing on tiny rails.

I say, "Bill—I'm assuming—is smashed?"

"More or less," she says. "He sort of turns everything into a party."

"That's Bill."

"He says you like a good time."

"I try," I say.

"The university loves him down here."

"Are you one of his students?"

"Really," she says. "You're too sweet. I teach Composition. Occasionally they let me teach a fiction workshop. I loved your book by the way. It was really dirty but really sweet, too."

"Thanks," I say. "Is there really a reading or am I just here for a party?"

"You'd have to talk to Bill about that. Why aren't you on a big publisher?" she says.

"Big publishers didn't like my book," I say.

"Silly big publishers," she says. "Their loss."

"You don't by chance have my money, do you?"

"Yes and no," she says. She pushes her hair back but it immediately falls forward. Her blouse is low-cut and I see her tanline, fading but still there, the white skin leading to a dark nipple. She says, "Were you supposed to get five hundred? Well, Bill cashed the check. I don't know how but he did. I think he spent two hundred, maybe a little less." She reaches into her purse. "Here's the rest. Sorry I couldn't stop him sooner." She hands me a pile of crumpled bills and goes back in her purse. "Here's your ticket home. Why the hell did he send you on a bus?"

I take the money. I take the ticket. It's been a long time since I've been away from work and my wife and my kids. Her purse holds a bottle I bet, maybe better things.

"Well," I say. "We might as well get fucked up."

"I'm about half way there," she says and laughs. "Carla," she says and we shake again.

Out in the parking lot, she talks some more about my book, saying nice things. I get the feeling she doesn't have the time to read a lot and Bill gave her my book and, as someone who loves books but doesn't have time for them, she wants to talk literature.

She says, "Do you like Henry Miller?"

"Sometimes," I say. "When he's not being cryptic."

"I like when he's being sexy."

"Me, too."

"Do you like sexy writers?" she says, looking away then back.

She's drunker than I thought, drunker than she admitted, as drunk as I wish I were.

"I like all the sexy writers," I say. "I'm working on a novel called *Sit On My Face*."

"Really?" she says and laughs.

"No," I say. "I'm just fucking with you."

"Bill said you were funny."

"I try."

She has beer in her trunk, bottles and ice packed in a blue Igloo cooler. The parking lot is empty. Pines trees stand on mountains and the mountains block out the sun but the sky is still bright. We keep the trunk open. I drink fast to catch up. The labels on the bottles slide off without being peeled.

She says, "What's it like being a writer?"

I say, "I don't know," because hardly anyone reads my

book. I chug half a bottle. I open another and say, "What about you? Do you write?"

"No," she says. "Essays, critical stuff, nothing real."

"Essays sound real."

"Can I kiss you? Bill said I could probably kiss you."

"You're fucking weird," I say, but funny, then I let her kiss me.

My rules about cheating are flexible, and they mostly revolve around not hurting my family. I try to have more rules than opportunities.

Carla and I drink some more and talk about Henry Miller and teaching. I lean against her car and she leans against me. I ask about West Virginia. It's a good state that lets you drink in the parking lot without arresting you for public intoxication.

I say, "You should unbutton your blouse another button. If you're going to wear a black bra, you should let people accidentally see it."

She unbuttons her blouse and adjusts her tits.

She says, "Look, I'm married. I have three kids who I love. I probably love my husband if I look hard enough. I get out once or twice a year—not a month, a year. My husband works construction. He drives the thing that makes the roads for the miners to go up the mountains. It pays great. He's gone for weeks at a time. I work and do everything with the kids." She stops and finishes her beer. She lets it fly across the parking lot so it lands in the grass near a garbage can. She says, "I'm not a whore and I don't care if you ever want to see me again but I really like your book and Bill says you're a great guy."

"Okay," I say. "Did Bill or you or the university that loves Bill get me a motel room?"

"Motel 6," she says. "It's a dump."

We kiss a little more in the parking lot. I feel her tits and they feel exactly like tits which is good but less than I was hoping for. When I'm home and being faithful, which is mostly what I do and love to do, I start to imagine miracle tits and miracle asses and miracle pussies, not whole women, just tits and asses and pussies, tits and asses so big and soft and pussies so wet and available they could never exist, and I know the miracle tits and asses and pussies are not real, but when I close my eyes on days I am overwhelmed, when I am teaching or making dinner or doing laundry or cutting grass or paying the electric bill, when I am stuck on everything else that is required to survive, I see miracles and start thinking about getting laid.

Now I want to get laid with Carla, even though I am close enough to Carla to see she is not a miracle. She is as common as the rest of us, as common as I always am, though it sounds like she has her own miracles to chase and, because she doesn't know me, I must appear holy.

I drive Carla's car to the Motel 6 and she checks me in.

I'm buzzed.

I'm horny.

My former student Bill is somewhere, smashed, overdosing, snot all over his face, blood foaming from his mouth, a man he barely knows punching his chest to start his heart. I won't hear from Bill for months. Then he'll tell me it was a suicide attempt, that he wanted me to be there for him when he finally did it. Bill will be in AA by then and NA and all the other groups that say you can't do anything fun or you will die.

In the room, Carla takes off my clothes.

I take off her clothes back.

She says, "Can we turn the lights down?"

She turns the lights down.

She says, "I'm sorry about my body. It's the three kids."

"You look great," I say, but it's dark and her body is like my body, barely there.

We're two people doing our best to not be who we are so we can go home and be our better selves. I turn the TV on for a little light. Carla has a lot of pubic hair.

She blows me and climbs on me before I can do anything back. It's a herky-jerky fuck, like high school, like she's trying too hard, like she wants me to be impressed, like she wants to impress herself, that she can still do it, bounce on a cock, show a man she can be a woman. But it's still fun. She kisses my ear and I like it.

I like it until we're done.

Then I like the beer and the TV with the volume up. She has cocaine waiting in her purse and I like that. I like the students I never have to see, the reading that never happens. I like the bus ride home, the three hundred dollars in my wallet. With my eyes closed, I imagine my beautiful wife and my two children and the happy noises they make inside our house.

I always think the miracle is leaving, but the miracle is coming home.

I

It's almost eight o'clock in the morning and I'm hiding in my office here at the university in Pittsburgh because I don't want to teach my class. Composition is bad but poetry is worse. All these fucking kids want to do is rhyme and write about their souls. Soul, old, black as mold. It's one big dreary pop song about how their parents make them want to commit suicide.

Last semester, I said, "You're all young, good-looking people. Doesn't anyone want to write about love? About getting laid?" They sat there. They shook their heads: no thanks.

Then they wrote a letter of complaint to the dean who passed it on to the head of the English Department who passed it on to the head of the Writing Department who pulled me aside after a meeting and said, "Real fucking nice," though he's an old alcoholic from eastern Kentucky with a thing for young girls and once, thirty-some years ago, he taught an entire workshop half-naked and drunk on moonshine while waving a pistol to emphasize the importance of geography and local color in fiction writing.

When there were complaints about the pistol, the dean said, "It was my understanding that the gun was unloaded," and the president said, "I don't agree with the pistol per se, but it is an interesting technique when you think of it in context," and people around the English Department in 1976 said, "It's just his personality," and no one mentioned the moonshine or the nakedness and everyone went back to teaching their own classes and the students studied with whoever else was teaching the next-level writing course without a pistol and moonshine and they probably missed the gun and the booze and their half-naked professor and were bored.

Thirty-some years later, and Kentucky Jim is still here, not writing, barely teaching, friendly and happy, drunk but clothed and not armed. The rest of the writers from 1976 and their tenure and their good paychecks have gone and those of us of who have replaced them don't bring guns to class or drink moonshine on campus or anything. We teach and hope to be invited back the following year to teach again. Every January I start thinking about my contract and the other people in the department and their contracts and if there are enough contracts to go around.

The amount of time I spend worrying about my job is significantly greater than the amount of time I spend doing my job.

When I step out of my office, I shake hands with a kid from last semester whose name I can't remember. He smiles but not much, his black-rimmed glasses very serious on his very serious artistic nose. I think I gave him a letter grade he didn't appreciate. I think I may have graded him on his glasses and artistic nose.

Now I pass the stairwell and see my officemate, James. He looks happy but very red and ruddy. He has on his own artistic glasses and a blazer, and I wonder if there's a meeting I've forgotten about. He's almost at the top of the stairs but I'm too late for questions. When I wave, he raises some sort of coffee mug and, simultaneously, falls backwards and takes the whole flight of stairs, something like twenty-two or twenty-three steps, straight down on his back.

I assume he is paralyzed or maybe dead, and this is not just my officemate but my best friend in the world, but he raises his head and his coffee and says, "I'm fine, no problem, catch me after class," and smiles through what must be excruciating pain.

I have six guys in my poetry writing class. There are thirteen girls. The girls speak. The guys do not. One of the guys wears an army jacket and has greasy hair and eyes as intense as pistols. He looks at me until I look back then he looks away.

Two of the girls, the best writers so far this semester, the ones who do not write rhyming poems, were smoking dope out behind the building right before class. I said, "Hello, ladies." One smiled. The other coughed. Dope smoke exploded from her nose. I said, "That's very literary," and they both laughed. It's okay if they get stoned as long as they come to class, as long as they read and write and know how to turn off the world and open a book.

The guy in the army jacket is named Samuel.

Three weeks into the semester, I called him Sam.

He mumbled something.

I said, "Sorry?"

He mumbled again, like he was eating his own face.

I said, "I'm sorry, Sam. I'm deaf."

He shook his head and looked down. Sam is never happy. He does not come to conferences and he does not do well on his quizzes. He does not do the assigned readings and his answer on the last essay quiz was, "I don't do readings."

I would like Sam to be happy. I would like him to do well. My class is not required and it is not biology and no one talks politics. I am not a nut-buster. We read books and the students make poems and maybe dream about making poems well enough to have a book of their own. If I sometimes grade on appearances, it's only the frat guys who pretend to be deep.

The girl next to him said, "He wants to be called Samuel."

I said, "Sure. Samuel." I said, "I'm sorry. I missed that."

Samuel put his face on his desk and covered the back of his head with his arms, the sleeves from his green coat like a tiny tent.

Today, we read Samuel's poems. The first line in his first poem says, "In my darkest darkness, I know that I will explode like the fires from Heaven and, oh yes, someday, even get even." It gets worse. Another line in another poem goes, "The aloneness of being alone drives the loneliness deeper into my soul."

It's almost six weeks into the semester, and I can't afford a bullet-proof vest. I can't afford anything. The students all think I'm in charge of their lives, but I make less money than a shoe store manager at the mall and with no job security. This year I have a job. Next year I may not. The students know they're customers and they know they're getting ripped off. They know learning to write poetry won't make them any money in the corporate world.

I hope Samuel doesn't kill me this semester.

I hope he finds a way out of all the darkness he's putting on the page.

Maybe it's nothing, the last dust of his teenage years, heavy metal and weed.

But I like it better when the girls show up at the end of the semester and lift their tops and inquire about grades. I've yet to be shot by a boob.

The next poet has written a series of poems relating to outer space. He calls the series: "My Nebula Masterpiece." It lacks concrete images. The most coherent line is, "The planets swirl like the human foot hopped up on meth, 360 degrees."

I say, "But the human foot really can't swirl 360 degrees, even if it's on speed."

The poet looks down. She has on a beret.

I say, "But I really like the idea of a foot being hopped up on meth."

The poet in the beret smiles.

We read on.

The cosmos does some weird, very implausible things.

I ask what she's been reading to inspire such work.

She says, "I watch a lot of B movies."

I say, "But in B movies we can tell who's who."

She says, "That was not my intention."

I say, "Oh," but I don't ask what her intention is.

I can't tell the difference between the planets and the astronauts; the aliens may or may not exist. There are more poems. I tell her to keep reading. Her classmates don't comment but I can see they think this is a masterpiece. I suggest a more coherent narrative and we move on.

The final poet has crammed his words together so they look like images, like Rorschach inkblots. They can't be read. The words have disappeared.

I say, "Maybe this is for painting class."

The kid, in black-rimmed glasses and a rock 'n' roll t-shirt like all the artistic kids with rich parents, says, "But they're made of words."

I say, "I can't see the words."

He says, "That's the point."

When I open the door and step inside the office, James says, "Surprise," and waves a bottle of Absolut Vodka in the air like he's just defused a bomb.

I say, "Really?"

He says, "Why not."

I say, "That was a rough fall. How's your head?"

He says, "What head?"

He opens the desk drawer and drops the bottle in like he's filing a bad grade. I close the door. It's nine in the morning, barely. James, another one of us who teaches here without tenure and makes about thirty grand, looks like his face has morphed into a damaged balloon. The cheeks are puffed. The eyes are sunken. I can't see the back of his head, the results of his crash, but he's hammered, possibly starting the second day of a bender. He's laughing then he's not. He hasn't had a drink in eleven years and now he's weeping at his desk, a vodka and Gatorade in one hand, a red pen in the other.

If I know anything about alcoholism, it's that you can't talk to an alcoholic about drinking when he's drunk.

I say, "Really, are the papers that bad?"

"I'm not even correcting the papers," he says. "I just write stuff in the margins."

"Why the weeping?"

"Because I'm drunk."

"Well," I say. "Stop drinking and you'll probably feel better."

"Doubt it," he says and wipes his eyes. "Why do we only have two desks in here when there are three of us sharing an office?"

The two desks are old and gray, metal and pressed wood, the tops coffee stained, the sides dented. The black phone in the corner is hard plastic and the ringer is down to one pingy bell. The only computer in the room is ancient and moves across the internet like a train pulling a mountain. There are no pictures on the walls. The walls need to be painted. We don't put up pictures because we are afraid to put the pictures up then have to take the pictures down then put the pictures up in another office at another college or have nowhere to hang our pictures when no one wants to hire us to teach.

"I don't think they could fit a third desk in here," I say.

"Where's Richard anyway?" James says.

Richard is our third officemate. Last year he was full-time. This year he is part-time. Last year he made thirty grand. This year he will make nine. The job is the same. The course load is the same. The pay is not. The benefits are not. Everyone is afraid to become Richard.

"He's not in today," I say. "You technically aren't either."

"They're firing Richard," he says.

"I know."

"They'll fire us, too."

I say, "I don't think they call it firing."

"What do they call it?"

"Nothing," I say, and it's true, they don't call it anything. They just don't hire us back at the end of the year, and they don't explain why, and the secretaries ask for your key.

He says, "They hired Richard back."

"But part-time," I say.

"How do they do that?"

"They can do whatever they want."

"How can they hike tuition every single year but never give us a raise?"

"They can do whatever they want," I say.

"So can we," James says. "Watch this."

He takes out the vodka and pours an extra spike in his

Gatorade. He uncaps his red pen. He checks his watch. He slugs a drink.

He says, "There are nineteen papers in front of me."

I say, "The university would say that is at least ten hours of work."

"Possibly twenty."

"Possibly thirty," I say.

"But would they pay me for even ten hours of work?"

"They would not," I say. Then I look at my own watch and say, "Ready, go."

James brings down his pen like a lightening bolt, marking every other page with a flash of red ink. Eight seconds for the first paper. Five for the second. What he's writing is not legible, but it appears to be positive. In under three minutes, he's completed the stack. The pen is capped. He raises his cocktail and drinks.

"That's impressive," I say.

"Yes," he says. "Fuck them."

James is in the bathroom, cleaning up, wiping his sweaty face on a brown paper towel. No one says I have to teach. As long as I teach enough to confuse the students, to keep them from complaining, I am perfection in khakis and scuffed-up loafers. I haven't cancelled a class in six years. Now I am going to, again and again.

My ten o'clock is something ugly. It's an intro course, fiction writing. The students are mostly video game addicts and one girl who talks endlessly about Joan Baez and folk rock. On the first day, when I passed out the syllabus and introduced myself and generally tried to be inspiring, no one was inspired.

No one laughed at my jokes. I mentioned Hemingway and one girl said, "Ugh," then spelled it, "U-G-H." We read the syllabus quietly. I took roll.

Someone said, "Do you really take attendance?"

I said, "Yes."

Someone else said, "This is like high school."

I said, "It's not."

We went around the room. Everyone had to state their major and name their favorite book or books. Six of the twenty-two students had majors. No one had a favorite book.

James comes back from the bathroom, cleaned up, shining.

He says, "Here's the plan."

M y class is on the third floor of the Cathedral, an enormous building, a skyscraper, a sort of giant academic hard-on pointing at the sky. It's ninety-one degrees on the third floor. It gets hotter as you go up. This is winter. I'm always covered in sweat.

I step into the classroom. Half the kids are there. I write something on the board about their next assignment. As I face the board, I count to ten. Ten seconds is the perfect length for a college writing course when the students hate to read.

James knocks on the door. A kid in the back of the room lets him in.

James says, "I'm sorry to interrupt." He looks at the class. He looks at me. Everyone can see the problem. The red necktie he added in the restroom makes it official. Administrative. He says, "They just called a department meeting." He's sincere as a drama student at a better college. He says, "I know. Don't blame me."

I say, "Now?"

"Now."

"I'm teaching."

James says, "So was I." He says, "It's mandatory."

I shake my head and look at the students, the ones who smile and the ones who try not to smile. I point to the blackboard.

"There's your assignment," I say. "I apologize for this."

Minutes later, James and I are outside in the snow, heading for a bar.

"Thanks for coming so soon," I say.

"No problem," he says. "I didn't want you to unpack your bag."

James says, "I wrecked my car."

"You're kidding?" I say.

Wrecking your car is the worst thing you can do when you teach college. Cars come with insurance and insurance comes with a deductible. Nobody I know, especially James, has money for a deductible. He barely has money for his first vodkas in more than a decade.

"Not kidding," he says.

"How bad?"

He says, "I don't know. Bad." He says, "Drive-me-to-vodka bad."

"A thousand bucks?"

"More, I think."

"Side or front?"

"Side, front, hood," he says. "I'm fucked."

James teaches another class, a travel writing class at another

college, a fairly prestigious private school. James makes 1500
dollars to teach this class. The class is six hours long for nine
Saturdays during the semester. He teaches six books. It takes
at least twenty hours to read a short book and write a lecture.
There are nine students in the class, and those nine students
turn in three papers each, ten or more pages per paper. That's
around three hundred pages. To read and comment on three
hundred pages of student writing takes fucking forever. To
teach this Saturday travel writing class, James makes, approxi-
mately, when you break it down, seven dollars an hour. We've
figured this out before. Sober.

I say, "What about the college? Maybe they have special
insurance for people who teach travel writing?"

He says, "No." He says, "Bartender."

The bartender brings another round.

It's 10:35 in the morning, and I have another class to
consider.

Third class same as the second. We're back at the bar. It's
good to be Friday. My wife calls. My cell phone is not paid
up but it still rings.

She says, "Townes needs shoes."

"I know," I say.

"You told me to call before I buy anything."

"I forgot I said that."

"He has basketball tonight."

I say, "His shoes won't last another day?"

"He feels bad," she says.

It's true. He feels bad. He's nine and he notices things. Everyone's been to Disneyland. Everyone has a new car. "Dude,"

he said, "get that fixed," speaking about the crumbling asphalt at the edge of our driveway. Now it's shoes.

"I'll get the shoes," I say.

"Really?" my wife says. "You don't have to. Just tell me how much."

My wife is no good with money. I'm worse. When one of us wants to buy something, we call the other person. The answer is always, "No." Then we buy whatever we want because it's usually something we need, usually something for one of our kids. Now I'm drinking bottled beer in a bar and skipping classes and worried about getting fired.

"I'll get the shoes," I say. "Not a problem."

I hang up the phone and order another round.

James says, "You having kids makes me want to kill myself."

"They're nice kids," I say.

"But all that stuff."

"When was the last time you stole anything?"

"Five minutes from now," he says.

"Good," I say. "Let's go cancel my last class."

James goes into my last class by himself. I wait in our office. He apologizes to the students and explains that I'm hung up in a meeting.

"Is he getting fired or something?" one girl asks.

"No," James says. "They're discussing the possibility of allowing certain exceptional students—ones who don't play video games—to skip over their Composition requirement."

"I don't play video games," the girl says.

"So, no class today?" a guy says.

"No class today," James says.

"Fucking awesome," someone else says and everyone laughs.

I f we're going to steal basketball shoes for my son, we need to be drunker. I wish James, with his wrecked car and eleven years of sobriety, was not drunk, but since he is drunk, I am happy to have someone to drink and steal with.

James says, "If I could make ten more thousand dollars a year, I'd be set."

"Then you could lend me money for my kid's shoes," I say.

"You know why I didn't come to your kid's last birthday party?"

"Because you hate small children?"

"Seriously," he says. "Don't pick on me. I'm drunk and sad enough."

"Because you didn't have money to buy him a present."

"Because I didn't have money to buy him a present, exactly."

"I told you not to bring a present."

He says, "Seriously." He says, "I'm not walking into a kid's ninth birthday party without a gift. Kids notice that shit. I want your kid to like me."

"He likes you."

"Kids like anyone," he says.

"Not poor people," I say.

"I don't think of us as being poor."

"No," I say. "We're sort of lower middle class."

"Lowest middle class."

"Yes," I say. "Lowest."

James says, "I'm going to have to get a roommate."

"You're forty years old," I say. "They're called wives."

James used to have a girlfriend, Heather. Heather was nice. She was chubby. She was chubby and she was always trying not to be chubby so she was constantly going to the gym or working out or parking a mile away from wherever she was supposed to be so she could walk and burn the extra calories. "Americans are the fattest people on the planet," she'd say. She didn't care about Americans. She wanted to lose her ass. Heather did not eat carbs. Then Heather did not eat meat. Then she ate yogurt. James was supposed to eat yogurt. "I'm not eating yogurt," he said. I suppose there were other things involved in their break-up, but on the surface, it was yogurt and Heather's ass. After she caught James eating a box of Mike and Ike, she moved out. She moved back in with her parents. James said, "Fuck yogurt." Heather gained thirty pounds. No one, especially James, considered the rent or the gas bill in winter.

James says, "Are you ever going to bartend again?"

I say, "I don't know."

We're standing on the corner of 5th and Atwood. I could go for a burrito. Mad Mex has a great chicken burrito and excellent black bean soup.

James says, "I should bartend."

I say, "You're an alcoholic."

He says, "But right now I'm drunk."

"Drunk is temporary," I say. "Tomorrow, you'll be sober and you won't want to be around drunks. Trust me. I'm a drunk and I can barely stand being around drunks."

"Mexican food always smells so good," James says. "It always makes me think of Ocean City, Maryland."

"Mexican food always makes me think of Mexican food," I say.

But I can't afford a burrito. I can't afford bottled beer in bars. I'm not supposed to be in bars, period, because I, we, my young family, am, are, is saving money. By saving money I mean not paying for this year's vacation to a crappy motel in Ocean City, Maryland with my Visa card so my kids can say, "Wouldn't it be cooler if this was Disneyland?"

We should have money. My wife teaches, too. Her job is better than mine. Why don't we have money? Nights, my wife waits tables. I used to bartend, but my tips were worse than her tips, and the coming and going was impossible with our small children.

My son is nine. My daughter is five.

Neither one is old enough to work.

It's winter, so I can fit two bottles of beer in the front pockets of my navy peacoat. Then, when I'm inside of Target and finished with the beers and drunk, I can ditch the bottles and make space for a new pair of basketball shoes, size 7.

James says, "The beer bottles will draw attention to us."

I say, "We'll be discreet."

We park in the side lot, by the buggy corral. James wants to smoke a joint. Even though he doesn't drink—except for now—he never stopped smoking pot.

Last summer, I read the new Ray Carver biography. Ray Carver was an alcoholic short story writer and poet who quit drinking but still smoked a lot of dope. James lights the joint. James is an alcoholic. He hits the end. I am not an alcoholic. I hit the end. When I'm stuck on the dives of my life and the wrong choices I've made, I often think of Carver and how he got famous, then sober, then abandoned his first family and found a new lover and how he married his new lover then signed over his entire literary estate to her, his new second wife, rumored witch and a lousy poet. I take another hit and hand the joint back to James. I open another beer. James blows on the end of the joint. He eats the smoke like a fish going for food.

It's important to think and act like this when you are going to steal something that you cannot afford. When James and I die, we will have nothing to leave anyone.

Ray Carver's kids got a couple grand. His first wife, who Carver almost killed when he beat her with a wine bottle and the jagged edge sliced her throat, got less.

So Ray Carver is dead and famous, and I am drunk and stoned, and James is drunk and stoned, and Ray Carver's kids have nothing, and I want my kids to have something, and Ray Carver's second wife, the lousy poet, gets to live off his royalties. I don't want a second wife. I want my first wife, my only wife, to have time and money and love. Carver's first wife, the one he almost killed, is out in the Northwest, collecting food stamps and delivering pizzas.

I can smell hot pretzels and popcorn. The light in Target is soothing. Target wants us to shop, and they trust us not to steal. At Walmart, they would expect us to steal and try to stop us with bright lights and undercover shoppers. Walmart hates me. But I hate Walmart so much, I would never steal from their shoe department.

It's almost dinner time, and James is hungry.

He says, "Do they have nacho dogs?"

"They have good popcorn," I say.

We stand in line at the concession stand.

I order a pretzel then say, "Never mind."

The woman at the counter is four feet, eleven inches. She has gray hair and purple teeth from drinking a blueberry Icee. She says, "Honey, you stink like booze."

I say, "In a good way or a bad way?"

She says, "Please."

James thinks we should abandon our plan to steal the basketball shoes, but I've already finished both my beers and stuffed the bottles inside an empty Dora the Explorer shoebox. The shoes stuffed inside my jacket are Chuck Taylor hightops, blue with a funky star. They don't offer much support, but they look cool. At nine, the support you need is not around your ankles.

My son's name is Townes. I named him for Townes Van Zandt, the brilliant songwriter, the country outlaw, the folk singer who liked to hammer dope and codeine. I was thirty years old when I named my son. I believed greatness transcended tragedy, or that tragedy was its own form of greatness. I don't believe that anymore.

Because I'm drunk and scared and sad and already burdened with shoes sticking out from my side like a tumor, I head to the toy section. All I can fit down my pants is a small box of Legos from the *Star Wars* collection. My son loves *Star Wars*, especially the force, the way our minds can move objects and control other minds.

I stick a couple tiny stuffed animals down the back of James' pants. My daughter hasn't started to ask for things yet, which makes me want to give her more things than she needs.

"That's probably not enough," I say and stuff two books down the front of James' jacket and zip him up and adjust the lumps. I say, "There."

He says, "This is definitely a bad idea."

"Of course it's a bad idea," I say, then we walk to the front of the store and out the automatic glass doors like men possessed by magic, by science fiction, by the force. Our minds control their minds. They will let us pass.

The bar is called Hemingway's. I didn't tell you that before because I was embarrassed. When I think of Hemingway, the writer, and I think of bars, I do not think of Hemingway's Bar on 5th Avenue in Pittsburgh. Hemingway's Bar is near the dormitories. At night, it gets packed with under-aged undergraduates who like to drink dollar drafts from plastic cups and dance to obnoxiously loud hiphop. Once, I saw a girl in yellow skirt and a blue sweater, her hair sprayed into some style I don't have a name for, squatting in the corner to piss because the lines to bathroom were too long. Another time, a young guy stuck his finger down his throat, gagged, then puked on his friend as a joke. In the backroom, a local women's group, The Mad Hatters, sponsors an open mic poetry reading. The reading, their brochure says, will satisfy your soul.

"What would Hemingway think of this place?" James says.

"Bad," I say.

"Worse than that," James says. "The drink special is a Sex on the Beach."

"That's not a Mojito," I say.

James says, "Look at all these tits."

I look. There are a lot of tits. I don't know if the bars Hemingway drank in were filled with tits or if those tits were on display like the tits are now.

James says, "Do you think Hemingway was an alcoholic?"

"No."

"Why am I an alcoholic?"

"Because god made you that way."

"You don't believe in god."

"I believe in Hemingway," I say.

"Hemingway believed in Hemingway," James says. "That was the problem at the end."

"Maybe," I say.

I get sad when I talk about Hemingway, the opposite of how I feel when I read his books. It doesn't matter that everywhere he drank became a tourist spot. The only reason Hemingway matters as a drinker is because he was such a great writer.

James says, "I think Hemingway was an alcoholic."

I shrug and finish my beer.

Even if you're an alcoholic, you can drink with dignity. But I don't think Hemingway was an alcoholic. He had time, and he was in pain, and he liked to drink. James is an alcoholic. He drank without time and without pain and he drank when he hated to drink. Hemingway had the money to drink. James did not and still doesn't. Hemingway liked rum and limes and mint leaves and crushed ice. He liked bartenders with faces you fall into. James liked Bankers Club Vodka, four dollars a bottle. The bartenders hated him because he was broke.

James says, "If I would have never read Hemingway, I would have never become a writer. I would have never taken this job."

"Are you blaming Hemingway?" I say.

"No," he says. "I'm praising him."

He's serious. James loves Hemingway. I love Hemingway. Every summer James and I re-read *A Moveable Feast* and remember why we aren't lawyers.

James says, "This place is getting packed."

"It's Happy Hour," I say.

Now the frat guys and the sophomore girls are coming into Hemingway's Bar. There are so many great things about Pittsburgh, but not the university and not this shithole bar where the menu offers Buns and Aps, not sandwiches and appetizers, no, just Buns and Aps.

"I'm never drinking here again," I say to James.

James says, "You should probably get those shoes on your kid's feet."

"I will, once I finish not drinking here," I say.

The basketball game is looming. Tonight, my son will jump and run with the confidence of a rich kid. He will soar in his new hightops, if only in his imagination.

The bartender comes by. The afternoon bartender was a woman and she looked tough, with rough hands and kind eyes. The evening bartender has a baseball hat on sideways. He has muscles. He's tan and the hair falling from his hat is streaked, maybe frosted, something most women quit doing when they're still teenage girls and don't start again until senility.

The bartender says, "You guys want another?"

I say, "This is a terrible bar."

James says, "It's the worst bar in Pittsburgh."

"A real shithole," I say.

"Even worse than that bar where they throw midgets," James says.

The bartender could easily beat us up, but he won't. He, like an entire generation of young men, has forgotten how to fight, has forgotten that fighting is even an option. All they know is what they get. If it doesn't flash across a screen, it doesn't exist.

I say, "You should get an education."

The bartender says, "I'm paying for my education by working in this shithole."

"Good," James says. "An education is important."

The bartender hands us two bottles of Corona Light and a small bowl filled with limes. He takes our old bottles and wipes down the bar. He offers us some pretzels.

The bartender says, "Those beers are on me." He says, "I hate this fucking place."

"And you should," I say.

"Do you read Ernest Hemingway?" James says.

"Read Ernest Hemingway," I say. "It will change your life."

"I need something," the bartender says and goes to wait on a guy who has, for no apparent reason, taken off his shirt to reveal a peace sign tattooed on his left pec.

James wants to stay and maybe get laid with a student. I'm not against professors getting laid by students and students flirting with and leading professors on, but James is very drunk, not stumbling drunk but reckless, so I load him in my 1999 Ford Focus and we start back towards my house. It's dinner time. My kids are home, eating whatever my wife has cooked. My wife is dressed in her evening work outfit, her uniform. I thought she would be embarrassed to waitress, that she would worry about seeing her students and her students seeing her dressed in a short black skirt and a white oxford with an extra button undone. My wife is not embarrassed. If anything, she would rather wait tables than teach college. If she could just get more tips. If she could just get summers off.

James says, "I've never seen little kids play basketball."

"It's great," I say. "They can't even get the ball through the hoop."

I love the way our house looks, the half whiskey barrels filled with flowers in the summer and a big yard for the kids to run through and throw things around and a huge fence to drink beer behind and a fire-pit to burn stuff to give light to see what we're drinking.

Now everything is covered with snow, the trees and the bushes and the pine trees, except the walks which I keep shoveled and salted so the mailman won't fall. The house is almost fifty-years old and looks it I guess, the outside a sort of dark-pink brick and weather-damaged siding I've painted gun-bolt gray.

It was my mother-in-law's house, the house my wife grew up in. Six years ago, when my mother-in-law, Bertie, was diagnosed with cancer, she signed the house over to my wife. Bertie was in the hospital and sick, and she wanted to die at home, so that's what we did. We took her home. My wife stayed with her mother, just like she'd stayed with her father when the cancer was in his lungs and brain. When Bertie died, my wife was there, just like she was there when her father said, "I see the light, and I don't know if it wants me."

Now we live here and paint the rooms funky colors and don't remodel because we can't afford it. The kitchen is ancient with old pressed-wood cabinets. The window frames are starting to rot, and the screens have holes we've patched with tape. All the faucets leak. You can't shower upstairs because the downstairs will flood. The rooms are small, the bedrooms are smaller, and the toilet in the back bathroom won't flush.

But we are happy, almost always happy here. There are books in every room, and the living room has bookshelves I bought from a rummage sale that look expensive. On one wall, we have a framed Phil Levine poem with a wood-cut image of a factory and a desolate city, a gift from a publisher who was supposed to publish my first book then, without telling me, didn't. The TVs are old but the pictures are good enough to watch the movies we love, the ones with people in them, talking about their lives. Once a year, my wife and I watch all of John Cassevettes' films. We make our kids watch the *Wizard of Oz* even if they would rather watch cartoons, and they always eat too much popcorn and get scared of the flying monkeys and learn something about home and what it means to lose that. It's the kind of house I would have dreamed if I would have ever dreamed of houses, but now we have kids and kids mean other kids and other kids mean parents, and these parents stop by to pick up their kids and says, "Oh, books," and look at our bookshelves and they see our kitchen and say, "Now, that's a red wall," but not in a nice way, then they look at our cheap-o cabinets.

I park the car and we step outside.

James says, "You have a nice house."

"It's a great house," I say, putting my key in the front door.

"It is," he says. "It's a great house. The best house. I don't know another house in the world where you can piss and look at a framed photograph of Charles Bukowski at the same time." Then he says, "Is your wife going to be mad that we're so drunk?"

I say, "Why would my wife be mad that we're drunk?"

My wife, Lori, forty-six years old, still beautiful, a college professor—a real college professor with tenure and evaluations and raises—but also a waitress at The Brillo Box Bar, and of course a writer with two books (one memoir and one book of poems), a great mother, a wonderful mother, and a great and wonderful wife, she sees James walking through our front door and how he's droopy and deflated, and she says, "Oh Honey, come here," and she takes him in her arms.

James is in the bathroom. He either needs a drink or he doesn't. The water is running, probably flooding or about to. In the dining room, my wife is in her usual chair, being rational. I am in the kitchen, looking for a beer. The beers appear to be in the garage.

"You can't drive Townes to his basketball game," my wife says from one room.

"I can," I say from the other.

I'm drunk, but I'm fine. I've explained this.

She says, "Trust me, you can't."

I find a Dogfish or some fancy beer hidden behind leftover pasta in a Tupperware container. I hate Dogfish. It's a Porter. I hate Porter. I like Coors Light. I love Hoegaarden. When we have money, there is Hoegaarden in the kegerator, what my kids call the beer machine, in the kitchen. I open the Dogfish. Lori bought me the kegerator for Father's Day. I can drink fancy Belgian beer for the price of Coors Light. It's a good deal. Kegs are half the price of bottles. The beer machine paid for itself after four kegs. But I hate to buy a keg, to pay one hundred fifty bucks all at once. I drink the Dogfish Porter and almost gag. I walk into the dining room and my wife looks sad.

She says, "Why do you drink Dogfish when you hate it?"

"It was the only thing in the fridge."

"Order a keg. We can afford it."

"We can't afford anything."

"We can," she says. "We can't afford much, but we can afford beer."

"Is there any Coors Light in the garage?"

"I think so."

"Where are the kids?"

"Downstairs, working on a Lego city."

"I got Townes a pair of Converse hightops from Target. They're canvas, but they look pretty cool."

She says, "He'll be so happy." She says, "How drunk is James? Why is James drunk?" She says, "I know you're fine to drive, but you can't take Townes to basketball like that. People will smell the alcohol on you and they'll put you in jail."

"How else is he going to get there?"

"I'll take him."

"You have to go to work," I say.

"I'll call off."

"You can't call off. We need the money. I'll eat some cinnamon gum or something."

"Trust me, you cannot take Townes."

James comes out of the bathroom. He looks better. Every time he disappears into a bathroom and reappears later after the sound of running water and a toilet flushing, he looks sharper and more defined. I thought it was the time alone, the mirror, even the water, but now I'm thinking there must have been cocaine on him somewhere and now it's up his nose.

James says, "I'll drive."

I say, "You can't drive. You're drunk."

Lori says, "Neither of you is driving. Trust me. I'll call in work and I'll tell them I'm going to be late. The game's only forty minutes long. We'll be one big happy family."

James says, "I could use a big happy family." He says, "I could use a mechanic, a better job, and a few thousand dollars." He says, "I could use a beer."

I say, "In the garage."

Lori says, "I'm not being a nag, but are you sure you don't want to stop drinking and think about it?"

"Tomorrow," James says and goes for the garage.

I say, "He got the kids some toys."

Lori says, "That's sweet, but he doesn't have any money."

I say, "He missed Townes' birthday. He feels bad."

Lori says, "He can come and not bring a present."

I say, "I told him that."

James comes back with a Coors Light. He says, "Are you talking about me?"

I give him a look and say, "I was just telling Lori that you got the kids some stuff."

"I did," he says, and he doesn't let on.

Lori says, "That's very sweet."

I say, "Where's Abby? Is she downstairs with Townes?"

"She's downstairs. She's been talking about being a cheer-leader. All day."

"That's what little girls do," I say. "They talk about being cheerleaders and wear pink stuff. Then they grow up to be doc-tors and support their poor struggling writer dad and his low-life friend and his lovely wife."

I stomp the floor and say my daughter's name.

Abby is five. She's named Abby after a character Gerald Locklin created. Gerald Locklin is one of my favorite writers. He's known mostly as a poet but he writes excellent fiction and in his fiction he calls himself Jimmy Abby. Jimmy Abby is a big rollicking poet and professor who drinks too much and womanizes and stumbles around Southern California reading poems and playing pool and getting laid. I liked the name so I took it. Then I gave it to my daughter so she would always understand the world and men and the kind of men that will make her happy and the kind that won't and the kind that can do both. Sometimes Abby calls herself Abby Popcorn. Gerald Locklin is not a surrealist, but I think he would appreciate that.

Abby hears my voice and her name and bolts up the stairs, flying a Lego airplane in one hand, reaching for me with the other. Her hair is blonde, to her shoulders, and it curls into round springs and ringlets.

"Daddy!" she says.

"Abby!" I say.

"I missed you!" she says.

I pick her up and spin her and kiss her belly and almost knock over my lousy Dogfish Porter. She lands the plane on the table and takes a seat on my lap.

Abby says, "I love you, Daddy! I missed you so much! We made brownies today." Then, realizing James is here when he hasn't been for months, she turns and happily screams, "Oh James Longo, you're finally here," like she's been doing nothing but making brownies and waiting for him to arrive.

James says, "Where have you been? You never call."

Abby says, "Oh James."

James says, "Oh Abby."

Lori says, "I'm going to go call work."

I say, "Are you sure?"

"I'm sure-sure," Lori says.

I kiss my daughter. James hands me his beer and I take a sip.

Abby says, "You should see the Lego city Townes is building."

"Is it great?" I say.

"It is so great," she says.

I can hear my wife on the phone in the other room. Her boss is a good guy. He knows Lori has kids and a husband and another job, but he likes having a writer working for him. It makes the bar arty and hip. Here's your drink. There's her book.

James mouths, "Should I give her the stuff?" meaning Abby, meaning the stuff we stole.

"Wait until after the game," I say.

He nods.

Lori comes in from the kitchen. She says, "Not a problem. No one's in tonight because of the weather. I can come in late or I don't have to come in at all."

James says, "If I owned a restaurant, I'd want you to run it for me."

Lori says, "I'd cook you whatever you want."

James says, "Scallops in lemon and butter."

Lori says, "I knew that's what you'd want."

All I want is money.

When I was in my twenties, all I wanted was to be a writer. I wrote and read and punched walls for it. My poems came out in little magazines. I had a story published in England, another one in Ireland. I wrote every day. Drafts piled up. I was a genius. I was the best ever. Then I was not. I was terrible. No writer had ever written as poorly as I wrote. It's a bad feeling to have read enough to know that your own writing is no good. But I wanted to get better. Then I didn't get better. The first three novels I wrote were junk. The next one was worse.

So I worked boring jobs and wrote and ran and wrote and

drank and wrote, and I fucked women I didn't have to talk to so I could get back to writing.

Then I met my wife. Then we wrote together. Not in the same room, but in the same life. My wife is lazy with her writing, so I said, "Write," and she did, and I knew I had to write, too, but more, better. She had talent. I had desire. She had writer friends who would help her. I did not. She published a book. I did not. I wrote books that I thought should have been published, but they weren't. I managed a bookstore. Nights, I bartended and sometimes drove truck. I wrote while I drove truck and tended bar.

My wife's book didn't sell. It was a great book, a book about her father, the millrite, the gambler. The publisher put a pink cover on it. They changed the title. It looked like a book for housewives. My wife was too sad to write.

I kept writing.

My wife got a teaching job. She got tenure.

Then we had kids. Then the kids could walk. Then they could talk and I wanted to talk with them and I wanted to have the right answers.

My wife published a book of poems.

I allowed myself to sleep twenty hours a week, but no more. When I wasn't sleeping and working and wrestling my son or playing with my daughter, I was writing. I took a lot of pills. I was sick from the pills and the writing.

Then I published a book, a novel, 176 pages long. I loved having a book published. The book didn't make any money, but so what. It was a little press. It wasn't supposed to make any money. I wanted to be a writer. I wrote. I became a writer. There's my book on the shelf.

As we pull into the parking lot, my son, in his new hightops, says, "Could I just call you James? Uncle James sounds weird."

My wife parks and we climb out. We're early. We'll get good seats, up high in the bleachers, away from the other parents. We'll cheer and clap and stink like booze.

Abby says, "He's Cookie Crumbles."

"I *am* Cookie Crumbles," James says.

Townes says, "Cookie Crumbles is a cool name. How'd you get it?"

"I was born with it," James says.

"You're awesome, Cookie Crumbles!" Abby says.

James was born James, then he got drunk and stayed drunk for years. When he was in his mid-twenties, he moved to Florida and went on a two-year bender. He worked as a waiter. He did a lot of coke. He made pilgrimages to Key West to think about Hemingway and he wrote coked-up stories about visiting Key West. When he had enough money, he drank full-time. Once, really wrecked on rum and blow, he hopped a boat for the Dominican Republic. From Santa Domingo, he mailed a letter that said, "James Longo is dead. I am now JoJo Crash." He was JoJo Crash for five more years. He drank until he puked blood. He kept drinking. He fell from a first floor window and broke his ear drum. He walked zigzags. He fell again on the sidewalk. When he got sober, he lived on sugar. All that sweetness that was in him as a kid returned and we took long walks around Pittsburgh until he wasn't always thinking about booze. He ate donuts. He drank Dr. Pepper. I started calling him Cookie. My wife suggested we start a band called The Cookie Crumbles. My kids heard the name and it stuck.

Townes says, "Cookie Crumbles, why didn't you come to my birthday party?"

James says, "Because I wanted to come to your basketball game tonight."

"That's right," Lori says.

"Yes," I say. "He's here now."

"Cool," Townes says.

"Pick me up, Cookie Crumbles," Abby says, and he does.

It's an old school, but it's been remodeled. The bricks are dirty. The windows are clean. Inside, the little kids, nine-and-ten-year olds, play in the practice gym. My son is on the floor now. He starts at point guard. He can barely dribble, but he dribbles better than most of the other kids. The referees very rarely call a foul. The hoops have been lowered to eight feet. They play quarters instead of halves. The score is 0-0.

Lori says, "Why is the other coach yelling?"

The other coach isn't yelling. He's talking loudly at the referee. You can tell the coach would like to yell. His face is a bag of red skin that's been puffed with air. He has on business clothes, a tie and slacks and a white shirt, but everything is rumpled and wet. He could be drunk or maybe he's hungover from a business lunch. If he is, I forgive him. Only a man with a job in sales would care this much about basketball and kids who can't shoot.

"Go Townes!" Abby yells.

Townes is nowhere near the ball.

"That coach does look pretty pissed," James says. "You didn't sneak in any beer?"

"No, I did not sneak in any beer," I say.

Abby is sitting on James' shoulders. She's hugging his head like a stuffed animal.

The coach yells, "Come on, Ref, you gotta call something. They ain't gonna learn from this." He turns to his assistant coach and says, "Jesus!" The coach wipes his face with a hand towel. He turns back to the referee and says, "They're hacking each other to death out there."

James says, "You should go beat that guy up."

I say, "He's not even my kid's coach. Townes' coach is the skinny guy in a green track suit who's always smiling. He's great."

Lori says, "I'm going to take Abby down to the concession stand."

Abby says, "Peanut butter cups!"

Lori says, "Hot dog," and they step down the bleachers.

When they're gone, I turn to James and whisper, "Where's the blow?"

"What blow?"

"What blow, come on."

"I did it," he said. "Sorry."

"Where'd you get it?"

"Ginelli."

"You're kidding? I didn't know he was alive."

Matt Ginelli was a guy that went to high school with my older brother. He was a football player, a prom king. He was class president. But he was stupid, couldn't get a scholarship because his SATs were too low. Teachers passed him because he was charming and the coaches needed him to pass. After high school, he went to the community college and failed out. He got a job at UPS, loading boxes. He started selling blow. That was twenty or more years ago. I thought someone had killed him or he'd killed himself.

James said, "I bumped into him at Toads. Two guys were beating him up over a gambling debt in the parking lot behind the bar. I walked over and they must have thought I was a cop or something and they ran. Ginelli was out of it. He stood up and sort of recognized me. He pulled out his wallet and gave me two teeners of blow and six bucks and said I'd saved his life."

"Then you did all the blow without me."

"You have a family, you can't be doing blow."

"I'm drunk, what's the difference?"

"Drunk's probably worse."

"You could have saved me some."

"There might be a couple lines left," he says.

I don't know if it's hot in the gym or if it's hot inside me. I take off my jacket. I wipe my face. Maybe I look like the other coach, but less angry. There are banners hanging from the ceiling. The banners are yellow with green lettering. A few are for championships, but most are for second or third place. I want Townes to play basketball now, so he can run and sweat, but I hope he quits before he gets to high school. All those banners mean something I hate.

James says, "There goes Townes," and stands up and starts to clap.

Townes has the ball. He dribbles down the court. No one really tries to stop him. Townes has a lane to the basket. No one is in his way. He keeps dribbling. He's looking down. He can't dribble without looking down. Then he's under the basket. Then he's back around. He looks up and passes to a teammate. The ball hits his teammate in the head and the kid stumbles back and the ball rolls out of bounds. The referee blows his whistle. The kid is okay.

"Good try, Jason," their coach says to the kid who caught the ball with his face. Then, "Nice pass, Townes. Don't be afraid to shoot." The coach stands, but away from the court.

He points to the kids and gives them a thumbs-up and Townes waves back.

The score is 2-2. Townes has his team's only basket. There's a minute left. The other coach has complained so much, the referee is calling fouls. When they call a foul, the clock stops. The other team has a kid at the foul line. He throws up his first shot and it doesn't make it to the hoop. The second shot he tries granny-style and the ball goes over the backboard.

Townes' teammate, the other guard, takes the ball out of bounds.

"This makes me so nervous," Lori says.

"Me, too," James says. "I wish I had a drink."

Lori looks at him.

"A little drunkard humor," he says.

I'm too nervous to talk so I pretend not to be nervous. I don't care if Townes makes another basket ever, but I want him to have fun and be healthy and if he doesn't make a basket, this all stinks. I stand up with the rest of the crowd. There are more people here than there should be. All these parents thinking their kids will turn pro.

"Show us how those new shoes work, Townes," the coach says, and I see Townes turn and smile and nod.

The other guard passes to Townes. Townes looks down at the ball and starts to dribble. It's amazing how hard these kids try. The other coach screams and yells.

"D-up on number 7! D-up!" he yells.

Townes is number 7. It's like he's dribbling an invisible ball. No one on either team seems to know who has what and where he's going. Townes makes it to the basket. Then he's under the basket. The other team is at the wrong end of the court. I'm really sweating. I know this means nothing, and yet because I'm the only one who knows this, it means everything. These kids are making their lives.

Lori screams, "Shoot Townes!"

Abby screams, "Townes!"

James screams, "Shoot!"

Townes dribbles under the basket. Time is running down. I watch the clock, then my son. Townes keeps dribbling. I hope he passes it. I want him to shoot and make it, but shooting's too much pressure. A pass is all he needs to do to survive.

Our coach yells, "Shoot Townes!"

The other coach yells, "D-up! D-up!"

Townes keeps dribbling, away from the basket, then back. He's underneath. He's in the lane. He turns and shoots. It's a terrible shot. It hits the underside of the basket. The ball slams back down. Townes gets the rebound and accidentally passes it to a kid on the other team who swats at the ball like it's a bug or a big round leather bird attacking his chest. The ball bounces back to Townes. One kid on Townes' team sits down on the court and quits. There's twenty seconds left. Townes shoots and misses. Fifteen seconds. I hope they don't have overtime for midget sports. A tie is great. When no one wins, everyone wins. Fuck the coaches, that coach. Townes has the ball. He's facing the wrong way. He stops and, without looking at the hoop or the backboard or his teammates, fires a shot back over his head. The ball is in the air for a long time. It's up. It's up. It's coming down. It hits the backboard and falls through the net as the seconds tick off the scoreboard and all the parents on our side start to scream.

"Time out!" the other coach shouts, but the referee ignores it and the buzzer goes off.

Everyone is excited, even me, especially me. James has Abby over his head, Abby is screaming, and I can see Lori looking at James, making sure he won't wobble and stumble and tumble down the bleachers with our daughter. James sets Abby down and everyone hugs. We are a jumble of arms and legs, cheering. This is all so stupid but we won so it's not.

James says, "Wow!"

Abby says, "Townes is the best!

Lori says, "That makes me want to cry."

"Please don't cry," I say, meaning it's stupid, but I could cry too.

It's winter and the weather won't break for another two months. My best friend, drunk and happy, looks like he could fall from the top row and mean it. No one here has any money, but my wife touches me, and my daughter hugs my legs, and James is alive, and there's my son with his two baskets and last second heroics and his new shoes. He's looking at us and waving and we're waving back like he's on a boat we don't ever want to leave.

'm doing the puzzle with Abby. James and Townes are in the other room playing video games. Lori is cooking something in the kitchen. It smells like bacon. Bedtime was an hour ago but James passed out the presents we stole and Townes built the Legos and now Abby and I are almost done with her first one-hundred piece puzzle.

Abby says, "We need a green piece for the frog."

I nudge the piece away from the pile so she can find it and think she did it herself. We are excellent at puzzles together. I find the pieces and she matches the holes. Outside, in the porch light, I can see snow falling. The kids could use a delay tomorrow. I could use a delay. I try to drink my beer, but I've lost it. I'm tired and dry, and the time at the game changed my focus. Like I want to finish this puzzle. Like I could sleep on this table.

James comes in from the living room and says, "Townes wants to play another game, is that okay or too late?"

"Too late," I tell him. Then I yell into the living room, "Townes, brush your teeth."

"It's bed time?" Abby says.

"Almost," I say.

"But Cookie Crumbles is here. I thought we were going to stay up."

She looks like she might cry, but it's fake, or if it's real, she's tired.

I say, "No crying."

"That's right, "James says. "No crying."

Abby sniffles and pulls herself together and says, "I just want to finish my puzzle."

"We'll finish your puzzle right now."

Townes sulks by, pissed that he has to go to bed. I can hear him in the bathroom, peeing. Then the water to brush his teeth.

James says, "Hey," and nods. He makes another gesture and says, "You want the last little bit?" He's talking about the coke.

I forgot about the coke. I'd like some bacon and eggs.

I says, "It's all you."

James says, "You sure?"

I say, "You want some bacon and eggs instead?"

"I couldn't eat," he says. "It would make everything worse." He says, "That was an amazing shot Townes made."

"I heard that," Townes yells from the bathroom.

"I'm just complimenting your excellence," James says.

Lori comes out with bacon and eggs. She says, "Sorry, it's all we have. I haven't had time to get to the grocery store."

James says, "I couldn't eat anything."

Lori says, "You should," but she's not pushy.

Townes comes from the bathroom and says, "Cool, bacon."

Abby finishes her puzzle and we high-five.

She says, "It's a magical forest."

I say, "You did a great job. One hundred pieces, too."

Lori says, "It looks great, Abby. You're the best puzzle-builder ever."

Townes says, "If you're into puzzles."

Townes is tired, and he's about to get mean.

That's how it is being nine. That's how it is being thirty-nine.

James goes to the bathroom.

I hear the water and know he's doing blow.

A t three in the morning, I hear a loud retching sound. I think it's one of the kids and roll out of bed with the covers on and fall. I stumble to the bathroom, hoping it's not Townes, a middle-of-the-night puker since birth. He shouldn't have had the bacon.

"Are you okay, big guy?" I say, turning on the hall light, but it's James and he sounds like he's trying to throw up a desert.

James says, "Sorry."

I say, "You're okay." I say, "I thought it was Townes."

He says, "Oh."

I feel sober. He looks wrecked. The days and the drinking and the drugs have caught him, and now he's on his knees, his cheek on the toilet seat. Then he shifts and throws up again.

It's not much, just red strings of snot or bile. My stomach hurts hearing his stomach.

He says, "I don't think this is good."

He's covered in sweat. It's like he's been working out—soaked hair, his shirt on the floor, his t-shirt drenched. His shoes are off, and one sock is missing.

I get a washcloth and turn on the faucet. I make it cold. I ask James if he wants a drink and then say, "Ginger Ale," to be clear.

He says, "No." He says, "Yes." He turns and does it again.

When he's finished I hold the washcloth to his forehead then wipe his face.

He says, "You make a good mom."

"Only some days," I say.

It's been so long since James has been drunk, I forgot. One time years ago, in the hospital, a nurse did what I'm doing for him now. James had jumped from a moving car and ended up in the emergency room. His blood alcohol level was .3, three times the legal limit. The doctor told James he couldn't drink again. James drank that night. Maybe that was fifteen years ago. Now I look in the toilet, and it's all blood.

I say, "When was the last time you ate?"

He says, "Cocaine."

"Right," I say. "We should get you to the hospital."

"Good," he says. "Hospitals have nurses and drugs," then he turns to throw up again.

II

I'm on the phone with one student when another student knocks on the open office door. It's Monday, always a busy day. The student sits down at my desk and pulls out a sheaf of poems. She's a pretty good poet but she never comes to class. I try to remember her name.

She says, "Are you going to be long?"

I whisper, "Two minutes."

The student on the phone wants to know why he has to read Bukowski. Bukowski is offensive. Reading Bukowski is counter to his upbringing.

"What's your upbringing?" I say.

"Not Bukowski," he says.

"Really?" I say. "That's an upbringing?"

He says, "Yes."

The Bukowski we're reading is not about sex. It's about work. Those are the two basic Bukowskian themes: work and sex. Fucking and earning, one critic said in the New York Times, but he meant it as an insult. I mean it as a compliment. You can get a lot of books out of sex and work. If you're good at either, you can build a pretty decent life.

The student says, "I'm waiting for your decision."

His voice is polite but filled with bile. He's no snarkier than my other worst students but he pretends to be respectful so it's worse.

"Give it a try," I say. "Once you get past the language, Bukowski can be very tender."

The girl in my office looks at her watch. She came here to show me her poems and now I'm doing something else. I smile at her and hold up one finger. She does not smile back.

The boy on the phone says, "Maybe I could do additional work."

"Additional work for what?" I say.

"In lieu of?"

"What's that mean?"

"You're the English teacher."

"I am the English teacher," I say, mock surprise.

"Right," he says. "Therefore, in lieu of the Bukowski, would it be possible to read another novel? I'd be willing to write a short paper."

"You'd be willing to write a *short* paper?" I say. "Hmm."

I'm just fucking with him now.

The girl in my office stands up. I tap the desk and motion for her to sit down. I smile and apologize with all my gestures. "One second," I mouth. I'm almost done with the student on the phone. The student in my office won't look at me. She packs up her poems in an expensive looking orange-and-brown backpack and she shakes the backpack and it's all very noisy and disgusted. The way she uses the zipper makes it sound like she's digging a grave.

The guy on the phone says, "Yes. Perhaps one-to-three pages."

"One page," I say. "Keep it concise."

"Do you have an author in mind or shall I choose?" he says.

"Let me think for a second," I say.

This is the same student who hated Chekov. "I don't get his endings," he said. Then he hated Dawn Powell. "Her characters are all sort of small towny," he said. I said, "The whole novel is set in a small town in Ohio." He said, "Yeah, that's probably what's not working." I try to remember if he liked any of the books. He didn't like any of the books.

"Have you read Joyce?" I say.

"James Joyce?" he says.

"Yes," I say. "They used to teach him in high school."

I don't know if that's true. In my high school, they taught Poe and Whitman but only the safe stuff. We read "A Tell-Tale Heart" and "When Lilacs Last in Dooryard Bloom'd" and that was it—a story about a heart beating underneath the floorboards of a house and a flowery poem for President Lincoln. We didn't read Joyce. Mostly we diagramed sentences.

The student says, "I believe we read Joyce, yes."

I say, "You probably read *Dubliners* or maybe a story from *Dubliners*."

The girl says, "Thanks for nothing."

I put the phone to my shoulder and say, "Don't leave yet. I'll be done with this student in one second."

She says, "I have class."

I say, "I've been on the phone for forty-five seconds."

She says, "You could have blocked out the time for me."

I say, "I didn't know you were coming."

She says, "Are these office hours? Is this your office?"

She looks around to check. Her red hair, long and straight to the collar of her sweater, moves with her sarcastic gestures.

"Leave me some poems then," I say. "I'll write you some comments."

"I didn't want comments," she says.

"What did you want then?"

I'm so used to all of this, I'm not even angry. I wanted to be a teacher, now I'm a counselor. I'm a punching bag. I'm in customer service.

She says, "Whatever," two words, and gives me the palm.

She slams the office door so it shakes my desk.

I go back to the phone.

The guy on the phone says, "What was that?"

"James Joyce," I say. "He wants you to read *Ulysses.*"

"Is that a story collection?" he says.

"Novel," I say. "Just write your one-page paper on the significance of subversive language in *Ulysses*, and you'll be fine."

"Can you say that again?" he says.

I say it again. When I'm done saying it, he hangs up. When he's done with *Ulysses*, he'll be out of my class. He'll be wishing he was brought up Bukowski.

"Professor Longo," I say, which is what I call James when I'm trying to be funny. Sometimes it's, "Professor Cookie Crumbles." Once and a while it's, "Professor Douchebag, emeritus."

It's between classes and he's coming down the hall. All the damage the alcohol and cocaine did, all the creases in his face and the wobble in his step, is gone. He's sober again, feeling guilty and ashamed. To alleviate the shame, he's been writing a lot, working on his novel. He's also been going to the coffee shop to hear students read their work, a tough thing to do when you can't drink alcohol.

James says, "You want to read some pages for me?"

I'm James' reader. I don't think he lets anyone else read his work. His work is almost always great by the time he shows it to me, but he hardly ever writes anymore. James makes Lori, my wife, who I always considered one of the laziest writers on the planet, look like a workaholic. It's been five years since James published a story. Most of the stories he writes never get finished. When he does finish a story, and it's not perfect, when I have comments that are not all glowing, he says, "I knew it was a piece of shit," then throws the story in a huge plastic container he keeps in his office. He says, "In the bucket," even though the story was a draft or so away from being done, from being publishable, from being great.

"I'll read some pages for you," I say.

"It's a Harold story," he says.

"I love Harold stories."

Harold is James' main character. Harold is a little James, but not really. Harold is more earnest, more naïve. He drinks but that's not his problem. Everything else is Harold's problem: women and work and his uncle who knew Andy Warhol when Warhol was still in Pittsburgh. James does not or cannot write autobiographical fiction. All this has something to do with alcoholism. James looks at his life and he can't tell what's an adventure and what's a drunken mess. "You can't worry about stuff you did in your twenties," I sometimes say. "Everyone was stupid in their twenties."

Now he digs for the pages in his bag, a sort of satchel that looks like a saddlebag, and says, "I was trying to write about that time I jumped from Florida and headed for the Dominican Republic when I was on one of my coke-and-rum benders. I found a draft—or maybe just a letter—I'd written from that time, and I figured I'd try to use it."

"Can't wait to read it," I say.

James hands me the pages.

He says, "You growing out your goatee?"

"A little," I say.

"Looks good," he says. "Sort of covers your double chin."

"Thanks," I say and give my goatee a tug.

I'm thirty-nine. I'm bored with my face. I'm not so bored with my face that I'd shave my head or get a Mohawk or pierce my nose, but I like tugging on my new long goatee in class, a gesture I've never been able to do before. I think it makes me look thoughtful, if not a little more intelligent, and it does sort of hide my fat face which isn't going to change until my kids get older and I can get to the gym more regularly and quit eating Hot Cheetos with my son late at night while we watch Superhero movies.

James says, "I need new shoes."

He looks down at his shoes and shakes his head.

He's in fancy jeans and a nice shirt and a tie, very handsome. But it's one of only three outfits he owns, and his shoes look like they've been chewed on.

I say, "If you had money, you'd be very fashionable."

"You're goddamn right," he says. "You have class?"

"Comp," I say.

"I'm pissed," he says. "You got a minute?"

"Car?"

"Yeah," he says. "It's out at some chopshop in Greensburg. It's that and the other."

The other is booze.

"Come over for dinner tonight," I say.

"All I can think about is getting drunk. The weird thing is, the better I feel the more I want to drink. It used to be the opposite. When I first got sober, I was so happy to feel good, the last thing I wanted to do is drink. Now I'm like: well, I feel pretty good, might as well get smashed and pulverize my liver."

"Don't drink," I say. "Come to my house and eat fried chicken."

An old student of mine, Britta, comes down the hall. She looks frantic. Britta was an accounting major, but she could write like a motherfucker.

"Danny," she says to me. All my best students call me by my first name. "Oh god, I'm so sorry to bug you." She sees James and says, "Hi Dr. Longo."

James says, "Hey Britta."

I say, "Why's he Dr. Longo and I'm Danny?"

Britta looks at us, not sure if she should be embarrassed.

I say, "I'm joking. What do you need?"

She says, "A letter of recommendation?"

I say, "Sure. Not a problem."

She says, "By five o'clock?"

"Five o'clock today?"

James starts to laugh and catches himself and says, "Sorry."

Britta says, "I know. I just…god."

I say, "Didn't I write you one before?"

She says, "Last year."

I say, "I have class now. Send me an email with all your new information and I'll touch up the old letter I wrote for you. I'll make you sound great."

"You're the best, Danny," Britta says and she wraps me up in a hug and kisses me on the cheek twice like I'm some sort of priest. Britta goes down the hall saying, "Thank you," and bowing and shaking her prayer hands at me.

"See that," I say to James.

"Stunning," James says. "A nice student."

"A great writer, too," I say.

"I'm almost too happy to complain that I can't get drunk

and I'm broke and my car is being repaired by a man with eight fingers."

"Just come over for dinner tonight, seriously."

"I think I will," he says. He looks down the hall towards Britta who is disappearing into an elevator and says, "See, there are still some good ones out there."

"There are," I say.

James says, "Go to class."

I touch his shoulder and say, "You sure you're going to be okay?"

"What's Lori making for dinner?"

"Fried chicken."

"I'll be fine," James say.

It's been two weeks since his bender, since I rolled him into the hospital in a wheelchair because he was too weak to stand. I'd cleaned him up in the bathroom at my house but I'd rushed and there was blood, little brown flecks on his chin and cheeks. The nurses hooked him up to an IV and they pumped him full of fluids. They gave him something else and he slept. They took his blood and when he woke they made him pee in a cup. In the morning, the doctor stopped in. He looked neither sympathetic nor impressed. He looked at James, the dark circles under his eyes and the popped blood vessels in his cheeks and nose. He picked up James' chart and said, "Your white blood cell count is way down," and James said, "What's that mean?" and the doctor set down the chart and said, "Don't drink," and James said, "Oh," and the doctor said, "Lay off the cocaine too."

Now James is going into the office. Now I'm going to class. Later we will meet up and, somehow, make better what we can make better and try not to worry about the rest.

We're talking about James Baldwin. This is my Comp class. All the students are freshmen, and they're not happy. Writing, to them, is like biology or calculus, something they have to take. They all, if asked, want to be doctors or pharmacists.

Maybe they can do math.

They can't read.

I'm talking about "Notes of a Native Son," James Baldwin's brilliant essay on race in America, set in Harlem in the early 1940s. It's a challenging essay. Baldwin is a challenging character. His writing is dense, and the narrative about his relationship to his father and his father's relationship to God and white people, then Baldwin's relationship to God and white people while the country is at war overseas and race riots are burning up American cities, is difficult but also, in a good way, emotionally devastating. The world Baldwin writes about is filled with distrust and violence, and everywhere he takes the reader something explodes. His father dies. Harlem burns. White cops and black people crash head on. There are bullets and more deaths. You can feel the impact of slavery, it's right there, a grandparent away. Baldwin, after losing his job because of the color of his skin, after not being served in restaurants because of the color of his skin, walks into one last diner, The American Diner, and before he can order, the waitress says, "We don't serve Negros here." Instantly, James wants to kill her. He wants to take her by the throat and choke her out. His father, who was bitter and miserable and sick and paranoid, was right: white people are evil. James wants to kill the waitress but she won't come close enough, so he picks up a water pitcher and hurls it at her head. The water pitcher misses the waitress and explodes against the wall. It's the dynamite inside all of us. James Baldwin will not— cannot—be denied. If he's denied, his world ends.

I'm explaining this to my class. I'm animated. I'm enthused. It's an essay, one of the few essays we're encouraged to teach, that I absolutely believe in.

I say, "Who do we side with here? As readers, who are we rooting for?"

I'm standing behind a podium. I do that in Comp. If I sit at the desk or even lean, they start talking and giggling. I have to be up high.

I say, "There's not a right or wrong answer."

Nobody says anything. One guy in the back is asleep. Two girls are texting. A couple other kids could be texting but they've piled their books on their desks and laps like guard walls. One girl has her laptop open. Another guy is playing with a piece of yarn.

I say, "The more you talk, the sooner we can leave. Help me out."

"Who are we talking about?" one guy says.

"James Baldwin," I say.

Someone else says, "We're not on the essay about Ray Carver and his dad anymore."

"No," I say. "This is definitely James Baldwin."

"But they both have fathers?" the first guy says.

"They both definitely have fathers."

I know they haven't read the essay. They probably haven't bought the book. If they can't get it for free on the internet, it barely exists. I gave a short essay quiz last class and half the students wrote about James Baldwin's father being ravaged by alcoholism, even though James Baldwin's father doesn't drink, even though he's a minister obsessed with God.

"Come on," I say. "Even if you haven't read the text, you know the situation. I just explained it to you. You have a white waitress not willing to serve a black guy, and the black guy throws a water pitcher at her head. Who are we sympathetic with and why?"

"I don't know," someone says. "The waitress?"

"The waitress," I say.

"Yeah, the waitress," someone else says and a couple students nod.

"Absolutely, the waitress," I say.

But I want them to think about it. I go over the same points again and again: slavery, segregation, the inability to get work based on your race.

"So why are we sympathetic to the waitress?" I say.

"Because the black dude throws a pitcher at her," someone says.

"Yes," I say. Then, "Now, why should we be sympathetic to James Baldwin?"

Someone else says, "We shouldn't."

I should mention that half the class, maybe less, is white. Of the twenty students, five are black. Five are Asian. One girl is from India.

"Okay," I say. "So what is James Baldwin supposed to do?"

"Leave."

"Complain."

"Take his business elsewhere."

"Anything but throw shit at the waitress."

"Exactly," I say. "And what would any of those things change?" No one says anything. "You're all right," I say. "There's no wrong answer. I'm just saying that if James Baldwin doesn't stand up for himself, if he doesn't throw the water pitcher, it's a lot more years before he can get a job and something to eat. Think about that. What would you do if someone wouldn't give you a job or let you eat in a restaurant because of your race? How would you react?"

They're so bored I can feel it in my teeth. But I'm so excited, I'm sweating. I still get worked up over James Baldwin, over books, over literature, that we can put our experiences, our worlds, into words and put those words on the page in a way that makes other brains come closer to the brains that first had the experience, that first push against the universe. I wipe my forehead and look out at the classroom. They're all here, twenty students. No one with an excuse, no dead dogs or swine flu or emails saying, "I thought you'd like to know I'm struggling with depression." It's a full class but I don't have anything left to say. Whatever I would say would embarrass us all.

I say, "Anyone sympathetic to James Baldwin now?" All eyes are everywhere but on me. No one even pretends to take notes. I say, "Last chance? Anyone?"

A young black girl, Shaniqua, takes out one of her earbuds. Her hair is thick and straightened and she wears it forward so, I'm assuming, professors can't see she's wearing headphones during their lectures.

Shaniqua says, "I'm for him. Wait." She thinks about it and says, "This is like a Tiger Woods thing, right? Kinda like the Tiger Woods thing, being a black golfer when most golfers are white, right?"

Tiger Woods has been in the news for banging a lot of women who are not his wife. He's taken a hiatus from golf to fix himself. None of the women Tiger Woods has been banging is black. Tiger is black and Asian. Maybe this is what Shaniqua is talking about. I don't know. Tiger Woods is a billionaire. He can't be about anything.

Shaniqua says, "Wait. That's not it. I don't know."

"I understand you're frustrated," I say. We're in my office. She has her poems and her backpack and her anger. I still can't remember her name. I say, "I just don't think you can pull off the 'jellyfish with a fungus attached' and the 'vulture with big tits' images in the same stanza. They sort of cancel each other out. It's a lot of science for one poem."

"But he was a douchebag," she says, speaking of her ex-boyfriend. "A real piece of shit." She says, "And that bitch he called a girlfriend was fucking worse."

I'm leaving campus when I bump into Richard. Richard waves. He always waves before he speaks, a nervous tic. Richard is shy and seldom makes eye contact.

"Richard," I say. "How's the rock 'n' roll treating you?"

"Better than teaching," Richard says. "I'm a mess."

Richard looks like a mess, even for Richard. He's almost shaking, like the weather outside has caught him and won't let go.

I put my hand on his shoulder.

Richard says, "It was a very rough class."

"At least it's over now," I say.

"It's never ending," he says. "That's the problem."

I look towards Schenley Park which is too far away to see. There are trees and bridges and another university and a library. The cloud factory that Michael Chabon so famously wrote about pumps smoke into the air. I used to take my son through the park and along the train tracks to watch the clouds steam out of the enormous brick stack and once he said, "It's like a canon that shoots fluff." There are mysteries here that would take a lifetime to discover and another lifetime to write about. I'd rather do that than teach. I'd rather do that than talk to Richard. A bus splashes by, hitting every puddle. Students head for their dorms. A man on the corner, wearing a sandwich board with a bible verse painted across the front, used to play right guard for the Pittsburgh Steelers until his brain went gray from concussion and he couldn't find his locker, let alone who to block.

Richard says, "You park at Schenley?"

"Yeah," I say. "Right where the kids sled ride."

He says, "Do kids even sled ride anymore?"

My kids do. Maybe others don't. We tried to buy a sled at Walmart, and the lady in the toy section said, "We don't carry sleds. Sleds are dangerous. Walmart cares about their customers, and their customers' children." She was eating a pretzel. We bought a floatie, a big tube for lounging in the swimming pool, and it was faster than any sled.

I look to Soldiers and Sailors Parking Garage, a giant concrete cave, one of the many buildings the university owns. I wish I could afford to park there. Parking there, even three days a week, would be more than my car payment.

Richard says, "I know you need to get going," but he stops before dismissing me.

I say, "It's okay," but it's not.

My bag is filled with work. I've been here since six in the morning. Now it's three-thirty. Any later and rush-hour traffic will kick in and I'll be stuck in a quarter-mile tunnel for thirty minutes. I know Richard needs something. But my son has basketball practice. My wife works tonight. I think my daughter needs to be signed up for dance class and I'm supposed to do it because I missed the sign-ups last weekend.

Richard says, "I know you're trying to leave, but can we talk?" He says, "I'm sorry."

"Sure," I say, because it's the only thing to say. "You want to go back into the office?"

"I need a cigarette," he says.

Concrete benches line the sidewalks beneath the trees that make a university in the city look like it has a campus. We sit down. Richard pulls out his wrappers and his loose-leaf tobacco. I know he's broke. I think I told you before: last year Richard was full-time; this year he teaches the same number of classes but as a part-time professor and makes nine grand. He has a wife and three kids. His kids are teenagers.

I say, "Don't let the students get you down. They're not worth it."

"I know," he says.

He's fumbling with his papers. It's windy in the city. The tree branches crack against each other and try to scratch out the human voices.

Richard says, "I just need to calm myself down a second." He says, "Sorry." Richard apologizes a lot. He's bald with a neatly trimmed beard. He wears thick, black-rimmed glasses and cardigan sweaters, sometimes with neckties, sometimes with a bowtie. He's not joking. His dress is as sincere as everything else about him, and it's sad that sometimes he speaks too thoughtfully, too intelligently, for students to understand.

Richard says, "I'd kill for a Marlboro," and smiles but doesn't look up.

Richard is forty-eight, maybe fifty. He plays in a rock band when he's not teaching. The band is The Rugged Richard Trio, though for years it was Rugged Richard and The Blazing Saddles. Richard was an indie rocker, still is.

Back in the early Nineties, when grunge and alternative music took off, major labels started courting Richard. Back then, he was doing a sort of punked-up alternative country, part rockabilly, part smash your guitar because your girlfriend fucked a guy in a business suit. His CDs got reviewed. The city papers and alternative zines interviewed him and *Guitar Magazine* did a piece they called, "Geeks Who Shred," and they talked to Richard about his guitars and amplifiers and a distortion pedal he'd wired himself.

Richard never got huge but he once told me he made almost thirty grand one year off touring and CD sales and t-shirts. He assumed it would keep growing. The van he was driving would finally become a tour bus, the tour bus would suddenly find itself driven by a real driver. There would be motel rooms for showers instead of truckstops and YMCAs. Maybe a roadie. It would never be glamorous, but bills would get paid. Happiness would abound. Richard would never have to work a day job. He would sing and play guitar in a band with his friends and if they stayed honest they might even end up with enough money for health insurance. Richard wouldn't have dreamed anything else. Anything else would have been an insult to his original dream to follow the music.

So when Geffen, the label that signed Nirvana and made them millionaire rockstars, called Richard, Richard went home, drank a six pack of Pabst and said, "Thanks, I'll pass." He didn't talk to his wife. He didn't talk to his band. He didn't say, "Fuck you," or, "Corporate rock sucks," and he ended the conversation by saying, "Thanks for calling." He booked the next tour himself. He opened for some bigger acts, bands that had jumped to major labels. Those guys and girls were all buying houses. They were touring Europe and not drinking Pabst in cans. Richard was jealous when he let himself but he seldom did and mostly he was happy. He had his plan. Richard wasn't religious but every night when he stepped on stage after unloading his own gear and doing his own soundcheck, he said thank you to someone, whoever was out there.

Then one day he called home and his wife said, "I'm pregnant."

Then kids, millions of them, started getting their music off the internet for free.

Richard finished the tour and headed home. He went back to school. He became a father. He got a job in a record store. Summers and weekends he still rocked, and there was the occasional five-city tour put together on a whim, but mostly it was bills and another kid then another kid then this teaching job then losing this teaching job and working part-time and rolling your own cigarettes in the wind.

Richard cups his hand and fires up his Bic lighter and gets some smoke into his lungs. He exhales and does it again.

"That helps," he says.

"So what's up with these kids?" I say.

"Well," Richard says. "I think... basically... pretty much... well, one threatened to beat me up after class today if I gave him another C."

I start to laugh. Richard smokes and laughs.

He says, "Funny, right, I know. But now what?"

"Could you take him?" I say.

"I'm not much of a fighter," Richard says. "But yes. These kids are all such pussies. When he said he was going to beat me up, I assumed he meant that his mom was going to come to class and beat me up while the kid watched and complained about our fighting techniques."

"What are you going to do?" I say.

"What is there to do?" he says.

"I don't know," I say

But there has to be something to do.

Richard says, "This ever happen to you?"

"My goatee is longer than yours. It makes me look like I know kung fu," I say.

He says, "I feel like I'm in junior high. That was the last time a bully threatened to kick my ass. Not high school. Junior high. It's ridiculous. Shouldn't he be expelled?"

"He should be."

"But he won't be?" Richard says and flicks his cigarette into a puddle.

"I don't know," I say.

"What if he has a gun?" Richard says.

"He doesn't have a gun," I say. "He's just an asshole."

"I know he doesn't have a gun, he probably thinks guns are joysticks with triggers for his X-Box or whatever, but what if he did? What if next time he threatens me with a gun?"

I say, "I honestly don't know."

I've had students threaten me but never with violence, and usually they're too scared to do it to my face. The semester ends and they get their grades and they shoot off emails demanding to know my supervisor's name and contact information.

The last one was this kid Randall. He wrote, "A C for my final grade? Frankly, I am appalled. At no point during the semester was I aware that I was doing 'average' work. I will need your supervisor's contact information so that I may register a formal complaint."

I wrote back, "Randall, you are remarkably talented. On your first story you received a B+ which I consider to be a very strong grade. You didn't turn in your next two stories. You didn't take any of the quizzes. You didn't do your presentation. You missed eleven classes. You are allowed to miss three without affecting your grade. Miss five classes and you fail. The C you received was my gift to you."

Then I gave him the writing program director's name.

Then I never heard from him again.

Then I went to my next class and wondered who was going to be the next Randall, and if the next Randall would really complain to my boss and if my boss would have my back or sell me out to the next Randall who believes he should get whatever grade he wants because he's paying tuition, because as one Randall said to me, "Look, dude, I'm paying your salary."

Richard says, "I just don't know."

I say, "Shoot Jim a line."

Jim is the director of the writing program. I mentioned him—the gun, the moonshine, the nakedness. He's an old-fashioned writer and drinker and lover of female graduate students who now, approaching seventy, walks with a cane and keeps a flask of vodka in his leather jacket. He refers to himself as Ol' Kentucky Jim. He doesn't give a shit about anything. If he's worried about anything, it's his next great sentence or his last great piece-of-ass or why the hell none of his students know who Richard Brautigan is.

Richard says, "You really think Jim would care?"

I say, "No."

Richard says, "Maybe he would."

I say, "Maybe."

Richard says, "No, you're right, he wouldn't care. No one cares, and that little shit is going to ruin me."

"That little shit is not going to beat you up," I say.

"I wish he would," Richard says. "It would give me something to show."

"It might give you some job security," I say, trying to make a joke, but Richard, not able to generate enough nicotine from his hand-rolled cigarette, is too tense to laugh.

I touch his bald head, something I've never done before,

and shine him up in a warm way. I put my arm around his shoulder and keep it there.

The problem is not that a student wants to beat Richard up.

It's not even a problem if the student actually beats Richard up.

The problem is that the students are our only means of evaluation. Once a semester a woman comes in and passes out a dot-survey and some #2 pencils and the students—good and bad, mature and immature, passing and failing—rate their professors. There's nothing else. We don't peer-critique. Neither the director of the Writing Program nor the head of the English Department evaluates our skills in the classroom. The dean never peeks in for a look. Not even the secretaries. Last year, Richard's student evaluations were down and he lost his full-time position. If he ever wants to get his full-time position back, he needs to improve his student evaluations. If he keeps giving students Cs and evaluating them on their actual performances rather than their dreams or what they think they deserve or the amount of cash they dole out in fees and tuition, his student evaluations will never improve.

That's why I tell a lot of jokes in class and take late work and give any student who appears both mean and competent one full letter grade higher than he or she deserves.

Richard, if he knew my grading techniques, would think I was a despicable sell-out.

I consider Richard to be incredibly naïve in his understanding of the system.

Come on Richard, I want to say, if you give a student a C you do it after evaluations.

Richard sits up straight. He gets out his tobacco and starts to roll a cigarette like he's trying to tune his guitar when he can't hear the notes.

I say, "What's up?" and move my arm away in case I'm making him uncomfortable.

"Not you," he says, "There, there he is," and Richard nods but doesn't raise his head.

Three young guys, all in hoodies and weird colorful hats, walk by. I know which one threatened Richard immediately by the way he turns backwards to make eye-contact with his pals then spins forward like he's dancing, like there's an audience. He talks loud and he's dressed in expensive clothes that make him look poor. He's maybe a buck-fifty, under six feet tall. The other guys are about the same. Three on two, and giving up twenty-plus years, Richard and I could still takes these guys.

"Is he looking?" Richard says.

"No," I say. "He's drinking an energy drink. I don't think he sees you."

"Thank god," Richard says. "I'm not prepared."

"There's nothing to be prepared for. The kid's a jerk."

"Maybe," Richard says, face down, puffing his cigarette like a smoke screen.

I'm sort of hoping the kid says something. I don't know why. I don't know what I'll do.

Richard says, "Tell me when he's passed."

"Almost," I say.

Then the kid leans back from his group. I mean, he really leans. He keeps walking but he's tilted so far back it's like he's falling in slow-motion and he's smiling and he points his can of energy drink at Richard and says, "How's that bow tie treating you, Professor Pussylips?"

There's a wreck on the Parkway. It's a fender-bender. The cars have pulled onto the berm, but everyone rubbernecks going by and traffic barely moves for three or four miles. I listen to NPR but they're having a pledge drive. I love public radio but it's painful when they're begging. I try another station and they're playing Bad Company. The next station plays Steve Miller. I turn off the radio. I crack the window. The cool breeze helps. The light snow helps. I turn up the heater and roll the window the rest of the way down.

When I step through the front door, Lori says, "I'm late."

I say, "Me, too. Sorry."

I want to tell her about Richard and the students who want to kill Richard, but I don't. She's moving with purpose, like a woman with two jobs and a family.

Lori's in her uniform. Her hair is wet. My daughter jumps into my arms and kisses my face. I kiss her back. I'm happy to be home. Then I'm not. My son is on the floor playing video games even though he's not allowed to play video games during the week.

My daughter, Abby, says, "Daddy, your ears are red," and tugs on each ear, up and down, like she's trying to milk my head.

"It's cold out," I say. "Brrr."

I stomp the snow off my feet. Lori looks like she's being hit with tiny jolts of electricity. When she walks, it's like she's trying to kill something on the floor.

"What's up with the video games?" I say.

"Please don't," she says. She's trying to find something in her purse. "I had papers to correct and it was the only way to get something done."

"I'm just saying."

"Well, please don't."

I give her a look. Our lives are a mad rush. I got lost with Richard and his angry students. Lori isn't ready for her second job. Everyone is hungry. It doesn't mean we should melt our kids' brains with video games when we've agreed that video games melt kids' brains.

She says, "Don't look at me like that. I had work to do. They wouldn't leave me alone."

I say, "Bullshit."

Townes doesn't hear me. He's moving Mario across the screen so Mario can eat mushrooms and double his size.

Abby says, "Oh Daddy, I missed you."

"I missed you too," I say and put her down.

I'm pissed at Lori. I know she's been running all day, preschool with Abby, lunch, cleaning, correcting papers, the bus stop for Townes, and now waitressing. I don't care.

Lori says, "Just stay away from me so I can get ready for work. That's all I'm asking."

This does not happen all the time, but it happens more than it should.

Townes says, "Dad?" like I've stepped from a cloud. He says, "Wow. You're home."

"Hey," I say. "Thanks for noticing."

Lori says, "What else was I supposed to do?"

I say, "Put him in his room. Make him read a book."

She says, "That'll work."

If she could take me in a fight, she would.

But she can't.

I would block her punches and take her in my arms and speak quietly and squeeze until she couldn't breathe.

I say, "Don't look at me like you want to punch me."

She points her keys at me and swallows whatever she was about to say.

I say, "Yeah, exactly."

She says, "Stop it." She says, "I'm dying here."

I say, "But you're not."

She says, "I am, I am," and drops her keys and bends to pick them up and stumbles and says, "Fucking great. Now I'm dizzy."

She could be dizzy. She is not dying.

The stress in our life is not as great as the stress she creates by being miserable with our stress. Last week, she sent a co-worker an email asking for his bio note for some brochure she was working on. He didn't send his bio. He didn't respond. She sent him another email. Then another. In bed that night, she said, "He's doing it on purpose." He may be. But he may not be, too. It doesn't matter. Problems are to be avoided, minimized. Lori confronts everything, escalates. Whatever is wrong becomes the focus. She takes what's bad and pulls it closer until it's the only thing she can touch.

A month ago, one of her old friends was in town for the day and wanted to know if they could get together for dinner. Lori couldn't. I was working. The kids had basketball and a play date. Lori said, "I'll see." She called everyone who had ever babysat for us and everyone who had ever babysat for us said, "I'm sorry," or, "I have to work," or, "Maybe I could do it tomorrow," but the friend was only in for six or eight hours. So Lori canceled the play date and basketball and had her friend over to the house and cooked dinner. They had some wine. It sounded fun. I came home and played with the kids and brushed their teeth and put them to bed. At ten o'clock, after the kids were asleep and the friend was on a plane, Lori said, "I can't believe I didn't correct my papers for memoir class." I knew what was happening. I started to vacuum and when I stopped she said, "Now I have to read eight chapters in the Joan Didion book." I put away the vacuum cleaner. I said, "Maybe take a bath," which is where she reads and corrects papers but she said, "I'm too tired," and she finished the dishes and stomped around the house muttering about lectures she needed to prepare and papers she needed to correct. She took off her make-up and cleaned her face with anger. She came to bed with a great thud and tossed and pulled at the covers. Then went to sleep. Then—and I'm guessing here—forgot everything that had destroyed the previous day and evening and bedtime. She woke up fine. Kissed me, made coffee, took a shower. She went to work, taught without notes or corrected papers to return, and came home in a good mood. A great mood. She poured a glass of wine. She sat down on the floor and wrapped up both our kids. I was still stunned from the previous night's stomping.

Now she moves to the bathroom. I hear the blow dryer, then the blow dryer on high. I wait for the pop, for the circuit breaker to go, and it does. The hair dryer stops and the lights go out and the music on the video game quiets.

"Shit," Lori says.

"The lights!" Abby says, but happy.

"My game!" Townes says. Then, "Mom!" drawn out in one long whine.

Lori steps from the bathroom. Her hair is frantic. She holds a purple hairbrush like a weapon. This is not all her fault. If I would have been home earlier, I could have contained the kids and she could have gotten ready at a reasonable pace. So I practice hating Richard and his stupid rock 'n' roll dreams and all the students that want to beat him senseless, but I only hate everything for a millisecond because I'm a very poor hater.

Abby says, "Tonight is dance class."

"I thought it was sign-ups," I say, but I feel like I might not sign her up. These dance studios know parents. There is often a make-up day for the make-up day.

Townes says, "Mom!"

Lori takes the brush through her hair, and I can hear it, like paper ripping.

Townes says her name again, longer, whinier.

Lori says, "Townes, don't. Do not."

He says, "But my game."

She says, "Do. Not." He starts to say something and she yells, "Not another word."

Now she's pissed at Townes for being upset that his video game was interrupted, and she's pissed at me because she thinks I'm happy that Townes is complaining about a video game that he wouldn't be playing except Lori let him play it.

I would like a nap.

I would like a sandwich and a can of diet Coke but that's unrealistic.

I say, "I'll get the lights."

Lori says, "No, I'll get it."

I say, "I'm sorry I'm pissed at you."

She says, "You're not sorry you're pissed at me."

"You're probably right," I say. "I hate when you're psycho."

I move for the stairs. Lori moves for the stairs. It would be so much easier to love each other if we could stand still for even a minute.

I say, "I have it."

She says, "No, I'm the dipshit," and she opens the door.

"I have it," I say and I head downstairs to the closet with the breakers.

It's always the same circuit, top left. I flip the switch and I hear the whole upstairs power on. Townes and Abby cheer and I hear the music Mario makes when he's on an adventure.

The lights are dim in the gameroom, only a hint of sun coming through an old glass-block window. I sit down on the couch and close my eyes. I find a pillow and get comfortable. It's easy to get comfortable. I could live down here, alone, so my family would only be noise and a few flashes at the top of the stairs.

I hear Abby call my name.

Townes yells down, "Dad, who's your favorite Mario character?"

I don't answer.

Lori is back on her hair, the blow dryer on low, the fan like a distant train. I could tell her I love her but I won't. She'll leave and I'll keep my eyes closed until the kids get hungry and remember where I am. Lori will call from work. The beers and the drunks and the waitresses will remind her to breathe and when she starts to breathe she'll remember what's important.

The bathroom door opens and Lori yells, "You better not be pissed off down there."

I say, "Make him turn off the video games."

There is Lori's voice and Townes' voice, neither happy, and Abby's singing a made-up song about something that has nothing to do with any of this. One door closes, then another.

I open my eyes. I think I could live down here on the couch in the basement but pretty soon the sun will quit shining through the block-glass window and the only sound will be the wind blowing down the chimney and out the flue. Upstairs, no matter what's happening, will start to sound like music.

'm in the kitchen making grilled cheeses when someone pounds on the door and rings the bell. Townes is off the video games. I'm making him read to Abby so they can recoup their brain losses. They're in my bedroom with a book called

Diary of a Short Fat Dork. I flip the sandwiches and turn down the heat on the stove and go to see who's calling.

It's James. He's in his work clothes, a new scarf around his neck.

"What's up?" he says.

"Not much," I say. "What's up with you?"

"Nothing at all."

"Nice scarf," I say.

"One of my students gave it to me."

James' students are always giving him scarves. They love him. The girls sometimes offer to buy him dinner. He often accepts. The guys invite him to keggers. He often declines. James, without a wife and kids or even a girlfriend, able to answer emails in the middle of the night, able to meet for coffee to discuss a story from an old student, is more like a friendly editor than a professor. He's more like a peer but smarter, the best and coolest student in the class.

I say, "What does one have to do to get a free scarf?"

He says, "I smile a lot."

"I smile a lot."

"Yeah, but you have that hideous goatee that makes you look mean. And you're fat too, that certainly doesn't help anything."

"All good points," I say. "So what's up?"

"Nothing much at all."

James never comes unannounced. He hardly comes at all. I'm happy to see him, but confused. He hasn't driven in from Pittsburgh to show me his new scarf. He hands me some sugar cookies in a plastic container from Giant Eagle and steps in from the cold. His car, still dented up, is parked at the end of the walk. The bumper appears to be tied on.

I say, "You got your car back?"

"Temporarily. I have to take it back in next week. The guy at the shop had to order a bumper or something, and I couldn't be without a ride for that long. It's a clusterfuck."

"But you're safe and sober," I say, a joke we always use.

"I'm safe even when I'm not sober," he says. Then, "That smells good."

I say, "The grilled cheeses?"

He says, "I thought Lori was making fried chicken," and I remember what I'm supposed to remember about dinner and James and his alcoholism and the trouble he's having being alone.

"Yeah," I say. "About dinner."

"Forget about dinner?"

"We have grilled cheeses," I say. "Lori had to work. I got confused. Plus, I thought you were suicidal and shouldn't be alone. Then I sort of forgot about you being suicidal. Between Lori and work and the kids, I completely forgot about you."

"That's all right," he says. "At home all I have is soup. It might not even be soup. It might be creamed corn."

"These are some great grilled cheeses," James says.

"It's the soup," I say.

We're having spicy tomato soup flavored with crushed red peppers. It's from Costco. It comes in a gallon jug. James and I are on our third and fourth bowls respectively. I'll send him home with the rest of the gallon. Maybe some cheese and bread and butter, too.

I say, "Why would you buy creamed corn?"

"I think it's from before."

Before is the word he uses for when he had a girlfriend. He is neither happy nor sad about this, just factual.

"So what's up with the alcoholism?" I say. "Are you craving all the time?"

The kids play in the other room. They've eaten their grilled cheeses and now are jumping from the coffee table to the couch to the floor so it sounds like an earthquake.

James says, "It's not the cravings. It's more like—I don't know—that I just gave in to the cravings after not drinking for eleven years. I know I wrecked my car and I've been living on this shitty salary from our job for years now so I've never been able to save any money but I'm still shocked I went on a bender." He finishes a grilled cheese. When James eats, he eats. I'll probably have to make him two more. He says, "It's more like scared. Frankly, that's it. I'm afraid of what I'll do even though I don't feel like doing anything right now but eating. Worse things have happened to me in the past, work stuff and love stuff, but it never set me off. Then the car and the money did. Part of being sober is being able to predict what will make you drink and avoiding it. I couldn't avoid getting in a wreck on an icy road. I can't avoid being broke. I don't know. Maybe I need an AA meeting."

"AA meetings are great," I say, though I know James hates AA meetings.

He says, "AA meetings are fucking ridiculous," and he picks up his soup bowl and slurps.

He tried AA when he first quit drinking but all the attention to a higher power and sharing stories and cookie trays and coffee with extra sugar made him want to lick the inside of a rum bottle and disappear. Writing and reading made him want to get healthy, to be lucid and productive. That was his AA, his therapy, his prayers, whatever. But now he hasn't been writing. He teaches books instead of reading them. To teach a book is to reduce it to a political speech, a pep rally. The essence is all scraped out. If you can't or don't read books and love them, then you can't write. If you depend on the reading and writing to be sober, you're fucked.

"AA is retarded," James says. "I'm dreading going."

I say, "I'll go with you."

"Really?"

"Sure."

"You'll hate it."

"I like it in movies," I say. "They always make it seem sort of sexy and desperate."

He says, "It's worse than drinking. It's the worst. Right now, I'm not thinking: I've relapsed with my drinking. I'm thinking: I'm about to relapse with my AA." He says, "You read my story yet?"

He's talking about the story he handed me earlier in the day, the one about his excellent main character Harold, the one I really wanted to read.

I say, "Honestly," and give him a look. "I forgot you were going to kill yourself."

We're playing hide and seek. I'm in the bathtub with Abby, the shower curtain pulled but not the whole way. We're having a very hard time being quiet. Abby's a giggler. I'm a giggler, too. Townes is under the bed in my room, wrapped in a blanket. It's his only hiding spot, but with the blanket and the darkness, it's a good one. James is seeking. I've read his story and it's great, Harold looking for work, Harold drunk and naked at the zoo. A few line edits and it will be ready to go out into the world. James is happy and confident. Maybe he will not need

AA. He steps into the bathroom and turns on the light.

James says, "Anyone in here?" It's a monster voice, a call from a cave.

I hold Abby tight. We manage not to giggle. We are sitting down, hunched over, Abby between my legs like I am her boat. I wish I could always be her boat. I press my lips to her head. James starts to move the shower curtain but stops. Abby reaches back and touches my face.

James says, "Hello in here?"

We say nothing back.

I am so happy to be with my family and my best friend, waiting for my wife to come home so I can be good to her when she is exhausted and needs it most. I will not get to correct my papers or do my lecture notes for school tomorrow, and I do not care and I will not care. I will get by on charm and authority and, if necessary, cruelty.

Abby turns and raises her eyebrows. I raise mine back.

James says, "Nobody in here?" He says, "I didn't think so," and turns out the light and moves down the hall.

Abby whispers, "We have to move."

I whisper back, "Shhh, this is perfect."

"We have to move, Daddy, to the closet."

I don't understand her logic but I move. We climb out of the tub and tiptoe across the bathroom floor but when we step into the hallway, James is there, in the dark, hiding, waiting.

He screams, "Got ya!" and it is so loud and unexpected that a short girl-scream flies out of my mouth like an unexpected cough.

Abby, really surprised, not used to adults playing to win, turns and screams and backs away from me, but not down the hall, across it, two steps to the open door that leads downstairs. For a second, she is perched on the edge, reaching forward, the soles of her feet split by the floor and the drop, moving so slow I can see her toes reaching, stretching out for something to balance or hold. I lunge but too late, she's gone, straight back, headfirst, like a sled going down a very steep hill, like James, drunk, down the stairs at the Cathedral, but Abby is soft on her head and back and everywhere else that matters.

"Abby!" I say, like my voice is a rope that will stop the fall. Nothing stops the fall.

Abby slides fast but it feels longer as she hits each stair, her screams like accordion sounds, until she turns at the bottom and her head collides with the wall.

"Abby!" I say and start down the stairs, jumping steps.

"I'm fine," Abby says, instantly standing up, holding her head, but she's crying. She's crying and saying, "I'm fine, I'm fine," and I pick her up, so glad she can stand, that it's not her neck or back, that all the muscles work, and she says, genuinely mad, "James, you scared me!"

James, still standing at the top of the stairs, scared and embarrassed as only someone without kids who has just scared a kid can be, says, "I'm so sorry, Abby, I didn't mean to."

"It's okay," she says, still crying, and hugs me with her arms and legs at the same time, her chin on my shoulder.

When I touch the top of her head, I can already feel a lump. When I carry her to the top of the stairs, I touch her head again and there is blood, not a lot, but blood.

James says, "I'm so sorry," but to me this time, then again to Abby.

"Hey," I say. "Can you watch Townes for a little? I'm going to take her to the hospital." I show James my hand so Abby can't see the blood.

"I'm going to get a shot," Abby says and starts to bawl. Kids hate shots. Abby hates shots. During flu season, when she hears us talking about vaccinations, she will sometimes cry until she passes out.

"You're not going to get a shot," I say, though she may need to get a get shot.

"Really?" Abby says, happy, relieved. Then, not believing, "I'm going to get a shot."

"They don't give shots for bumped heads," I say.

"I'm going to get a shot," she says, bawling.

This is how it goes until we get to the hospital, shot and no shot, screaming and not screaming, until the young doctor in glasses with thick black hipster frames assures her she will not get a shot and the nurse gives Abby a stuffed animal to distract her while the doctor goes behind Abby and gives her a shot with a long terrifying needle which Abby either doesn't feel or notice. The needle comes out. The doctor puts it under a white towel, out of sight.

The doctor says, "That boo-boo isn't too bad."

"Not too bad," Abby says, holding a stuffed bear. "Can I get some ice?"

The doctor laughs and says, "For your head? Sure."

"Thank you," I say.

"Not a problem," he says.

Doctors are like magicians sometimes, strange men in funny outfits with tricks for everything our imaginations need.

"Really, thank you," I say.

"She's a good one," he says. "Is she always this happy?"

"Mostly," I say.

"Am I all better?" Abby says to the doctor.

"Almost," the doctor says. "I'll get you some ice. Then in one minute I want to put a string band-aid right across your boo-boo then we'll be all done."

"Oh that's great, Doctor," Abby says. "Thank you!"

The doctor tells me he wants to make sure it's numb, that we'll give it a minute or two extra. He leaves the room. Everything is so fast, so professional. The tools are all on a small table, little props off camera so Abby can't see the points and edges.

I hold Abby's hand.

The nurse, probably fifty, skinny yet flabby in her scrubs, sits in a chair and says, "My feet are so tired. How are your feet?" and she hugs Abby's feet with her nurse hands.

"My feet are so tired, too," Abby says and yawns.

"We should get a feet nap," the nurse says.

Abby says, "Yes, a feet nap," then talks and laughs, about her feet, about her fall, about James and Townes and school and her toys. Anything. The hospital is like a playdate, a game.

I think about Townes, how hard this would be for him, how, like his mother, he goes towards the darkness, the harshest of realities. He couldn't be tricked into a shot. He wouldn't have ever let the doctor behind his back.

"What do you do?" the nurse says to me.

"I teach," I say.

"Oh, where at?"

"Down at Pitt."

"Oh," she says and smiles. "You're a professor."

"Something like that," I say.

"Isn't your daddy modest?" she says to Abby.

"My daddy is awesome," Abby says.

The doctor comes back and says, "Are we almost done?"

"Almost done," Abby says.

He walks behind her and in seconds puts in three stitches while Abby talks about her Littlest Petshop collection with the nurse who, despite her wrinkled face, looks like I remember feeling when I was a much younger man.

close the front door with my foot. Abby is in my arms, sound asleep. Outside, the doors on the minivan are open. When we left the hospital, Abby said, "Daddy, that was so great," and, "I can't wait to tell Mommy." Someone needs to tell Mommy, but not now, not until Mommy is home and can see everything is fine, can touch her daughter and see the stitches and know the bad is over and the rest is the healing.

Inside, I smell soup. I smell the grilled cheeses, too, but they're cold, distant. I am hungrier than I should be.

Townes is out on the couch, snoring little puffs, his head in James' lap. James rubs Townes' ears, probably afraid to stop, probably afraid to break another child. It's 10:30, past everyone's bedtimes. The TV is on, cartoons. James looks white and blind, his glasses folded on the table, his eyes red and glossy in the dim light.

James points at Abby.

I nod: okay, everything is fine.

James mouths, "Thank god."

I carry Abby to bed. She's easy to undress and get into pajamas. I turn her on her side, one ear and cheek on the pillow, her stitches not against anything. I kiss her shoulder, the safest spot, and tell her I love her.

Townes is a ton, ninety pounds. I have to lift with my back to get him off James, off the couch. He barely fits down the hall in my arms. When I put him to bed, he wakes up.

He says, "Is Abby okay?"

Townes loves his sister like he loves nothing else or no one else in this world.

I say, "She's fine. Just a bump."

"Any blood?" he says.

"No blood," I say.

"I was really scared for her."

"She's going to be fine," I say.

"I have to pee," he says.

Townes stumbles down the hall and into the bathroom. He pees. I can hear him hit the water, one loud stream. He probably needs to brush his teeth, but I let it go. Back in bed, I fix his blanket. I tell him I love him but he's already gone.

In the living room, I tell James, "I have to eat something."

"Jesus, yes," he says.

"Grilled cheeses?" I say.

"Yes," he says. "With some more of that good tomato soup."

"It's not your fault," I say.

"Tell me that again," he says.

It's almost one when Lori gets home. I'm back in bed, wide-awake, exhausted, bored, trying to read an old collection of Chinese poetry but unable to concentrate. I've been up ten times in the last two hours to check on Abby and every time I check on Abby, I check on Townes.

In the dining room, Lori drops her keys on the table. Maybe it's a handful of change, the tips she couldn't turn into bills. On the best days, I know everything everyone does in this house by sound. Today is not that day. I can still see Abby falling.

I put down my book. I turn on the TV.

Lori steps into the bedroom and says, "I'm sorry I was so grumpy. I'm sorry about the video games. I'm sorry about everything."

"It's okay," I say.

She comes near the bed and I pull her in, on top of me, then over me so I can pin her down with my thigh. She's in my arms. I squeeze, hard, until she laughs, until she says, "Okay," and knows everything is fine.

She says, "Watch it, big guy," and kisses my nose.

I kiss her nose back. She closes her eyes. Some nights we fall asleep with the TV on, with the lights on, like we're at an airport, like we've been exhausted by travel.

I mean to tell her about Abby but Abby is fine. Abby is dreaming. In the morning she will tell me what she always tells me, "I dreamed about unicorns." But Lori has been ready for night since evening or maybe afternoon or even morning, and she will not sleep if she knows Abby has stitches, if she knows there was a fall and blood and a doctor with a needle and thread. I'm already nervous and awake, and I'll be nervous and awake all night. I kiss Lori. I don't mind being awake with the kids. There are nights when I want nothing but to be awake with my kids.

She says, "I get so grumpy some days."

"You do," I say. "You can be a miserable twat," but I say it nice.

She says, "I need to make more money."

I say, "I need to make more money."

She says, "We should sell books and get famous."

"Or sell books and become recluses."

"Or sell books and not become recluses. We could just sell books and get famous and have legendary parties and then promote our friends until they sell books and get famous."

"Yeah," I say. "Or you can just go get a shower and come back to bed and I'll eat your pussy while I squeeze your ass."

"You are a good good man," she says.

"You are a good good woman," I say, "when you're not a miserable turd bitch."

She stands up and starts to undress. Her shirt is off, her

bra comes off. Her tits are out. I've never grown tired of her tits, the way she fluffs each breast every time she gets naked, even now on a terrible day when I'm tired of almost everything else. If I could come on her nipples, things would be better. She double-fluffs her breasts. I lean over the bed like a lizard and lick her stomach. How awake we are about to become.

How exhausted tomorrow.

She says, "I'm done being a grump." She says, "Seriously." She says, "I was embarrassed the whole time I was at work. I felt like everyone knew I was a terrible wife and mother."

"You are a great wife and mother," I say.

"Here," she says and she strips off her pants and turns and bends over and shows me her ass as she leaves our room and heads for the bath.

It's a great ass.

She's a great wife.

It's morning. Early, not quite light. I hear Lori's voice but when I reach for her, she's not there. I am naked from last night, the covers across my middle. I try the other side of the bed. Lori says my name again. I open my eyes.

Lori is above me, Abby in her arms. Abby is asleep or sleepy. Lori points at Abby's head and mouths some words. Lori looks scared. She's in her red pajamas. Her hair is lopsided like a crazy person's or a bad wig.

"It's fine," I say in a whisper. "Is she awake?"

Lori whispers, "Are these stitches?" She says, "Is this a cut?" Lori could be crying.

"Yes," I say, standing up.

It's lighter out than I thought, the sun pushing through the clouds, pushing through our wooden shades. I take Abby in my arms. Lori resists for a second, then gives over. Abby's sound asleep, a gentle snore coming from her nose. My eyes adjust. The stitches look great, no bleeding, nothing. On and off all night, I've been up, checking. I look at the clock. It's barely six. I get my legs and walk. Abby breathes deep but doesn't wake. I am so sleepy, everything's an effort. I've been out for less than two hours and before that it was one hour and so on. In the hall I adjust Abby in my arms and open her door with my foot. If she wakes up, no one will sleep. There will be cereal and stuffed animals and she'll want to get ready for preschool even though preschool is hours away. I move into her room and get her back in bed. I check her pillow for blood, but nothing, not a drop. Abby still doesn't wake. I listen to her breathe. Normal. All the falling and hospital moments and her fears and the healing have kept her asleep. I touch her forehead. I fix the covers and the doll she shares her bed with. I move away like a spy, like I've been moving all night.

Lori says, "What happened?"

I finish closing Abby's door and head back to our bedroom where we can talk. Even Townes, an early riser, won't be up for at least an hour or more.

Lori says, "Those are stitches, right?"

I say, "She fell down the stairs and bumped her head. I took her to the hospital to make sure everything was okay. The doctor gave her three tiny stitches."

Lori says, "Oh my god. I'm nauseous."

She goes white, weak. I wait for her to fall. She doesn't. She steps to the bed and sits on the edge. I'm still trying to fall back to sleep. Lori hugs herself, confused. I know her thoughts: I am a terrible mother; I should have been here; no one told me my daughter fell down the stairs and got stitches because I am a terrible mother and I wasn't here; they should have told me; he should have told me; he thinks I'm a terrible mother.

"It's not a big deal," I say. "Come back to bed."

"It is a big deal," she says, but quietly. "I'm so scared."

"It's not," I say. "I would have told you." I prop myself up with pillows. I say, "You needed sleep. I wanted you to sleep. You wouldn't have slept if you'd known Abby had stitches. I was happy to get up and check on her last night. Everything was fine. I would have woken you up if it wasn't."

"God," she says but getting back in bed. "Okay. Everything is fine. Okay." She pulls up some covers. I pull her close. She says, "My heart's going crazy."

I want this to be a test. I want us to pass this then to pass every other test we have to take. I want us to do better. We cannot live in a constant state of panic.

Lori says, "Okay, I'm calming." She says, "Thank you." She says, "Did I say that yet? Thank you? Thank you. I can't believe you took her to the hospital by yourself."

"It was all fine," I say.

I close my eyes and hold Lori, one hand under her head, one hand over.

Lori says, "Thank you," and kisses me. "Thank you again."

"It's okay," I say. "Go to sleep."

"I just wish I was here all the time. I wish I could clone myself."

"I was here," I say. "I'm good at this stuff."

"But you're not the mother."

"No," I say. "You're right. I'm not the mother," which is what she needs to hear, but what I mean, I think, is: no, I'm not the mother; I'm something new, a father; a father can be as good as a mother or better or just a father; let's not pretend we don't need that.

III

Six kids come to my first class. Nineteen are enrolled. I give everyone ten bonus points for showing up. They seem happy. They don't look at me but they smile.

I say, "Why don't we just talk about the poems today. What you guys liked and didn't like or what was inspiring or what pissed you off. I'll save my lecture for next class when the rest of the students show up. How's that sound?"

Nobody says anything.

I look towards my two smart students, the girls who smoke weed before class. Both are diligently flipping through their books, either trying to find something to say or putting up a force-field to keep me from asking questions. Even the great students here often don't do the readings. The average students do the readings and don't understand what they've read. The bad students don't buy the books. Most of the students are bad.

I pick up my own book, the one covered in notes.

It's *The Lunch Poems* by Frank O'Hara. I want to talk about pop culture and the city and how poetry can hold both these things and still be fun.

"Which book are we doing?" someone says.

"Frank O'Hara," I say.

"My roommate says he's a fag."

"He's actually dead," I say. "But when he was alive, he was gay."

"Right, so he was a fag."

"Right, we call it gay now."

"Yeah," he says and laughs.

I look around the room for help.

No one looks back.

So Frank O'Hara was gay. Frank O'Hara was everything. He was a social butterfly in New York, rushing from party to party, writing poems in between. He drank and got laid and made everyone fall in love with him. A critic said, "To read a Frank O'Hara poem is take the subway to the museum, see a Jackson Pollock, rush downtown for a movie, stopping only long enough to grab a Coke." I tell this to my students. They nod, sort of. I can't remember the critic's name. My students don't know there are critics, that there are people who read and interpret books and get paid for it. Maybe there won't be critics soon. Maybe there won't be books.

Angie, one of my good students, adjusts her knit Rastafarian beret and says, "I just got him. Like, got him got him, you know? I really understood him. Like, I don't know who Lana Turner is in that one poem, but I know who Lana Turner is because he shows me who Lana Turner is. If that makes sense."

I say, "It makes sense. Anyone else? Who is Lana Turner?"

Angie says, "She's like an actress, right?"

"Definitely," I say. "Lana Turner was a femme fatale."

"What's a femme fatale?" someone says.

"It's a Velvet Underground song," Sam says. Sam is my student in a green Army jacket who writes poems about darkness and suicide and sometimes moans when he disagrees with another student or something I say.

"It's true," I say. "It's a great Velvet Underground song. Thanks, Sam."

Sam grunts at me and shows his teeth, the bottom row. His entire forehead is three thick lines. Then I remember: he wants to be called Samuel. I don't feel like calling him Samuel. I feel like he should quit grunting in my class and baring his fangs.

"Sam," I say. "I didn't hear you."

He puts his face down on the desk. He covers his head with his arms. He talks to the desk in a low voice. The voice is either scary or it's supposed to be scary.

Angie, being kind, says, "I think Samuel isn't feeling well today." She looks at me when she says Samuel like I need to be reminded.

I shake my head. Samuel moans. He slaps the back of his own head with his palms, three times in quick succession, like an angry gorilla. I am over Samuel. I think of ways to get Samuel alone and beat him with my fists then tell security he threatened me.

I say, "Maybe Samuel should go home if he's not feeling well today."

Angie looks at me like I am making it worse.

I say, "Sam, go home."

Sam doesn't say anything.

The class, four other people and Angie, look at me like I'm throwing rocks at a rabid dog. Sam is either a rabid dog or not, I don't know, and I'm not sure I care. I do care. I hate him. I hate him more than someone my age should hate someone his age.

I say, "Sam, either pick your head up and talk like a normal person or leave the class."

Sam picks his head up. He pushes his hair from his face. He nods, not peaceful, but not sarcastic, not confrontational.

I say, "Do you want to be here?"

He says, "Yeah." He says, "This is the only class I come to."

"Here's the deal," I say. "Attendance is no longer mandatory. If you don't want to come, don't come. It won't hurt your grade. Get the assignments from another student, turn them in to me, and that's fine. That's it. I will grade your assignment even if I don't know who you are."

Sam keeps nodding, like I am being reasonable, like it's my job to degrade students and treat them like 4th graders. Everyone nods, the whole class.

I say, "But if you come to class, there's no more moaning and grunting. This is for everyone. If you come to class, come to class. Buy the book. Read the book. Have something to say. That's it. No more messing around. If you want to learn, learn. If you don't want to learn, leave. I cannot force you to learn. If I could force you to learn, I wouldn't."

Sam, looking sane, looking like he's been drugged back to reality, looking like he's been to rehab and therapy and bootcamp, all in six seconds, says, "Fair enough."

No one else says anything.

I say, "Class dismissed."

No one moves.

I say, "Leave." I say, "Now."

Jim, Kentucky Jim, the alcoholic head of the writing department, steps from the elevator I'm trying to enter. I hope he doesn't see me but he does. I can smell the whiskey. I know he is not supposed to drink whiskey. He's a diabetic. If he drinks, he's supposed drink vodka and diet Sprite or vodka and Crystal Light Lemonade or vodka and whatever else that does not have sugar. Kentucky Jim has three toes on his left foot. He showed me his big toe on his right foot once. It was brown and stunk. Right now he has on jeans and boots and some sort of flannel. His head is shaved to a crew and he has a short, unkempt beard.

"Old Danny Charles," he says. "You pussyhound. When did you start working here?"

I look around. It's not 1967. It's not 1977. You can't walk around drunk with your balls out and expect to keep your job. I know this. Kentucky Jim does not.

Kentucky Jim got hired in 1971 without a book. He published one crappy collection of short stories about moonshiners and got tenure. For the next forty years, he smoked dope with every degenerate grad student (myself included) to pass through the university, and seldom wrote. There was a rumor he had a three-volume fictitious biography of Richard Brautigan written and stacked on a shelf in his office, but I've never seen it. No one has.

Mostly it was a lifestyle. Kentucky Jim lived like a writer, like what a writer, a beatnik I guess, was supposed to live like. He drank and got philosophical and tried to get laid. The parties at his farm outside the city were supposedly legendary. He owned a llama. Occasionally a local entertainment journalist would show up, get drunk, and mention something in his column in the book section of the Pittsburgh Press. "Professor Jim Rayger pulled out the stops last night, roasting a pig and serving homemade wine for his friend, the fellow writer T.S. McClasky, in town for a reading tonight at the Cathedral of Learning."

The roasted pig was there, but not much else. The rest was chatter and cigarette smoke. The older adult writers stayed in one place while the student writers drank and acted silly in another. When everyone got drunk, there would be some mixing, some idol worshipping, but not much, and as the years came on, the parties became boring to the point of stuffiness.

The roasted pigs were long gone. So was the wine. Now it was vegan pizzas and fancy micro-brewed beer. There were still writers around but mostly it operated like a business lunch. People with jobs at the university made sure to come by and flatter Jim to keep their jobs. People without jobs—local writers and recently finished grad students—flattered Jim hoping to get the jobs that the other writers were so desperate to keep. It was all degrading, all the antithesis of what writing and teaching was supposed to be, what we imagined it to be when we all started reading books and going to school and publishing and getting drunk at Jim's farm.

I hung around sometimes when I was younger. I brought my own beer, seldom smoked dope. I hoped for something, some university job that paid the bills, but never asked, thinking my work, my publishing, would get me noticed. It never did. I applied for jobs. Jim never hired me. He hired other people, people who played in bands and other people who liked to smoke dope at his house and other people who knew people Jim had drank and doped with years ago. When I got hired, Jim was on sabbatical, and it was a black woman who was interested in black poets who hired me. I didn't ask why. But I didn't feel obligated to pretend to be Jim's pal anymore. I felt stupid that I'd ever tried to be his friend.

Now Jim has his arm on my shoulder.

He says, "You look like a man who needs a drink."

"I have a class to teach," I say.

"Who's the boss here?" he says and laughs.

"I'd love to have a drink with you later," I say.

"Later might not exist for me," he says. "I'm old. And I'm a drunk."

This is all charming but it's not. Jim can be the drunk writer. It's not a shtick. He's true to it. One of his pals, after a quadruple bypass, went back to drinking and cocaine and went on a bender that wiped his life away—stroked out at sixty-six, dead in a bar in San Francisco. "A champion," Jim said. "That guy was a warrior." Jim was right. The guy was a warrior. Went down like he wanted to. Died drunk where he planned. Jim is a warrior, too. He's allowed to be. He has tenure and can't be fired. He has money, lots of it, and not from writing, but from teaching, from pretending to teach, from fucking around with students and being a pal and getting young people who like to read Kurt Vonnegut stoned on Kentucky grass.

But Jim would step over me if I were in trouble with the department. If a student reported me drunk, Jim would write me up and pretend like it was the system. He once warned me, "You teach a lot of that druggie lit in your classes. Don't expect me to bail you out when the stiffs in the Literature Department start to complain." Last year, he didn't renew Richard's contract, Richard my officemate, the one making nine grand and getting threatened by students. Richard sent Jim an email asking why or if there was anything he could do. Jim wrote back, "Out of my hands." Jim is a wild man when it is convenient to be a wild man. He is the professorial head of the Writing Department when he needs that. You don't know what you get. He gives you whatever is best for Kentucky Jim.

Now Jim says, "You need a drink, you old pussyhound. How's that beautiful wife of yours? She hasn't left you yet?"

"Not yet," I say.

"Let's have that drink."

"I really have class."

"Not anymore," he says. He yells to the secretaries' office down the hall, door open but far away, "Stephanie, cancel Dan

Charles' classes for this afternoon. We are about to have an important meeting."

Stephanie sticks her head out into the hall. She is maybe fifty, smart, a former nurse, working for the university for less money so her kids can go to college on the cheap.

She says, "Jim, did you just call me?" Then, "Hi Dan."

I say, "Hi Stephanie."

Jim says, "Stephanie, could you please cancel this man's afternoon classes? He and I are about to engage in a meeting that may save this department."

Stephanie looks at me. Her hair is gray. My hair is going gray. If I keep this job, my kids will go to school for free too. I wave, meaning: whatever, okay, I'm sorry.

She says, "Sure, classes cancelled."

Jim says, "That's what I'm talking about."

I say, "Thanks Stephanie."

She says, "You guys have a good meeting."

I talk Jim out of his office and into a bar. Jim walks with a cane so I pick him up in front of the Cathedral and drive south to Carson Street, to Dee's Bar, the best dive in the city, open at eleven and only a little crowded. We try the barstools, but they're bad for Jim's circulation. We move to a booth. The booths are new, newish. They used to be ripped vinyl. Now the vinyl has been replaced and the color toned down from red to beige. I get a bottle of Coors Light. Jim gets a whiskey. I pay for the round. I was hoping Jim had some sort of department credit card. Jim probably doesn't even know that almost everyone in the department is broke or he doesn't care or like so many writers with money he thinks being a broke writer is romantic.

"Should you be drinking that whiskey?" I say.

"What are you, my third wife?" Jim says. He looks around the bar. Jim is not a bar person or he hasn't been for years. Real people drink in bars, ones who would step on his diabetic toes. Jim says, "What the fuck kind of jukebox is that thing? It looks like a video game. You can't get country music on that fucker."

"That is an internet jukebox," I say.

"I don't even know what that means."

"It means it plays country music and whatever other music you want it to play."

"Yeah?" Jim says. He sips his whiskey.

"Give me a buck and I'll play you some Hank Williams."

Jim goes for his wallet. He's not flexible, even to get his arm behind his back, and it's an awkward minute before he pulls out a wad of cash.

I say, "You always keep that much dough on you?"

"Just when I'm drunk," he says.

"You must be pretty drunk," I say.

There are fifties and twenties galore wrapped around fives and tens and ones. It must be a couple thousand dollars shaped into a warped green paper egg held together with a rubber band. I take two fives. I take three fifties.

I say, "That'll take care of the Hank Williams and I'll get you a bottle of whiskey."

Jim says, "Get yourself something more than a Coors Light."

"I'll do that," I say

The clock on the wall says 11:11. When I'm done with the jukebox, it sings "I Saw the Light" and "The Angel of Death" and, while we're on God and dying, "You Gotta Move" by Mississippi Fred McDowell. I place an order and the bartender delivers a bottle of whiskey, a bottle of vodka, ice, limes, glasses, and a beer to our table. Everything top shelf.

Jim says, "Cheers, you young motherfucker. I'll be dead when you're getting started." Jim raises his whiskey glass.

"You should have been dead years ago, you hideous old hillbilly fuck," I say and raise my beer bottle in one hand and my vodka-lime in the other.

Jim is ranting. He's sweating. He's not being loud, but intense. Every drink or so, he stands up and stretches his legs. It's the circulation. Or he needs a hip replacement. Or he's just old and drunk and needs to stand. I've never listened so much in my life. When I can't listen anymore, I take Jim's money and plug it into the jukebox. You can get a lot of songs about death and god on a jukebox that connects to the world. I play as many as I can. Now it's Johnny Cash. He's singing "Do Lord," which I remember from vacation bible school when I was six or seven. I buy bags of Hot Fries and Herr's Barbecue Chips from the snack machine and give them to the old men at the bar. I get another beer. I tip the bartender a five on a two-dollar bottle. At the table, Jim's pile of bills has barely diminished.

I don't know the time. If I look at my watch again, Jim will say, "I see, I see. Someone's got something better to do than drink with Ol' Jim." I guess it's after lunch. People were here eating fish sandwiches and fries and now they're gone.

Jim says, "You're my best friend." Then, "Not my real best friend, but for this afternoon." He says, "My best friend in the department which isn't saying a lot, but I like you, you old cunt-lapper." He says, "You drink. No one drinks anymore. If I'm going to have a best friend, he has to drink." He says, "Work on that bottle, you diabolical madman. Try snorting it.

It's faster." Jim's pretty funny. I'm drunk enough to like it, to dismiss it, to live with it and know it's better than teaching Introduction to Fiction. Jim says, "You're about the only one I can trust." He doesn't trust me. I trust him less. His whiskey bottle is half gone. I'm about the same with my vodka bottle, maybe a little less, plus four or five beer bottles lined up in the corner of the table like a make-shift town.

Jim says, "You want me to tell you a story?"

"Sure," I say. "It's about time you start making sense."

"I'm making sense."

"The fuck you are," I say.

"Well, I'm trying," he says and raises his whiskey and I clink it with my bottle.

Jim says, "Thanks for drinking with an old man."

"Any time, you fucking letch," I say.

The more sarcastic I am, the more Jim likes me. The meaner I am, the nicer he gets. I could punch him in the liver and get promoted. But all I want is to keep my job. It's that time of the year, late winter, when all of us, most of us in the department, have to apply for the same jobs we already hold. Then, for reasons unknown, some of us are kept and some are not. I assume this meeting means something, that I have been summoned and crowned. My job will keep being my job. The rest is a formality. All my credentials aside, I have drunk enough vodka and listened to enough bullshit to maintain my employment. Jim does this every March. He singles out a couple lecturers, usually women he wants to screw, and buys them drinks and flirts and tells them Ol' Jim has it taken care of, their jobs are secure.

Jim says, "You know how I got into teaching?"

"You got a degree and applied, then after an interview they hired you?"

"Bullshit!" he says and almost spills his drink. "There was nothing like that back then. I've had two real teaching jobs in my life. Two. This one and another one down in Florida. You know how I got the one down in Florida?"

"You sucked someone's dick."

"I have never sucked a dick in my life," Jim says. "But I do not judge those who do."

I say, "I'm guessing you didn't apply for it like a normal person."

"You're fucking right," he says and drinks. His mustache, which is longer than the rest of his scraggly beard, is filled with whiskey. I can see the brown drops in the white hairs before Jim wipes them away with the back of his fist. He says, "You know Harry Crews?"

I say, "I've read his books."

"See, I knew I picked the right person. Nobody fucking reads Harry Crews anymore. Harry Crews is a saint, a fucking moral titan."

Harry Crews is a Southern writer. He holds a black belt in karate and was, from what I've read, a serious weightlifter. I imagine he is Jim's age and like Jim almost dead from drinking and drugging. Crews was popular in the 70s. He wrote novels and he wrote a column for *Esquire*. Some of his novels, weird as they are, were exceptional, especially *The Gypsy's Curse*, a novel narrated by a deaf-mute with stumps for legs who walks on his hands. The columns were always outrageous and fun, and Crews would go anywhere to find a story: dog fights, cock fights, even out on the Appalachian Trail, drunk and taking acid.

I say, "I like Harry Crews but are you really going to call him a moral titan?"

"A moral titan," Jim says. "Absolutely."

"Did you see that documentary they did on him?"

"Hell no. They did a documentary on Harry Crews?"

"I saw a clip from it a couple years ago. He was raving about being drunk every day for thirty years. He looked crippled."

"He's a tough motherfucker."

"Not exactly a moral titan."

"Try being drunk every day for thirty years," Jim says.

"I'd love to."

Jim says, "Ah, you made me lose my fucking point."

I know his point, but I'm not ready to steer him back. I want to talk some more about Harry Crews. I want to talk about drinking and drugs. I want to ask Jim why he hasn't written another book since he got tenure thirty-some years ago. I want to ask why Harry Crews, after years of writing brilliant books, starting writing shit and hasn't stopped. All his recent novels are populated by caricatures who do violence to other caricatures who walk around trailer parks shitting themselves and having sex with midgets.

I say, "Harry Crews hasn't written a good novel in thirty years."

Jim says, "You believe that?"

"Hell yes."

"Like what?"

"Like that last one," I say. "Whatever the hell it was called. *The Mulching of America* if that was the last one. It was unreadable. It starts with a soap salesman getting his ass kicked—and I don't mean beat-up, I mean literally someone kicking his ass over and over while he tries to walk home—until he shits himself. It's like undergraduate writing, frat-boy writing." I'm not even sure I'm remembering the novel exactly, except that it was awful and that Harry Crews should have been ashamed. I say, "It's like he started reading Chuck Palahnuik at seventy years old and got inspired to fuck a donkey with a pool hose or something."

"I think I might have missed that one," Jim says.

"You should read it," I say. "It'll fuck up your whole week."

Jim says, "Maybe he didn't need to keep writing great books. He wrote great books. Great books forgive terrible books. Maybe what Harry Crews needs to do is die. I hope not, but that's probably true. Once he's gone, we'll know what's great, and the bad books will get buried with their author, that moral titan Harry Crews."

"Maybe," I say because it's the most sense Jim has made in hours. Maybe Harry Crews is already dead, and we haven't heard because nobody cares about books anymore. Maybe tomorrow Jim and I will wake up and pull the best Harry Crews books from our shelves and give them to the people who need them most. I say, "Your first teaching job. That was your point."

"Yes, my first teaching job!" Jim says and rubs his buzzed hair with a paper napkin. "Harry Crews. That's it. Harry Crews got me my first teaching job down in Florida. No interview. Not a fucking thing. I had a story in *The North Florida Review*, which Harry edited, and I was driving around that summer and I got to Florida and called Harry up. I told him I loved his novels and he'd just published my story and would he like to get a drink or two. So we got a drink. We got about ten thousand drinks. Harry had an old motorcycle and I had a big Harley I'd won in a poker game somewhere in New Orleans and we drove from shit bar to shit bar, terrorizing Floridians."

I say, "So how'd Harry Crews get you the job?"

Jim takes a long pull on his whiskey. I like this more than I should. Old writers. Old stories. If I could terrorize Floridians, I would terrorize Floridians, with or without Harry Crews.

Jim says, "I need limes. This whiskey is getting old.

Sometimes a lime will bring it back to life." He stands up.

I say, "I'll get your limes."

Jim can barely stand. He leans on the table. It's the booze, but it's his body. All that sugar in the whiskey is doing something to his blood. Or his hips are not used to being crammed in a booth and his knees are busted and barely bend.

He says, "A man needs to earn his keep."

"I don't know if getting a lime is earning your keep."

"Probably not," he says and straightens up. "But I still have to do it." Jim moves towards the bar like an old three-legged horse. Nothing—his feet, his legs, his spine—appears to work well together anymore. He's more like a door that's been ripped from the hinges than a person. When he gets to the bar, he's out of breath. When he gets back, he falls into the booth, not spilling a single lime wedge from the bowl the bartender filled.

Jim says, "Okay." He says, "My breath." He says, "I think you stole my breath, you old cunt-lapper. What a terrible thing to do."

"That was a fucking adventure," I say. "I thought I was going to have to catch you."

"No," he says. "But you might have to carry me out of here, Rio-Bravo style, my arm over your shoulder while you help me gimp along."

"I've been waiting to help you gimp along," I say.

Jim takes a breath. He squeezes three tiny lime wedges into his whiskey. He adds some water from an Aquafina bottle I bought from the machine an hour ago.

He says, "Harry Crews. Okay. So we start drinking on a Thursday. I remember it was a Thursday because it wasn't the weekend. By the weekend, we were best friends. Stayed drunk on Friday and Saturday. Saturday night we're in this biker place in Georgia, I think. We may have crossed state lines.

"Anyway, Harry asks me if I'd like a teaching gig with him. The university is hiring a professor for a one-year appointment and he'd like it to be me. Of course I was flattered as hell. Harry Crews was only a couple years older than me, but he was big time. He had two or three novels on big presses. Tenured teaching job. I don't think he was writing for *Esquire* yet, but he was publishing essays in the little magazines about what a bad-ass he was. I'd taught one semester out at Iowa, a sort of student thing, and that was it. So I figured, hell yeah, I'd apply for this job with Harry Crews, the greatest American writer since Flannery O'Connor."

I can see Jim doesn't need my questions anymore. He's on his story, and he's chasing it, finding the memories, turning them to fit his life. I squeeze a couple limes in my vodka. I add a handful of melting ice. Jim keeps on. Maybe this is why he doesn't write. All his stories appear magically, headlights pulled from the fog when he's drunk and stoned. At home, in front of a computer or typewriter, this wouldn't fly. He needs his audience present and drunk.

Jim says, "So I think I need to get a resume, a CV, whatever the fuck they're called, together and give it to Harry. But Harry says no. We just need to slow down on the drinking. Sunday will be our taper off day and we'll go in to see the head of the department on Monday, and he'll get me that job.

You know what he did?"

"Got you that job?"

"Fucking right he got me that job! Here's the fucking kicker. We go in Monday. Well, first I get up early Monday, before Harry who's sleeping naked on the couch, and I've never been so hungover in my life, but I get up and I go and get some coffee. On the way home I see this pawnshop, a Salvation Army I guess, and I go in and I buy a suit, not a nice suit, but it's

Florida, so what the fuck. I don't have to be perfect. I get back
to the place and I wake Harry up and I give him a coffee and
he says, 'What? Are you applying to be my pastor?' and falls
off the couch laughing, almost spilled coffee on his own nuts.

"Now, I don't know if he always dressed like this or what,
but he gets into like a fucking tennis outfit, like a jogging-ten-
nis outfit, like he's going to work out or something, and we
drive to the university like that. I'm worried. I'm not as worried as I am hungover, but I'm worried. I say, 'Harry, are you
sure you should be dressed like this?' Harry says, 'Ain't gonna
take but five minutes. I don't know why they hired that other
fucker first without asking me anyway.' I don't know what he's
talking about and I'm afraid to ask. So I just keep on sweating
in my ridiculous Salvation Army suit and drinking my coffee
which Harry has spiked with whiskey and we finally make it to
the university office.

"Inside, there's a man dressed in a real nice suit, a real
Southern gentleman type. He sees Harry and me, and especially Harry in these fucking exercise clothes, and he says, 'Harry,'
and this is in a real sophisticated Southern voice, 'Harry, I didn't
know you were a practicing homosexual,' and Harry says, 'You
too, you old faggot. I'd like you to meet Jim Rayger. He got a
new suit for this interview so I was thinking we'd hire him as
our new writer-in-residence.' The old pro thinks about that for
a second and says, 'Harry, we've already made that hire.' Harry
says, 'Well, unhire him.' The head of the department looks at
me and says, 'Thank you for wearing a suit. Someone needs to
take better care of Harry,' and he sits down and we walk out,
and that's it. Ol' Jim Rayger had his first full-time teaching job,
all with the help of the great Harry Crews. I love that fucking
Harry Crews. He got me that job, and that job got me this job,
and I haven't worked a day in my fucking life since, and my

daddy was a coal miner, no shit. Harry Crews. I will say that man's name as long as I have the breath. Harry Crews, Harry Crews, Harry beautiful Crews."

"A moral titan," I say.

"A fucking moral titan," Jim says then pulls out a cigar.

I throw up in the bathroom. It's mostly beer and vodka. No one is around. I don't feel like I'm drunk enough to be throwing up in the bathroom, but here I am, locked in a stall.

When I get back to the table, Jim is wobbly in the booth. His eyes are large and shiny enough to be pickled and served as eggs.

"If you're worried about your job, don't," he says. "Ain't nobody in that department likes a white man, least of all you, but they're afraid to say it in front of me."

"I always thought I was pretty well liked," I say.

"It's probably me they hate, you're right," Jim says. Then, messing with his money, which is down three or so hundred, easy, he says, "You want any of this?"

"Yes," I say. "I have children."

I scoop up the money, about half.

Jim says, "Ah, fuck it, take it all, you ol' whistle dick. If we would have been in a better bar instead of this shithole I would have spent it all anyways."

"That's true," I say, gathering up the rest of the money, straightening the bills like cards in a deck. "You might have even had to break out a credit card."

Jim says, "I haven't passed out in a bar in thirty years."

"Let's not start now," I say.

Jim says, "Your officemate there, ol' pussy-humping James

Longo, why the hell did he quit drinking? I don't get that."

"It's wasn't doing him any good," I say.

"It wasn't doing him any good," Jim says, like he's repeating something in a language he doesn't remotely understand. "I doubt it would hurt him to have a drink."

"It would," I say.

I could mention that James was shitfaced drunk only weeks ago, cancelling classes and lying to students, shoplifting from Target, but Jim would miss the message.

I say, "Well."

Jim looks at his empty whiskey glass. There's more in the bottle. There's more in my vodka bottle. There are hundreds of bottles of beer behind the bar in a cooler. I could throw up again, but I won't. I'll sit here with Jim until he can't sit here anymore, until he can find a way to stand and walk or stumble to my car.

If I can get some cool air on my face, I think, I'll be fine to drive.

But it's early.

But there's more.

If I could get Jim's money somewhere else, I could buy some cocaine. I could buy some cocaine and go to a whorehouse. I could snort and fuck and pretend nothing matters. I could forget Jim and every place he reaches.

I have these thoughts when I'm drunk in the daylight hours without purpose.

My wife and children feel distant and unreachable, or distant and safe, like they don't need me, like they'd rather I just stayed drunk and did drugs.

But then I see myself in a whorehouse, doing a line with some chick who barely speaks English, then there's a cop there, and he's arresting me, and my balls are out, and it's bad.

I should go home.

I think my wife has to work. Or she doesn't. She's preparing us a nice dinner. Or not. She's with the kids somewhere, being a great mother. She will find it ridiculous that I had to spend the day in a bar with Jim. But she will be happy I am employed for the following year, that my academic career, sad as it is, has been extended.

Jim says, "Shit. My blood's all fucked up. The sugar gets me when I'm drinking whiskey. I should have had a nice vodka and diet Sprite but it's downright pussified for a grown man of my credentials to order a vodka and diet Sprite out in public."

"Vodka and diet Sprite is a fine drink."

"Sucking dick is a fine profession, but you don't see me taking it up."

"No," I say. "That doesn't seem like something you would do for money."

Jim says, "Huh?"

I say, "So why the hell did you only write one book?"

Jim says, "If I could answer that question, I'd have written another."

Jim's blood is bothered by sugar. Mine is bothered by something else. I'm either bitter or sad or happy or angry or jealous or just drunk. Just drunk. No, everything. I hate teaching and I hate that I am paid so poorly to teach. I like to drink and I hate that I can't afford to drink. I could like Jim, but I don't want to like him because he's wrong. He's a writer who doesn't write. He's a teacher who doesn't teach. He's a rebel who doesn't rebel. Jim is, somehow, my boss.

Jim says, "It'd be nice if Harry Crews were here."

"Yeah," I say. "But is Harry Crews a dick-sucker?"

"Harry Crews is no more a dick-sucker than Ol' Jim right here."

"Ol' Jim might be a dick-sucker," I say.

"Ol' Jim is a professional do-nothing."

"Dick-sucking is something," I say. "You should take it up."

"Not professionally," he says.

It takes a second but I manage to stand up in the booth like a crows nest and I look out over the bar and say, "Ol' Kentucky Jim, legendary writer and teacher of legendary writers, whiskey drinker against the odds, friend of the moral titan and literary legend Harry Crews, does not suck dick as a profession. Is that clear? Kentucky Jim, legendary author of one book of short stories published four decades ago, does not fellate for profit. Anyone here accusing this man of drinking diet Sprite and vodka will be immediately pulverized. Is that right, Kentucky Jim?"

"I guess that's right," Jim says. Then, quieter, "Though probably unnecessary."

The bar is almost empty. One of the old men turns and winks. He's wearing a black-and-gold cowboy hat that looks smashed then unsmashed. I raise my bottle. He raises a bag of chips. I go in my pocket for some of Jim's money to put on the bar for the old guys to drink on when we're gone. The bartender motions for me to sit down. I hop from the booth to the bar.

I say, "Let's buy these gentlemen a round or two," and I put down some bills.

The bartender says, "You don't have to do that."

I say, "I'm drunk and it's not my money."

"Fair enough," he says. "But no more dirty talk."

I move from the bar back to my perch on the booth.

"Last chance," I say. "Any accusers making accusations about Kentucky Jim's sexuality and / or career choice, speak now." I say, "No one?"

The bartender looks bored. I give him a salute. He raises the wad of cash.

Jim says, "Sit down, pimple dick."

I sit down.

"That really wasn't necessary," he says.

"I think it was."

"My blood sugar is all messed up. My mother had this shit. Always kept a bag of orange candies with her."

"And probably didn't drink whiskey."

"Didn't drink anything," Jim says. "Give me a second. I'm just a touch dizzy-drunk."

He's dizzy-drunk and I'm angry. My mouth tastes like gum and puke and vodka and, possibly, cheese crackers, though I don't recall eating cheese crackers or barbecue chips from the open bag on the table. I sip a beer and try to be less of everything.

I say, "You want me to call a doctor?"

"Are you kidding me?"

"Not really."

Jim says, "Fuck."

He takes a second. I close my eyes. I've slept in bars before. I like bars that allow people to sleep in the booths or face down on a table. I open my eyes. Jim's eyes are closed. His head moves like a balloon that has lost most of its air. He's a bag, barely, and I'm over with this.

Jim says, "We should leave," and tries to stand.

I should do something.

I don't know what.

Jim says, "Harry Crews, Harry Crews."

Getting Jim from the bar is bad.

The ride home is worse.

do what I always do when I have money: I buy my children stuff. It's barely three o'clock in the afternoon and I am drunk, not just drunk but sick, so I sit down in an oversized pink chair in the bedroom furniture section of Toys R Us.

A woman in a blue smock says, "Do you need some help, sir?"

"Just re-grouping," I say.

She's old, all the women who work here are old, and her spine is bent and she has to hold her head up to look down at me in the chair. Her glasses are huge. Her hair is jet-black, permed, possibly a wig. I try to smile. I glance around the store for security. I don't think they have security in Toys R Us except at Christmas time.

The woman says, "Could I get you something?"

I doubt she's strong enough to lift a taser to fill me with electricity.

I say, "Yes."

She says, "Okay?"

"Let me think."

"Take your time."

"Thank you," I say.

Kentucky Jim is home. He's on the couch, the TV on AMC, playing some black-and-white movie I didn't recognize. His breath was puke and blood. I put a diet Pepsi on the table, near his reach. I covered him with a blanket. Before that, leaving the bar, he was fat and clumsy. He fell once, bouncing his face off the bottom of a stop sign as he tumbled then, probably, bruising his hip. "Fine, I'm fine," he said and willed himself to his feet. I put his arm over my shoulder. I took his weight. We made three steps. I said, "Jim, this isn't working." Jim said, "Carry me." So I did. I turned him and put him over my shoulder and hustled him to my car like we were teenagers doing a football drill. Did I say Jim was fat? It was like carrying a life-sized whiskey bottle. Inside the car, I rolled the window down and buckled his seatbelt. Jim talked some more about Harry Crews. He was slurring and openly a mess. "You're my best friend," he said. I said, "No, I'm not." I drove as well as I could, swerving when it couldn't be helped. I found his house and parked on the lawn, near the front porch. I said, "Jim, you have to walk. You're too fucking fat for me to carry," and he did, he walked, some version of it. Then he puked in the bushes.

Now the woman in the blue smock at Toys R Us says, "There are cold sodas for sale in the coolers by the service desk."

I say, "Is there a cart anywhere around here? I could use a cart."

"I would love to get you a cart," she says and walks off.

I close my eyes. It's great to be a writer, I think. Then I think, No it's not.

She says, "Are you ready for your cart?"

"That was fast," I say. "Thank you."

I stand up and do not wobble. I take the cart, blue plastic and dirty metal. It's nice to have something to hold, to push, to lean on. My head is better than my stomach which feels like I've been drinking daggers.

The woman extends her old white hand to pass me a card.

She says, "It's a 5% discount card. Also, if you mention my name, it will help."

"Sure," I say. "Thank you. Help with what?"

"Customer service," she says.

"You're great," I say.

"If we don't give out these cards and if people don't mention our names, we don't get our bonuses in our paychecks."

"Sure," I say. "What's your name?"

"Lydia," she says. "Like the flower."

"Perfect," I say. "Lydia."

She touches me and moves off. I don't know the exact amount of money in my pocket. Maybe a thousand. Maybe more. I do not know what Jim will remember tomorrow or if he even remembers anything anymore. "What the hell happened?" he might say and I'll say, "We celebrated the life and times of Harry Crews and you were very eloquent." I'll say, "Remember, Ol' Jim, you promised me a job, you dirty ball lapper."

I move from the bedroom department to the clothing department, thinking: my kids. There are sales, pink and blue signs knocking off twenty-five percent, fifty perfect, even seventy-five. It's mostly winter clothing, so I go large for next year. I get goofy pajamas, superheroes and fairies, things we would never buy, brands we could never afford. I buy jeans and skirts. I buy underwear and socks. I buy shorts and t-shirts that aren't on sale. My kids won't care about this stuff, but they'll need it. They need it now. They'll need it next year.

But what they love, what makes them happy, is toys, so I go there. My son gets Legos, mostly Star Wars but also some blocks to build his own city. My daughter gets another puzzle and a princess dress and shoes that shine. I buy her some pink Legos to build with, starter blocks. I buy my son a book and some penguin cards for a game he's been talking about. I buy them each a movie. I buy a video game for them to share.

All this stuff makes me feel better. I'm drunk and sick but I don't feel drunk and sick or drunk and sick is bearable because of all this stuff. I can see why America lives this way. I would like to live this way, buying when you feel like buying, giving when you want to give. I keep pushing the cart. I keep grabbing.

But there's nothing here for my wife.

My wife needs something.

On her birthday, because we were broke, we drank cheap wine and I rubbed her feet. No presents. No card. We always buy for the kids. She always buys for the kids. Instead of make-up, we go to the zoo. Instead of shoes, we see movies about drag-ons and aliens and ogres and donkeys. My wife needs clothes. She needs flowers. She hates flowers, but when you don't get flowers, when your husband can't afford flowers, flowers are something. I pick up a pink stuffed dinosaur. My wife would be happy with a pink stuffed dinosaur. But I wouldn't.

But there are other stores, stores that are filled with things for loving wives. I stretch my eyes. The light in Toys R Us is white, harsh. I stare until I see spots. The spots go to my brain and I tell myself that these are the pills that make a man sober. I push the cart. My driving is fine. It's all about the reflexes. If I can steer a cart, I can steer my car. I will go slow and watch for cops and enjoy the sunshine.

When I get to the register, the manager, a big fat guy with sweat on his forehead, says, "Did anybody assist you with your shopping experience today?"

"Did anyone assist me with my shopping experience to-day?" I say. "Yes, her name was Lydia, like the flower, and she was excellent."

The jewelry store is empty. One woman, more like a girl, maybe a teenager, is behind the glass counter. She has blonde hair down to her waist and it shines. Her outfit is something business, a bank teller. She is out and on me before I get to the first display case.

"Can I help you with anything?" she says.

"I'm just looking," I say.

Up close the girl is older, maybe late twenties. She's thin and together with tasteful jewelry everywhere, even a diamond on the tip of her fingernail. I smile and look away. I try the first case. There are watches and rings and necklaces. Everything is silver or white gold, I can't tell. There are price tags but they are neatly tucked under the merchandise. I know I stink like booze. My eyes burn with smoke and bright light.

The woman says, "Is it a birthday?" She is excited and fake but good at it.

"No birthday," I say.

"Anniversary?"

"Not exactly."

I don't know why I'm here. Lori hates jewelry. When we were first married I bought her diamond earrings and her earlobes turned blue with infection. All of this metal is junk. Lori would like the electric bill paid on time or the property tax paid early, but I can't accept a life where paying bills is a gift. I see a necklace with a diamond pendant that Lori would think is positively hideous. I try another case, one filled exclusively with watches.

"What exactly are you looking for?" the clerk says.

"I don't know," I say.

I'm sweating. I do this when I'm drunk and tired and lost and embarrassed. The woman takes my hand. She is so professional she doesn't mind that I stink like a wino. She doesn't mind my wet face or sweaty palms or that I'm parked half on the curb outside her store, the flashers on my car barely visible in the late afternoon sun. She touches my fingers and finds my wedding band. She lifts my hand like she's going to kiss it then examines the design of the ring.

She says, "I see you're married. Tell me about your lovely wife."

I can't imagine telling anyone I don't know about my lovely wife like my lovely wife was something I was trying to sell and not buy for.

The woman says, "Blond or brunette?"

"Writer," I say, taking my hand back. "With a great big beautiful ass," and I form something like my wife's ass with my hands, like I'm holding it here, like it's the size of a wrecking ball. "I need some ass jewelry. Do they even make that?"

"I'm sure they do," the woman says.

"Good," I say. "I should leave before I throw up."

"That's always a good idea," she says and steps back from me. "Don't hurt anyone."

"Huh?" I say.

"Violence is never the answer, no matter how bad it gets between men and women."

"I'm not violent," I say. Then amend that to, "I'm not violent with my wife."

"You can get her back with jewelry. But you can get her back with other things, too, if you don't have the money. Like a foot rub. Women love foot rubs."

"I do foot rubs," I say.

"And salt scrubs," she says.

"You're right," I say and I bow because I don't know why, because my wife would rather have money than anything in this store, because my wife never has money, because money is always the answer when you don't have money and I should deliver it to her so she can take the night off work and go get her nails done or her feet massaged or buy some new shoes I could never pick out because I'm fucking stupid that way.

I love you, Lori.

I'm sorry I'm so drunk.

IV

'm trying to unlock the office door. My key is stuck. It's an ugly, drab hallway. The walls are institutional yellow and lime green. James stands behind me. He's speaking to my class today, reading his excellent new story about Harold. I hope the attention does something, tweaks something in him. Focuses him. Tonight we are going to an AA meeting. I think it will be good for James. James does not think it will be good for James but he wants to drink and he doesn't know what else to do.

"You should try that pill," I say.

"What pill?" he says. "Why are you not opening that door?"

"I'm afraid to break my key."

"What pill?"

"That pill that doesn't allow you to drink. It blocks something or suppresses something. I don't know. I saw an ad for it in *People* magazine."

James says, "Antabuse?"

"Is that it?"

"Antabuse has been around forever. It doesn't stop the cravings. It just makes you violently ill when you do drink."

"That sounds like something they give to mental patients."

"Mental patients who are alcoholics," he says and laughs.

"Take your fucking key out of the lock. I'll try mine."

"This wasn't Antabuse. This was something else. It actually blocks the cravings."

James says, "All of those pills are bad ideas. For one, our insurance probably wouldn't pay for it. Two, it probably makes your dick limp. Three, it doesn't make sense to take a pill to stop taking a drink. But what the fuck do I know? In eight hours, I'll be eating donuts with a bunch of other shitbrains who also can't stop drinking."

I take my keys. I look at the door. It's 429. Our office is 431. James is digging through his bag. I touch his shoulder and point at the numbers.

James says, "That's embarrassing for everybody."

"It's the alcohol," I say. "It's damaged your brain."

"It was your key," he says. "The hamburgers have damaged your brain."

"You make a lot of fat jokes at my expense," I say.

"I know," he says, "You should lose some weight."

We're moving towards the next door, barely five feet away, when Carrie Polinski, a tenured fiction writer, steps into the hallway. Carrie Polinski's office is upstairs with the other writers and professors who make good money and teach fewer classes. Down here is slumming. She's either handing off work she doesn't want to do to someone who has to do it, or she's looking for someone to teach her new book.

Carrie's new book is about love and football. Carrie's new book is a self-help memoir and one of the main characters, the character who kicks off the narrative, is James.

James, at the university's suggestion, was Carrie's tour guide when she first moved to Pittsburgh. He was still in grad school then. He took Carrie to dinner. He showed her the sights. They drove down the streets of the safe neighborhoods with the low rents until Carrie found an apartment. James asked a lot of friendly, inquisitive questions. Carrie didn't. They talked a lot about Carrie's first book, a fictionalized account of the 1934 Kentucky Derby. James thought Carrie might be possessed by genius. He'd read the novel three times, and it'd only been out a year. He loved the characters and the story and the language. He wanted to know how she'd combined all three so perfectly.

Carrie didn't want to talk about character and story and language. She talked a lot about work, the academy. Occasionally, she talked about publishing, "the professional side," she called it. When James asked about the professional side—agents and publishers and the rest of that world he didn't know—Carrie scrunched up her forehead. She said, "You write so you can teach. Make a book to get the job. Otherwise, manage a Gap." James didn't want to manage a Gap. He'd been working with autistic people before he'd come back to grad school. Now, close to graduation, he wanted to teach full time. Carrie seemed to have answers but James never knew exactly what she was saying. James, talking it out, said, "She's really nice and I think she's trying to be helpful but she says mean things about everyone she meets."

They kept going to dinner. Carrie was lonely. She talked a lot about love. They went to a hockey game and saw a couple art films.

James wanted Carrie to read his stories. Carrie said, "I'm swamped," then gave James one of her stories to read before she sent it out. James was flattered to be her reader. She said, "It's the best thing I've written." He said, "Great." It was about Cain and Abel, but set in contemporary Louisiana. James said, "It's good." But it wasn't. Carrie's agent said, "Write something I can sell." Carrie called James crying. There was a long walk and a hug.

Carrie started to think James was her boyfriend even though James already had a girlfriend. James loved his girlfriend. She'd been there when he was drunk and she'd helped him stop drinking and she'd helped him find a job and get back into school. James' girlfriend was beautiful and kind. Carrie was not. James didn't know how to tell this to Carrie. Carrie said, "You need to be more serious about your career and stop worrying about your writing all the time." Carrie was taking pills for migraines. The pills were making her fat and miserable. Carrie got aggressive. She said, "You need to tell me what's up." James said, "Nothing's up." James, newly sober, didn't like confrontation. He thought he was being kind to a lonely woman in a new city. Maybe he liked being around a successful writer. Carrie thought something else. She thought this was about love, then deception. She said, "You need to make up your mind."

James quit taking Carrie's calls. Carrie started giving James looks at parties and around the English Department. She told one of her girlfriends that James was a fucking liar. James, being James, being a kind heart, simply endured. Time passed. James got his job, the same one he has now. Carrie kept her job. James wrote and published a few stories. Carrie didn't. One year passed, then two. Her tenure was coming. She needed another book. Her agent suggested she write something about sports, something less literary, something that might sell.

So Carrie turned all of this—her move to Pittsburgh and her relationship with James—into a book that somehow connected her search for love with the New Orleans Saints football season. James' name in the book was The Punter, as in: he had a chance for love but he chose to punt. The metaphors got worse. The sports clichés were too numerous to count. In the book's introduction, Carrie said she was inspired not only by

Drew Brees and the Saints but also by the TV show *#1 Single*, a reality dating show based on the life of Lisa Loeb, a former folk singer who had a video on MTV for about six seconds twenty years ago. The book's afterward is written as a sideline interview where Carrie discusses her love life with a fictional version of herself that she calls Carrie Cleats. My second least favorite line in the book is, "Football and dating are played on a postmodern playing field dominated by Generation Y technology." My least favorite line is, "Drew Brees is a postmodern genius. Drew Brees is my avatar."

The things she said about James in the book were probably true, but she completely avoided any truths about her own narrative and motivation. Like she didn't mention she was a professor and James was still a grad student. She didn't mention helping James with his resume when he applied for this job. She didn't mention telling James these jobs were for losers, for "townies who were too scared to leave Pittsburgh," once she realized James wasn't going to marry her. She didn't, for example, write the sentence, "Then I broke down and cried—wept really—and told James, The Punter, that all I really wanted was to be a stay-at-home wife, that I'd never write again and I'd quit teaching if I could just find a man to take care of me and love me." And she also didn't write, "James, The Punter, looked at me like I was insane, said he was having a nicotine craving, went to the corner store for cigarettes and didn't talk to me for at least three days." She didn't write, "I'm a mean-spirited person who would get James fired for not loving me if I could, then I'd write another self-help memoir about it and compare myself to boxing great, Rocky Balboa."

Now I turn to James and say, "Don't look."

James looks and says, "It's Carrie. Kill me."

"Just smile," I say.

The office door finally opens. I toss my bag on the desk. James steps into the office. I wait for him to slam the door and hide. He doesn't. He sets down his bag. He takes a breath. I'm trying not to be hungover. Being a friend is more important than my hangover.

James says, "So."

I say, "Exactly. No big deal."

He says, "You look sick."

I haven't told James about Kentucky Jim and Harry Crews and my job and the presents for my kids and how I bought six roses at a convenience store then stuffed two grand into the flowers with the baby's breath and put the bouquet in my wife's bathroom because that was the funniest place I could imagine.

James says, "Really sick. You look a mess."

"Focus on that," I say. "Forget Carrie Polinski."

"Fucking Carrie Polinski. Why is she not dead?"

"Pretend to be on the phone. I'll cover."

"I can't," he says. "She's the only person who has ever hated me for being nice."

We both move to the doorway, neither in the office nor in the hall.

Carrie Polinski, dressed in a flowing silky outfit that clings to her cinder blocks thighs, has seen us and waves and smiles. She has on her glasses, the stylish black ones. Her long brown hair is pulled into some kind of bun. Her make-up is pronounced, the rouge too dark and thick. The whole outfit, the whole look, is a sham, some imagined idea of how a professor should dress. When Carrie is away from the university, she wears Official NFL gear.

James, under his breath, says, "You talk to her."

"Just look busy," I say. "It'll be fast."

"Danny and James," she says, waving some paper at us.

"Hold on, guys."

"How's it going, Carrie?" James says and steps away from the office and into the hall and meets Carrie with an extended hand for a shake.

Carrie fills James' hand with a paper rolled-up like a scroll. It's either busy work or something promoting her new book, maybe a postmodern scorecard.

James says, "Is this biblical? Because it looks biblical."

"Let me take a look at that," I say and relieve James of the scroll.

Carrie says, "I've barely seen either of you this semester."

James says, "I know. I haven't seen you either."

She says, "How's classes?"

"Good," we both say.

"You guys teaching three each?" she says.

"Four each," James says.

"How's the new book doing?" I say.

"Great," Carrie says, smiling, professional. "Absolutely fantastic."

"Good," I say.

"Yeah," she says. "Through-the-roof buzz."

"Good," I say. "Congratulations."

"Absolutely, congratulations," James says and he sounds sincere.

"Yeah," she says. "I'm calling it a novel now."

She looks at James. James shrugs. I shrug.

"Memoir, novel," Carrie says, but like those are social words—hello, goodbye.

"Novel, memoir," I say.

"Right," she says. "Novel, memoir. Sure."

I can see her starting to tweak. One of her shoulders moves a little forward then back, subtle but nervous. She knows that

James knows he's The Punter, and she knows that we both read the *Publisher's Weekly* review that called her "small and arrogant."

"So what's up, Carrie?" I say.

"Not much," she says and tweaks again, both shoulders this time.

Carrie was on Prozac then she wasn't, then she was against anyone taking Prozac because Prozac was an evil drug made by evil people and prescribed by evil doctors, then she was on Prozac again. I don't know if she's on Prozac now. I think not.

She said, "The semester is busy. The book is good." She nods her head, up and down, still smiling, still professional, then starts bobbing her head the opposite way, suddenly frowning, suddenly sad. She says, "There's been some bumps in the road, sure, but you know, if the publisher has lost all hope, and I believe the publisher has lost all hope, I still believe in the book. My agent still believes in it. And there's always the paperback. Right? The paperback can still be a bestseller?" She looks demoralized, confronting the life of her own book. But then happy. She says, "A little adversity, right? Makes everything worth it." She raises her arm and flexes her bicep. "Stronger," she says and makes a noise that could be a growl. Then it's like she's actually selling demoralization as a good thing when she says, "In some ways, the book's failure is actually the book's success or at least the book's buzz. It's an angle for reviewers when the paperback comes out. If, of course, the paperback comes out." She says, "We're really hoping next football season throws some new life into the book. As long as the Saints are on top, the book should be okay. Go Saints!"

"I don't think the Saints are technically on top," I say.

"Drew Brees was the league MVP," she says.

James says, "Doesn't anyone watch hockey anymore?"

Carrie says, "No, I don't think anyone does watch hockey anymore."

James says, "Right. My bad."

Carrie adjusts her scarf. She shifts her weight from one foot to the other like an uncomfortable teenage boy who's wearing his mother's chunky high heels.

James says, "New outfit?"

Carrie says, "No." Carrie says, "Yes."

She doesn't look at James.

I look at James. He is as red as Carrie's scarf and he's sweating. It's embarrassment. It's anger. Behind his eyes is a brain that wants watered with alcohol.

I hold up the scroll and say, "Should we read this?"

Carrie says, "I was going to ask you guys to do something, but I think I'll be okay."

"Are you sure?" I say.

"Gentlemen," she says. Then, stepping between us but making sure not to touch, "Excuse me if you don't mind," and she starts off down the hall, her chunky ass somehow flat as a board.

Neither James nor I speak until Carrie is through the door and up the stairs. When I turn to James, he looks like a candle, burnt and melted down.

"Don't even let her bother you," I say.

"How can I not?" he says.

"Just come to my class and read. The students will love you."

"I can't read in your class," he says. "I need a drink."

"You don't need a drink."

"What if she makes me lose my job?"

"She can't get you fired for not loving her."

"She probably can. She has tenure."

I pull James in the office and check the clock. Now I need to get to class. Now I have nothing to teach because James and his new story were my lesson plan.

I say, "Come to my class."

He says, "I can't. I know I'm screwing you. I'm sorry."

"Look," I say, lying, "I talked to Kentucky Jim yesterday and he says we both have our jobs for next year."

"Really?"

"Yes."

James says, "That's great, but I still feel like shit." He has on a tie today, something from the thrift store. It looks awful, the texture clashing with his shirt. He says, "I really need a drink."

"Don't drink," I say.

"Kentucky Jim said we have our jobs?" he says.

"Yes," I say. "We were in a bar, talking about Harry Crews."

James says, "Kentucky Jim and Harry Crews, two assholes."

I say, "Better than Carrie Polinski."

He says, "Don't be pissed at me."

"It's no big deal," I say. "I'll read your story."

"I'm getting drunk. Don't be pissed for that."

"We have an AA meeting to attend."

"We can still attend our AA meeting."

"Drunk?" I say.

"That's how you're supposed to go to the first one."

"You have to call my wife and tell her you got me loaded."

He says, "Tell me more about Kentucky Jim and our jobs."

I say, "We're in."

But Kentucky Jim didn't mention James. Kentucky Jim is sick of James. Kentucky Jim is sick of writers who don't know writing is all about whiskey and weed. Kentucky Jim is fucking sick of James and his new-aged sobriety.

But when James and I stumble into his office today, drunk

but with purpose, we will all slap backs and talk about the system and screwing it and how Ol' Jim is going to help us out just like Harry Crews saved his wretched hillbilly life back in 1974, the year of our Lord.

I read James' story to my class. It takes about fifteen minutes. The students don't talk. I think they are mostly paying attention, though a couple girls quietly text-message and one guy opens his laptop and surfs the web. No one walks out. No says, "Yeah, and what's the point of this?"

After I finish, I say, "I want to talk about structure and a little bit about character but before we do that, before we get too academic and suck the life out of the narrative, maybe someone could say something more emotionally based, just what you liked about the story."

The guy who was surfing the web, Reg, says, "I liked it, and I haven't liked anything we've read in here this whole semester."

"Good," I say. "We're on to something. Now what did you like about the story? What caught your attention? Be specific."

Reg says, "My dad used to drink in a bar like the one in the story. I remember a bunch of old men sitting around, eating peanuts just like that. It's good stuff."

"It is good stuff," I say and wish James was here and hope he is still in the office, calming, not rising up for some fantastic drunk, though I know it would be good for him to stumble hammered into Kentucky Jim's office and secure his job for the following year by reeking of booze and incoherence. I say, "What else about the story?"

"Just that the characters were real," Jen says. Jen is a great writer but never talks. She has three fingers on one hand from a lawnmower accident and always positions herself to hide the stumps. She says, "I didn't feel like I was listening to some made up story. It felt real."

"Tell me why," I say.

She says, "Like the character had a job, he worked with autistic people. And how he was figuring out how much money he could spend until payday. It just felt real. It reminded me of early-period Kerouac."

"It did," another girl says. "It definitely had a Kerouac feel to it."

All the good students compare everything to Kerouac, especially the stories and novels they like that have nothing to do with Kerouac. I love when they talk. I'm happy to make connections that don't exist to keep them interested in something, anything, involving books.

I say, "Kerouac, definitely. Let's not forget that all of those characters in Kerouac were working class. Between cross-country car trips, they held jobs and went to school. So Kerouac and James Longo both create characters that need employment to pay for their kicks."

"Does he have a novel?" Jen says.

"Kerouac?" I say, making a joke.

No one laughs. Jen laughs a little. I see her bury her hand under the desk.

"Kerouac has novels," I say. "Does James Longo have a novel? Not yet. He's just finished a story collection, and it's going in the mail to a publisher."

James really hasn't finished a story collection and when he does it may not go in the mail to a publisher, but if he saw the way these students were reacting, he would. He would write and not drink and write again until he was done.

Jen says, "How do you publish a story collection?"

"Send it out," I say, being simple.

If the students knew James' collection could reach a publisher and be shredded and returned with a note that says, "Not for us," they would never write again.

Reg says, "And this dude teaches here?"

"He does," I say. "I would highly recommend his classes."

Reg says, "Cool," and closes his computer.

Jen says, "Do you have a book?"

I say, "I do."

Jen says, "Really?"

I never talk about my own writing with my students. Back in college, I never liked the professors who forced us to buy their books. They were arrogant and self-absorbed. They stood in front of the room, reading from their own novels and poetry collections, laughing in all the right places, being sad when they wanted us to be sad. That's parenting, not teaching. It's okay to be desperate about writing, the process and desire. It's not okay to be desperate with your books, the selling and promoting and teaching.

Jen says, "Can you buy it?"

"Can I buy my own novel?" I say.

"Like, can I buy it?" she says.

"Sure," I say. "Anyone can buy it. But back to Professor Longo's story."

"Look," someone says. "He's embarrassed."

"I'm not embarrassed," I say, though I am a little. "It's just…" and I can't think. Then I can when I say, "Professors who force their work on students are sad people. The books are out there, mine and everyone else's books. Students should read their professors' books so they can understand where their professors are coming from, but it would be silly for me to talk about it in class. Agreed? Yes? I think we can all agree on that."

"What's your book called?"

"It's called *Book*," I say. "You should all buy at least one hundred copies."

"Shit, man," someone says. "You're like a fucking rockstar."

"Rockstars are shit," someone else says.

"I'd rather be a writer than a rockstar," Jen say.

Reg says, "True that."

I say, "Everyone think of one thing relating to the characters in Longo's story and write it down for next class. We'll pick up there."

The class has clearly gone over to something else, and I still need to find James and follow him to a safe place or keep him safe while he does what he has to do.

One of the cashiers down in the cafeteria is crippled. His arm is gimped-up, and he might have some sort of compulsion too, like he lays out your money on the counter before and after he puts it in the cash register. It takes a while. His line, even at lunchtime, even when the other lines are backed up, is always short or empty. Everyone knows. I know. But I always get in his line, thinking I will distract him from his gimped-up arm and his compulsion and the students who avoid his defects and quirks.

So I get in his line with my chicken sandwich and Diet Pepsi. I see James over at a table, talking to a pretty girl. I think it's Jen with the two fingers on her left-hand and a Kerouac obsession. James looks sober. He has a drink in front of him and it could be Coke and it might not be mixed with booze. Jen is smiling. I think she might be telling him how much she loved his story and how much it reminded her of *On The Road*.

The guy with the gimped-up arm says, "What's in the cup?"

I always keep a big refillable mug with me. Right now, it's filled with watered-down iced tea. The mug is from Sheetz, a local convenience store. Every day the guy with the gimped-up arm wants to know what's in my mug.

"Iced tea," I say. "Three pink sweeteners and a little lemon."

"I knew it!" he says and almost shakes he's so happy. "Sheetz is the best!"

"They make a good iced tea," I say.

He says, "Back in college when they first started serving French fries—" and he stops.

I say, "Yeah?"

He says, "I loved those French fries."

"They have good fries."

"And awesome spicy chicken sandwiches."

"I've never had the spicy chicken sandwich."

I look at James. He sees me and starts to separate from Jen.

When James gets closer, I say, "Hey, hold on."

The guy with the gimped-up arm says, "You get the spicy chicken sandwich with the hot pepper cheese. Then, if you're feeling really wild, you get the buffalo sauce on the side and dip."

"I'll try that," I say and hand him a five even though he hasn't told me that my bill is, like every single day, $4.94.

"Oh," he says, "$4.94."

He lays out the five flat. He turns it sideways. Maybe he's reading some of the numbers or looking for a mark. He smoothes the bill with his good hand. The gimp arm is close to his side, his hand frozen against his chest. He puts the five in the cash drawer.

James says, "You ready?"

"Almost," I say. "We're discussing the fine art of culinary entertainment at Sheetz."

"Fine art of culinary entertainment?" the gimp says and laughs and almost knocks the cash drawer out of the register. He says, "You must teach advertising."

James puts his arm around me and says, "Gym. You're looking at the fattest PE instructor the university has ever hired."

I could lose some weight, but I'm not that fat. Gym teachers have been wearing blubber around their midsections like nametags for years.

James says, "He's quicker than he looks."

The guy with the gimped-up arm doesn't care. My six pennies are on the counter. They are being counted. Then counted again. He scoops them up with his one good hand, rips the receipt from the register, and hands me the paper and the coins in a crumpled-up pile.

"Thanks," I say. "I'll catch you tomorrow."

"Sheetz," he says.

"Sheetz," I say and start to walk.

James follows me and says, "What, do you guys talk in code?"

"It's the language of Sheetz," I say. "It's like the language of love."

We're outside the dining area. Students are everywhere. They are all colors and sizes and sexes and dressed both fashionably and terribly not. I'd like to get away before some student sees us and wants to complain about a grade or talk about their self-diagnosed ball cancer. James goes into his bag for a pack of cigarettes. He taps the pack and pops a smoke in his mouth even though there are No Smoking signs everywhere.

I say, "Sober?"

He says, "For now. I'm starving for some nicotine."

"Let's get outside."

"Thanks for reading my story. I'm sorry I was so wigged out. It's just that seeing Carrie Polinski makes me nauseous."

"Not a problem."

"The girl I was talking to was from your class. She said she really loved my piece. She wants to take me for class next semester."

"I told you," I say. "What else?"

"She says I'm like Kerouac."

"You hate Kerouac."

"I do hate Kerouac. Even when I was young and drunk all the time I hated Kerouac. He wrote like a big dumb jock."

"I like Kerouac," I say. "He's a gateway drug to literature for the youth of America."

James says, "Really? Then I like him, too. We need a gateway drug to literature." He says, "Hey, what happened to that girl's hand? She had like a thumb and a pinkie."

"Her hand isn't important. What's important is that they liked your story."

"Thanks," he says. "But why'd you tell them I couldn't make it in to read for myself because I was in a car crash?"

"It was either that," I say, "or I tell them you were sorting through your feelings for sometime novelist, slash, sometime memoirist Carrie Polinski."

Richard, of The Rugged Richard Trio, my other officemate, formerly a full-time employee of the university, now a part-time lecturer, the one being threatened by students, steps from the Cathedral into the sun. He's crying, or he's been crying and his eyes are still wet behind his glasses. He's red around the face and ears and even his bald head glows with embarrassment. His bowtie is crooked like it's been spun like a propeller.

James is smoking a Marlboro. I'm at the other end of the concrete bench, the same bench where I sat with Richard while a student walked by and shouted, "Professor Pussylips!"

Never, since I've been at the university, have I had a good spring semester, one where I could focus on teaching and writing and not worry about keeping my job. But this is something else, a hole that's opened after years of pollution.

James' smoke drifts and I fan it with my hand.

Richard wipes his eyes with his thumb and forefinger, raising his glasses.

James says, "Someday they'll invent a smokeless cigarette."

"They already have," I say.

I think I know what's happened to Richard but I don't know how bad. It doesn't look like he's been punched. His nose is straight. Nothing bleeds. Maybe he's been slapped. Maybe he's been shoved. I hope it's his nerves, that he hasn't been touched, that the color is shame.

James says, "They've invented a smokeless cigarette?"

Richard moves away from the revolving doors, away from the students rushing to class. He adjusts his bowtie and his shirt. He fixes what's left of his hair. He removes his glasses and cleans them with a tissue from his pocket.

James says, "Is that Richard? Is he crying?"

I say, "Yes. Both."

James says, "Should we run and hide or should we do something?" He says, "That was a terrible question," and digs for another cigarette.

"We should do something," I say but I don't move.

Then I think Richard sees us so I wave him over.

He waves back. He wipes his nose with the cuff of his blazer. The distance between us is filled with a freeway of students. Richard waits. He waits some more. If this was a packed club, a hundred-seater, Richard would be onstage and I would be in the back row. He would be an earnest indie rock 'n' roller, a guy who once traded licks with J. Mascis from Dinosaur Jr. He would sing and strum and not be afraid of the crowd. I would be a writer with enough time to sit back and cheer and push my way to the front if I felt like pushing.

But I haven't been to a show since my son started school.

But I can't imagine Richard with a guitar anymore. His shoulders are as sloped as the hills around Pittsburgh, the hills that separate the rich and the poor, and his chest is sunk deep enough for a lake. Gravity catches us all but Richard is lower than anyone I've seen. If you saw him on stage, you'd boo. If he took the next seat, you'd leave.

"Richard," I say, like nothing's up so, if it's better, he can pretend like nothing's up.

He takes two steps, wipes his nose again. He looks behind him to make sure he's not being followed by anything or anyone violent.

"How's it going?" I say.

"Bad," he says. "Terrible."

"Students?" I say. "That student?"

"Yes," he says and takes out his pouch of tobacco and rolling papers.

James says, "Don't do that."

James hands Richard a Marlboro. Richard nods. I stand up so he can sit down and we won't be three devastated professors on one bench outside a building that holds hundreds of classrooms and thousands of students who think we are purposely ruining their lives for a ridiculously high tuition rate. Richard sits. He stands and pats his pockets. He sits again without finding a lighter. He puts the Marlboro in his mouth but takes it out before James can light it.

James says, "Take a second."

Richard takes a second. He puts his face in his hands and weeps. It's a loud constant sob that goes at least five seconds.

Richard says, "Fuck fuck fuck." He says, "Sorry. Sorry. Sorry."

I stand and don't do anything. I look down. The red marks on his head aren't welts but they're close. James looks around Richard to see me but I don't have anything.

"You want to talk?" I say.

"No," he says through his hands. "Yes."

James says, "We were thinking about getting a beer," and I can see he's decided.

I've decided, too.

"Exactly," I say. "We were thinking about getting a beer."

Richard quits using his hands like a mask, like a disguise, and snorts and wipes his nose and flicks the snot to the ground. It's too sad to be gross.

He says, "Dan, I thought you had to teach another class?"

Richard knows our schedules and office hours. He likes to be in the office alone now that he's part-time. To be in there with James and me makes him feel sad and ashamed, a failure.

"I do have another class," I say. "I'd be happy to teach them drunk."

"What about you, James?" Richard says.

James says, "I'm miserable. I just saw Carrie Polinski."

Richard says, "She makes you miserable?"

James says, "Did you read her newest book?"

Richard says, "Yes." He says, "No." He says, "I think I was the wrong audience. It looked like it was for lonely women or single men. I'm neither. But I am teaching it in my Composition II course next semester."

"Really?" I say. "Why?"

"Because Carrie asked me to," Richard says. "Told me to."

"Let's go get beers," James says. "And whiskey."

Richard stands up and says, "James." He steps to James and, at arms length, puts his hands on James' shoulders so they look like a bizarre statue, Hugging Man. He says, "James, you can't drink. Think about it."

James says, "I can do anything."

Richard says, "Really?" He says, "Can you lend me five cigarettes and ten bucks?"

"I'll buy you a pack," I say. "And some beers."

"How did you get money?" Richard says.

"Yeah really," James says.

"Ol' Kentucky Jim," I say.

"That old cunt-lapper gave you money to buy me cigarettes and beer?" Richard says in mock-tones and laughs for what might be the first time this semester.

"Something like that," I say.

"Really?" James says. "Did he give you any money to buy me anything?"

"Sure," I say. "I have one hundred dollars to spend on both of you."

James says, "This is like a dream. I'm becoming an alcoholic, and for free."

"You really shouldn't become an alcoholic," Richard says and he's serious.

"I'll only be an alcoholic for a day," James says.

They step ahead like they've already decided on the bar and their brands. I go slow. Traffic is busy around the Cathedral, students and professors in the crosswalks slowing everything down. Buses stop and start with black smoke. A woman pushes a cart filled with blankets and cans. Sorority girls dressed like summer in short-shorts hold out cans for charity, scarves around their necks, their nipples poking through their sweaters.

The light turns red. None of the good bars are open yet. I don't think James knows what's happened to Richard. He thinks this is some sort of general humiliation and not a specific one. I would like to leave these two, my best friend and my fine co-worker, to solve their own mysteries like detectives in an old noir, Sam Spade and Phillip Marlow, but one can't drink and the other hates violence. James makes the corner. Richard pushes the button for the crosswalk. If I ran, they wouldn't immediately notice. I could be gone before they turned.

But where exactly would someone like me run to at eleven in the morning on a Wednesday when my kids are in school and my wife is at work and my students would rather I didn't teach them anyway?

James and Richard turns to see if I'm following. The traffic stops, a mail truck in the middle of the crosswalk, other cars beeping to get around. James raps on the mailman's hood and waves. The mailman waves back. I know his face from the local bars. One time, smashed, he let me wear his mailman hat.

The three of us step into Hemingway's Bar. The bar is as trivial and embarrassing and has as little to do with Hemingway the man as the last time we were here, but this morning, it's empty. The alcoholics know better dives off-campus. The students who know how to drink are still in bed. It's 11:15 and the neon behind the bar is still dark. When we take our stools, Richard gets the middle, his bag safe across his lap, me to his right, James to his left.

I order a Coors Light bottle.

James orders a Jack Daniels on the rocks.

Richard gets a glass of red wine.

James says, "Really? Wine?"

Richard says, "My stomach is melting from nerves. A glass of wine first helps."

The bartender says, "Let's call it an even ten."

I hand him my Visa and say, "Okay we start a tab?"

The card is full but I have two one-hundred dollar bills left in my wallet.

"Sure," he says. "But you can't cash out until at least noon when the regular girl comes in and opens the credit card machine thing. I'm the cash-only guy."

The bartender might be the owner. Hemingway's has been bought and sold so many times I can't remember. This guy is retirement age with pockmarks and thick gray hair slicked back with some sort of cream. The brown slacks and orange shirt are new or freshly laundered but nothing matches, especially the red suspenders. He's fat like he eats pasta every hour and scotch all evening. If I were cynical, I'd say he's hungover and the morning shift called off.

James says to Richard, "So why the boo-boo face, big guy?"

Richard says, "Danny didn't tell you?"

I know this makes Richard feel bad, that I haven't passed along his misery, that I haven't spread the word that his students are threatening to pummel him.

"I'm sorry," I say. "This is the first time I've seen James and then Carrie Polinski showed up and then just everything else, the whole world."

Richard sighs like it's the only way he knows how to breathe and says, "Shit. Where do I begin?" and drinks his wine like it's a shot.

The bartender notices and gets off his stool.

He says, "You guys are gonna make me work."

James says, "You don't even know."

Richard says, "I'll have a Pabst this time, thanks."

The bartender flexes his suspenders and says, "What kind of grown man in a bow tie drinks Pabst Blue Ribbon?"

Richard says, "In a can if you have it, thanks."

"Another Coors Light," I say and motion with my bottle.

The bartender says, "That's half full."

"It'll save you a trip," I say.

"I'm just jagging you guys," he says. "Drink up. I need the exercise."

I finish my beer anyway, and the bartender brings another round. I wait for him to add it to our tab or write it down for later but he doesn't. He opens the Post Gazette sports section and gets comfortable on a stool beneath the mounted TV.

James says, "I'm either drunk in one drink or I'm disoriented."

Richard says, "Probably both."

James says, "I hope not."

Richard says, "I once walked off stage stone sober, drank two beers and passed out drunk. I was dehydrated from the lights or something."

James says, "I used to pass out a lot of ways, but never that."

Richard says, "I'm calming down."

James says, "Good."

Richard is weird, but James is weird around Richard. Or Richard brings out the weird in James. If I don't talk soon, if I don't start directing the conversation, the talk will stop.

Richard will start nodding like he's autistic. James will nod back like Richard is autistic.

James gets out his cigarettes. He counts out five. They lay on the bar like pieces of chalk.

Richard says, "I was joking. I don't want your cigarettes."

James says, "I thought you needed cigarettes."

Richard says, "I'll just roll my own."

James says, "You're fine."

I hear them but I try not to. I drink. I act like I'm watching CNN on the TV above the bar and start making a mental list of what I need to do to survive:

1.) call home

2.) get drunk

3.) make it back to campus to cancel my classes

4.) make it back to the bar

5.) help Richard somehow

6.) keep getting drunk

7.) get James to Kentucky Jim's office so Kentucky Jim can guarantee James a job

8.) call home and apologize for something

9.) get James to an AA meeting

10.) go home

11.) never do any of this again

12.) never do any of this again

I turn back to James and Richard. James is smoking. The bar doesn't have beer in cans. Richard tears at the label of his Pabst non-returnable with his thumbnail. The silence sits between them like an empty bottle, past closing.

I say, "Sorry. I zoned out there."

Richard says, "Where should I start, Dan?"

I say, "Start with the asshole student who threatened you."

"Threatened you how?" James says.

Richard tells him. He tells James what he told me before, then picks up with today.

It was eight o'clock this morning and Richard was in the library. He had work to do, papers to correct. He knew he was welcome in the office but we were full-time and he was part-time and it doesn't matter if he's welcome in the office. There's a code: full-timers before part-timers. "It's my pride," Richard says. "It's not you two."

"Good," James says.

"Anyway," Richard says. "I have three papers to correct in two hours. I've read them, I just haven't marked them." He drinks from his Pabst. Pabst is a horrible beer for teenagers. It tastes like metal and other things awful. Richard says, "I have ballpark grades in my head but I haven't made any concrete decisions, and I haven't written any comments. So three papers in two hours, I'm rushed."

I can do three papers in thirty minutes.

James, on a tizzy, can do twenty papers in fifty seconds.

It's like we teach on different planets with different laws for success. If we were the models, physics wouldn't exist.

Richard says, "I want to be accurate with my comments."

"Of course," I say.

James says, "Get to the threatening-student part."

Richard says, "I know I ramble. Can you bear with me today?"

James says, "I am doing my best to bear with you today," but he's not and he sounds sarcastic. James wants to drink and, because he never drinks, wants to enjoy it. If enjoying it is miserable, then he wants it to be his own misery.

I nod with a bottle in my mouth.

Richard says, "I had my papers spread out in the library. I'm reading and concentrating."

James says, "Go on."

Richard was at a big table. He had a pen, a pencil, and a highlighter. The first paper, something that discussed the influence of Chinese poetry on American Independent Cinema, was the best essay he'd read all semester. He gave it an A-, mainly because he wasn't familiar enough with Chinese poetry to know if the student was being accurate; otherwise: B+. The next paper, a compare-and-contrast essay that related Fox News to *The Bible*, was average. Richard gave it a C+ even though it deserved a C because he didn't want the student to think he was prejudiced against Fox News (even though he was). Paper three was written by Carson Phillips, the kid who'd been threatening Richard. Richard read the paper. It was one page. It was three lines. The three lines said, "This deserves an A. I saw your band on YouTube. Fucking geeks."

James says, "I didn't know you were on YouTube. That part is interesting."

Richard looks at James. He raises his hands to explain it all again then stops. Richard cannot understand why someone like James cannot understand him.

James says, "I know. I'm just trying to be positive."

Richard says, "It gets worse."

I say, "Richard, you have a bruise the size of a quarter on your neck."

"Where?" he says.

"Right behind your ear."

He touches behind his ear like he can see with his fingers. The bruise is small but dark and violent, a blackberry that's been squeezed into his skin.

"He had me by the throat," Richard says.

"Who?" James says.

"Carson," Richard says. "Are you understanding anything?"

Richard's voice goes up. I've never heard him yell but this is it. He gets red, the ears, the bald spots. The bruise deepens. I think he may hit James.

He doesn't hit James.

Richard says, "I should use the bathroom."

He finishes his beer and stands.

I say, "You want me to get you another?"

He says, "I would appreciate that."

Richard takes his bag and heads to the restroom in the back of the bar.

James waits then says, "Am I being an asshole? Am I missing something? I get that this student is fucking with him. I'm not trying to make a joke out of that. He's just so fucking slow."

"He's upset," I say. "You might want to focus on the asshole student and not ask any more questions about Richard and his band being on YouTube."

"I didn't think Richard had ever made a video," he says and pauses. "Now I hear myself. I sound like an asshole. I need to drink faster. I'm in a very bad, selfish mood."

I say, "When you get drunk, we need to go see Kentucky Jim."

"Why?"

"It's a long story, but basically he pulled me out of class yesterday and took me to a bar. I think he was on a bender. He's sick of the university and writers who don't drink and his usual stuff. He was raving about Harry Crews. I got smashed on vodka and he guaranteed me my job. If he sees you drunk, he'll guarantee you your job, too."

James finishes his Jack Daniels in a long disgusted swallow and says, "I thought you said he guaranteed my job already."

"Yeah," I say. "I lied. He's very confused by your sobriety. He knows you're a good teacher and a good guy but he can't believe that a good teacher and a good guy would never get fall-down drunk. It would be good for him to see you shitfaced."

James says, "He's more of an asshole than I imagined."

The bartender says, "Asshole? Who called my name?" and he laughs and climbs down from his stool as I finish my beer. "Another round?" he says. He's at his suspenders again, like he's trying to make them fit.

"Sure," I say. "What's your name?"

"Hemingway," he says. "I'm the owner."

"No relation to the real Hemingway?" I say.

"No no," he says. "I'm him."

"The real Hemingway?" James says.

"It's an honor," I say and reach out and shake his hand.

James doesn't shake his hand. He says, "How about you reel me in a real big one this time? Best drink in the ocean, okay Papa?"

Hemingway says, "Double Jack, Coors Light, and another Pabst for the gentleman in the bowtie who looks like he went to cry in my restroom."

"That'd be great," I say. "Put it on the tab."

Hemingway says, "Is that gentleman a poofter or what?"

I say, "He's sensitive."

Hemingway says, "That's what I said. Sensitive. He looks like a mob lawyer, a bad one. And a drinker of Pabst."

Richard comes back. He's focused and ready to talk. His glasses are clear. His bowtie is straight. I think we're going to get to the bruise on his neck but we're back in the library, at the table, with his thoughts and his red pen.

In the library, he'd crumbled up Carson Phillips' paper and

thrown it in the trash. Then he dug it out and wrote F in red marker on the paper. He wrote, "See me after class."

Carson Phillips saw him after class.

"Devastated," Richard says. "I thought the kid was going to cry."

Richard invited Carson to the library for an impromptu conference. Richard said, "Carson, there's still a chance you can pass." He told Carson he needed to grow up and do the work. College wasn't high school. Carson said, "I know. I'm screwing up." Carson said he had a cubby in the basement of the Cathedral, two floors down. Cubbies are study rooms students can rent. It was closer than the library. They went there. The room was tiny, a desk and two chairs. Richard sat down. Carson closed the door. Richard said, "Can I talk straight?" Carson opened the desk drawer. He pulled out a pen, a gold, engraved, ballpoint pen. Carson said, "Talk." Richard noticed how the tone had changed in Carson's voice, but he didn't think it was much. It was nothing. Richard was in charge. Carson was afraid. Richard was the adult. Carson was not. Besides, Carson was at his worst around other students, his friends. This was the two of them. Richard was the professor. He said, "Look, you can still pass." Carson said, "Look, I can still pass." Richard paused. What he wanted to say, he wanted to mean. But he didn't know what he wanted to say. He couldn't say what he meant. Carson said, "Look, you can still pass," but in a whiny voice. Richard said, "Are you mocking me?" Carson did the voice. He said, "Are you mocking me?" Then he hit Richard on the head with the ballpoint pen. It hurt. Richard said, "Jesus," and ducked and covered up. His bag fell.

Richard says, "I shouldn't have ducked. It was showing weakness."

James and I don't say anything.

Back in the cubby, Carson said, "A. That's my final offer."
Richard picked up his bag. He tried to stand. Grades were
not negotiable. Carson said, "A. That's my final offer," and
whapped Richard again with the pen. Again, Richard ducked.
He stayed seated. Richard touched his head. He wanted to kill
this student. He could kill this student. No matter what Richard felt about violence or how he'd been born or the taunts
he'd endured as a kid, he was a man, and a man, any man, could
destroy a Carson. But destroying Carson would cost Richard
his job. It had gone too far. Richard couldn't explain this. If he
had acted according to policy, some policy he'd never read,
some policy never written, he wouldn't have ended up in a
cubby with Carson, being repeatedly rapped with a pen that
looked like it was a gift from a very wealthy aunt. This was
inexplicable, like Richard turning down a record deal from
David Geffen.

Richard says, "I've made so many bad choices with my life."
I say, "You've made good choices, too."
James says, "Yeah."
Richard says, "He kept hitting me with that fucking pen."
Carson threw the pen this time. It hit Richard and fell to
the ground and Carson picked it up. Richard stood and said, "I
have to leave." He said, "That's it." He covered his head so Car-
son couldn't hit him again. He stepped towards the door. Car-
son said, "Who said you could stand, Pussylips?" and grabbed
Richard by the throat. It was a weak grip. It was nothing. Rich-
ard, without even meaning to, broke the hold and knocked
Carson to the floor. "Stay down," Richard said and Carson did.
I say, "That kid should be arrested."
Richard says, "Really?"
James says, "Probably not." He says, "I'm just being
realistic."

Richard says, "I know." He says, "When I pushed him, he fell like a girl."

I say, "Fuck that guy."

Richard says, "I never wanted to be a rockstar like everyone else. I just wanted to make a living playing music. That was all."

James says, "I'm glad you pushed him down."

Richard says, "It was an accident."

I try to imagine Carson, first choking Richard then falling back. I can and I can't.

James says, "Another Jack Daniels."

Richard says, "Pabst."

I say, "Sure, another Coors Light bottle."

The bartender gets the round and makes four shots, all whiskey.

He says, "I like you guys."

Richard says, "A student tried to kill me."

The bartender, Hemingway, says, "You look like a scientist."

James says, "He is."

We drink our shots. No one makes a toast. I'm drunk but only because I was drunk yesterday. Richard goes back to his story, the misery of it.

Carson stayed down and Richard, in tears, made his way out of the Cathedral and to the lawn where he found me, where he found James.

But now we're here, in Hemingway's Bar, with the real Hemingway bartending, and James and I look at the marks on Richard's head and the bruise on his neck like a birthmark and say, "That's awful," but we don't know what else to do.

"You kick his ass," Hemingway says. "That's what you do."

James and I are at the bar. I've been to class, canceled without explanation, and come back, my Coors Light still cool on a wet napkin. Richard is somewhere in the Cathedral, his head bruised and slightly disfigured, teaching.

James says, "What the fuck is wrong with him?"

"Integrity," I say. "Discipline."

James says, "Neither." He says, "Naiveté. Stupidity."

"He's a glutton for punishment," I say.

"His head looks like it's been attacked by bees. The guy is retarded. You can't get beat up by a student then go back and teach more students. It's illogical."

James is drinking me two-to-one. I have a beer. He has a beer and a whiskey. When he finishes the whiskey, he knocks the glass on the wood bar like it's a door to somewhere he wants to be. The bartender doesn't like it. He hears the sound like James is ringing a bell in his direction and he sighs and shakes his head.

James says, "Do you have your cell phone?"

"I think it's turned off," I say. "Either I forgot to pay the bill or I forgot to charge it or probably both. Richard has a cell phone. You should have asked him."

"I don't want to use Richard's cell phone."

"When I say I forgot to pay the bill, I mean I was broke. Who do you need to call?"

James says, "Kentucky Jim. I'm not walking over there if he's not in his office."

"He'll be in his office," I say. "Even if he's not, I still have to cancel my last class. We can head over then go drink somewhere else then head to that AA meeting."

"You're still serious about that AA meeting?"

"You don't have to believe it. Just go."

James says, "I wish we had some cocaine."

I say, "I was thinking the same thing yesterday."

We talk about James' car, the one he wrecked, the one with the five-hundred dollar deductible. I'd forgotten such a car existed. James hasn't.

He says, "It's still in the shop."

"That's a little long," I say.

"It's a lot long," James says. "But my mechanic had to break a couple things—or make a couple things appear broken—so he could jack up the rate to cover my deductible."

"Your mechanic sounds like a good guy."

"He's not. He broke a couple things that couldn't be broken in the wreck so he could make some extra dough for himself, and now the insurance company is coming back out to take a look. It's pathetic. I'm pathetic."

"You're great and God loves you," I say.

"It's a scam gone awry," he says. "Was that just AA talk?"

"Maybe," I say. "How are you getting around?"

"I'm not," he says. "I'm walking."

James does his thing with his whiskey glass, two raps this time. He reaches over the bar for an extra napkin and wipes his mouth. He sucks air and says, "Wow," but to himself. All those tough guys in the movies swallow whiskey without a look but James shows the burn.

Hemingway says, "You guys want another round before I leave? The new girl should have been here twenty-five minutes ago."

"Sure," I say.

"You lose the poof with bowtie?" he says.

"He's gone to teach," I say.

"You know who my great teacher was?"

"Jack London?" James says. "Knut Hamsun?"

If you don't know Knut Hamsun, the great Norwegian

writer who almost starved to death while writing his first book, his name sounds like a dessert.

When the bartender doesn't respond to James' joke, James says it again with an English, maybe Australian, possibly Scottish accent.

I say, "Tell me about this teacher."

The bartender, Hemingway, says, "As I was saying," and picks up a rag and wipes around the bar in circles, moving up our drinks and throwing away our napkins. "You want to take a guess who my great teacher was? Remember, I was born in 1941."

I say, "Are we talking elementary school, college, what?"

Hemingway says, "College!" and laughs.

"Not college," I say.

"College was for poofters," James says.

Hemingway has started to ignore James like he has a bowtie on. With every drink, the volume on James goes up, the sarcasm gets more sincere. It's not bad yet, maybe it won't get bad, but bartenders have an ear for this kind of music. They listen for it to get too loud, loud enough to bother the other customers, then they throw the radio out into the street.

I say, "Assuming you're a Pittsburgh guy, I'll go with Art Rooney, Sr."

Art Rooney, Sr. was the original owner of the Pittsburgh Steelers. He was a cigar-chomping Irish Catholic who loved horse racing and backroom card games. He had blubbery lips and the kind of eyes that see joy and pain and nothing else. He died on the North Side of Pittsburgh in the same neighborhood where he grew up but many million dollars richer.

Hemingway says, "Art Rooney, Sr.?" and smiles and points at me with his rag. He says, "I *wish* Art Rooney, Sr. That's good. But I did drink with his kid Danny once at a tavern down by the yacht club. He was a nice enough guy, but I think he was drinking club soda."

James says, "Club soda? That's unacceptable. He must have been a poofter."

"You should try a little club soda," Hemingway says. "Or a lot of club soda." Then, back to me, "My father was my teacher, and I don't mean that in some metaphysical afternoon talk show way. I mean the guy was my teacher. When I was in school, first through sixth grade were all in the same building. No kindergarten. Men didn't teach then. Teaching was a women's profession. But my father built the school house and when he was done building it, he taught. He worked in a sawmill before that, drove to Ohio every day. That's why he wasn't in the war. He was a saw mill filer and that was considered essential work. He did that and came home every night and read books. A book was something then, solid. Looked like a box with pages in it. My father read the big ones too. Everything Dickens wrote. He read a *Christmas Carol* to us every December. Then, when I was old enough for school and my brother was almost old enough for school, he built our school house. A big barn-looking thing. He went to the church, and the church bought us books. I guess the state or the church or someone paid him some sort of salary because he eventually quit the saw mill. He taught us every day, five days a week, long days, bring your own lunch. If you weren't there, you better have been working on your family farm. My old man was a no-bullshit guy. If you mouthed off in class, he let it slide until phys ed class, then he cancelled whatever activity we were doing and taught wrestling. Wrestling back then was like fist-fighting without your fists. My father could pick up the biggest kids, guys fifteen and sixteen years old, and slam them to the ground like nothing, like they were potatoes." He says, "This was up in

Beaver County. It was all farmland then." He motions like it's just outside the bar. "My father didn't take any bullshit. He'd kick my ass right now if he knew I was running a bar. The man never drank."

James says, "Made Dan Rooney look like a real man, even with his club soda."

Hemingway turns away from me. He fixes his suspenders and breathes deeps. He takes his rag off the bar like it's a weapon, like he's going to make James eat it or put it around his neck and choke him out or maybe blind James with a locker-room flick.

I say, "He didn't mean anything."

James says, "I didn't *say* anything," and you can hear his voice crackle with meanness.

Hemingway picks up James' whiskey, wipes underneath. Instead of returning the drink to the bar or topping it off, he turns and tosses the glass, half-full, into the trash. He picks up James' half-full beer bottle and does the same. The glass and the bottle hit then settle into the trash with the other bottles, all making glass noises. Hemingway leans on the bar.

James doesn't say anything. I haven't seen him cornered like this in years, though it was common when he was a drunk, when he was picking up strangers' drinks and drinking them in a sip and pretending like the drinks were his own while the customers went for the bartenders and the bartenders went for the bouncers and James tried to steal another glass of booze.

A youngish woman walks through the front door. She's rushed, dressed in black slacks and a white shirt, obviously an employee, obviously the bartender who's running late.

She says, "Hey George. I'm so sorry. The bus never came." She stops to adjust her shirt. She says, "I walked. I'm covered in sweat. Can you stay three more minutes? Please?"

George, Hemingway, says, "Not a problem," still staring at James.

The woman goes off towards the bathroom, digging in her purse for something.

George, Hemingway, says, "There are people who can drink and people who can't. It's important to know which one you are and it's important to know before it's too late." He goes to the cash register and hands me my Visa. He says, "Drinks are on me this morning. I've enjoyed your company." He tosses his rag on the bar, not at James but near.

I stand and push in my stool. I know better than to argue or make excuses. James is melting his own personality down with booze and it's not the way Hemingway wants to make his money this morning or, probably, any morning.

"Thanks," I say, putting my card in my wallet. "We appreciate it."

"No problem," Hemingway says. "Stop back."

"Fuck you," James says.

"Okay," I say. "Don't."

James stands up, ready to fight or leave or get thrown through the glass.

"Fuck me," Hemingway says, calmly. "You got it."

Then he gets his newspaper.

Then he gets his stool and starts to read.

We're outside Kentucky Jim's office on the sixth floor of the Cathedral. I've just cancelled my class. I didn't go to the podium or write on the board. With the door cracked open, I poked my head inside the room and said, "Sorry, I have a meeting that just came up. We'll pick up next class." I didn't wait for questions. I didn't pretend to care. I've cancelled more classes this semester than I have in my entire academic career.

James plays drums on Kentucky Jim's door. James is happy to be drunk now that he knows getting drunk will help his job. He is loud, louder than the bar. I can see the aggression on his face like a line, like a wrinkle. The last time he was drunk, at my son's basketball game, was some kind of joyful fluke. This is the James I remember from the end of his drinking days: vicious. He presses his ear to the glass on Kentucky Jim's door. He knocks with the side of his head like he's a ram.

James says, "Where is that old fuckhead?" but happy, happy and angry. He says, "We should kick this door down and see if that old fuckhead is in there."

I say, "Hey," and motion with my hands. "There are other people around."

He says, "Where?" and he's right, the hall is empty. He says, "I would like to take a huge dump right outside Kentucky Jim's door."

"Yeah," I say. "Don't do that."

"What was up with that old-man bartender at Hemingway's?"

"You mean Hemingway?"

"I mean George," James says. "That guy was an asshole."

I think about George, about Hemingway, about what a kind man he was, and how it must be painful to own such a terrible bar when you know better.

"He wasn't an asshole," I say. "You should probably tone it down."

"I know I should tone it down," he says.

"Well?" I say.

"Well, let's just have a good time. I'm stupid. I know that.

Let's not ruin my future plans for sobriety by being rational tonight."

"Or something," I say.

"Come on," he says, sincere. "Let's just—" and he pauses and makes a motion with his hand like he's landing a plane on still water.

"Okay," I say.

"I know I'm being an asshole. I just…I'll settle in. You have my word."

"Okay," I say.

James turns and knocks on Kentucky Jim's door with his chest, a sort of belly-flop. The wood and glass rattle and echo down the hall.

"See, that's not okay," I say.

"You're absolutely right," he says.

"I know I'm right."

"Don't hate me."

He's doing a better job of hating himself than I ever could.

"Sure," I say. "We'll find Kentucky Jim and make it a night."

"I would like to hear some music," James says.

"I could sing to you."

A door opens at the bottom of the stairwell and we hear steps.

If it's Kentucky Jim, we're fine. James is more than drunk enough to be reappointed to the position of Visiting Lecturer in Creative Writing. Kentucky Jim will be impressed with James' slurred speech and head-knocking. James might fall or puke and get promoted.

If it's a student, we're okay. Students don't think their professors drink. We're like high school teachers or priests, parents with books and rules, not lives and ideas.

But anything else is bad. Secretaries are bad. Other

professors are worse. Even a nosy janitor could smell our boozy stink and spread the gossip.

James looks at me and puts his fingers to his lips, shh.

I nod, right, quiet.

Lila, one of the secretaries' work-studies, comes up the stairs and around the bend. Lila is maybe twenty-five, a writing major, serious about her school and work. She'd been living in South Korea, teaching English as a second language. Now she's on a scholarship and working part-time, stuffing mailboxes and delivering messages.

James shouts, "Lila!"

Lila shouts, "James!"

Everyone likes Lila. The other students wish they could write like her, and the professors are happy to have someone so talented, so mature, in class. Lila is from West Virginia. She writes about West Virginia and moonshine and hillbillies who grow pot and make bathtub crystal meth. Kentucky Jim thinks Lila is one of his protégés. He's loves her stories and her writing, but he loves her looks and southern-ness, too. "Ol' fucking Lila," Kentucky Jim says, a compliment. Lila has tits out to here and she was raised by a coal-mining uncle who got drunk and played Hazel Dickens songs on guitar. She wears jeans, sometimes overalls, and flannel shirts, which is a schtick. She's not on the mountain. She hasn't even been in America for the past two years. But the university is like this. Everyone must be identifiable. Black people must write about black people and wear at least one piece of tribal clothing. Writers from West Virginia, even students, must wear overalls. Lila also wears shit-kicking boots.

Lila says, "Hey, Professor Charles."

I wave and smile.

James picks up Lila and swings her like the war is over and

she's his girl. She has on a skirt today, a little country but not much, blue and flowing but feminine.

I say, "Where's your mountain clothes?"

Lila says, "I left them in the holler." She says, "You guys are drunk," and laughs.

James puts her down and says, "Shh."

I say, "Do you know where Kentucky Jim is?"

James says, "Yes, where is that ol' fuckhole?"

Lila says, "He's having eye surgery today, right? Or is that tomorrow?" She looks at us like we should know. She says, "I think it's today." She says, "Maybe not. I saw him yesterday and he was smashed and that was in the morning. So maybe the surgery is tomorrow. I think he'd need a day to sober up before surgery."

"Maybe it's a laser thing," James says and makes a laser sound that he fires from his finger.

Lila says, "You're funny when you're drunk." Then, "You guys should probably get out of here. Carrie Polinski is making the rounds, trying to get people to teach her friend's book or something. Everyone is hiding from her."

I say, "We should go. Good idea."

James says, "I should take a big dump in front of Carrie Polinski's door."

Lila says, "That's probably a bad idea."

I say, "No more talk of taking dumps."

"It's low class," James says but like he's talking about someone else.

"Yes," I say.

Lila says, "What time did you guys start drinking?"

James says, "Excellent question."

I say, "A while ago."

Lila says, "Why do you hate Carrie Polinski?"

James says, "I don't hate her. I just want to take a huge dump in front of her door."

"Stop," I say but I laugh which makes it worse. To Lila, I say, "Carrie Polinski wrote a book and James was a character."

Lila says, "I thought her last book was a memoir."

"It was," James says. "That's why I hate her."

"You're not The Punter, are you?" Lila says. "Oh god, you should sue her or something. I can't believe she'd do that."

"Write about him or call him The Punter?" I say.

"Both," Lila says.

James says, "She should have called me The Poofter. That would have been fine."

Lila says, "What's a poofter?"

I say, "It's someone who wears a bowtie."

James says, "I'm getting sick in the stomach thinking about Carrie Polinski."

Lila says, "You should." She says, "Did you guys really date?"

James says, "No."

I say, "Definitely not."

Lila says, "The book was terrible. I couldn't get through it."

"That helps," James says.

Lila says, "Carrie Cleats—I mean, what the fuck was that?"

James says, "Fuck Carrie Polinski. I was just trying to be nice."

Lila says, "No one would fuck her back where I'm from. She looks like a man."

"Okay," I say. "Chill out you two," though I'm there, thinking the same.

Lila says, "That probably sounded meaner than I intended."

I say, quietly, "We're not in a bar."

"But we should be," James says.

Lila says, "A bar would be fun," and she bumps me with her hip.

"Not getting fired would be fun," I say and bump her back. "Don't repeat any of this stuff, okay? I'm serious."

"I wouldn't," she says. "Everyone sort of knows Kentucky Jim is an asshole. Everyone thinks Carrie Polinski's book is self-help shit."

"That's good to know," I say.

"You know what's good to know?" James says. "My balls."

Lila says, "You're like my drunk uncle."

"It's possible I am your uncle," James says. "I have kin in West Virginia. We could be cousin or brother and sister or both."

Lila says, "You inbred son of a bitch," and laughs. Then, "You guys should really go. You're too drunk to be at work, and I'm pretty sure Jim isn't here."

I knock lightly on Kentucky Jim's door to make certain. I rub my knuckles on the wood. The answer is nothing, boredom, an empty office. There's a poster on the door for a movie by Lance Corbin, something about Appalachia and music. A woman is dancing in a long skirt. A man plays the fiddle. It's probably a fine movie that no one saw. Kentucky Jim sees all the movies about Appalachia that no one sees.

It's two o'clock. Kentucky Jim will not see James drunk and be impressed. He's either in the hospital or going there soon. He's either resting and drinking diet Pepsi or wearing a hospital gown and rubbing his eyes. I am drunk and tired and inappropriate. James is drunker, more tired, and more inappropriate. Lila is a terrific young writer. Lila knows our secrets. Carrie Polinski is somewhere, lurking. My bad ideas about employment have gotten worse. James and I are not going to any Alcoholics Anonymous meeting, ever.

James says, "Lila, you should come and drink with us."

Lila says, "I work until three."

James says, "We'll still be drunk then."

Lila says, "Really? Maybe I could get off early."

I say, "We were thinking about going to an AA meeting," just to say it.

Lila says, "That's different."

James says, "We were hoping to get drunk with Ol' hump master Kentucky Jim."

Lila says, "Maybe go to the AA meeting?"

James says, "You're being a downer."

Lila says, "I'll drink with you guys. You guys look like fun."

"We are fun," I say.

W e stop at the O, a dirty hotdog shop and French fry restaurant in Oakland. James runs in and gets a six pack of Mike's Hard Lemonade. I drive around the block until he comes out. He jumps in the backseat with Lila.

I say, "Am I the chauffeur?"

Lila says, "Mike's Hard? Are you kidding?"

James says, "I can't drink any more beer. I'm out of practice."

Lila says, "Those hurt my tummy."

James says, "My tummy is numb."

I say, "Give me one of those." I say, "Seriously, I'm supposed to sit up here by myself? You're terrible people."

"We're not," Lila says.

"You both are," I say. "I've known it about James since he was five. Lila, I thought you were better than this."

Lila hands me a Mike's Hard. I know she's a good person because she twists the cap off before she hands me the bottle over my shoulder. I look in the rearview mirror but it's too early for cops or at least cops paying attention. I could be wrecking my life.

Lila says, "Let's go to a strip bar."

James says, "No."

Lila says, "Why not?"

James says, "I am a serious academic at a serious university. I can't be seen in a nasty-ass strip club with a student and a fellow serious academic."

"Really?" Lila says.

"Not really," James says. "But drinks are too expensive."

"But the girlies are hot," Lila says.

I try to remember if Lila writes about strip clubs. I try to remember if she writes about girls or lesbians or being bi. I can't. It's all moonshine and reefer grown in the holler and Boone County police pumping shotguns outside the barn.

"I do like hot girlies," James says. "But not as much as I hate ten-dollar drinks."

"Boobies and shaved pussies," Lila says.

"Your mouth," James says. "It's horrible."

I look at Lila in the rearview mirror and she's smiling, probably imagining this is what writers do or what teachers do, happy to be pursuing a degree in English.

Lila says, "What do you think, Professor Charles?"

"I don't," I say. "Think. Not when I've been drinking this much."

I don't feel like going to a strip club.

But I could easily be convinced to go to a strip club.

Lila says, "You drive great."

"Thanks," I say.

James says, "I doubt I want to drink a Sex On The Beach at a strip club. If I were rich, yes, a Sex On The Beach and a couple Alabama Slammers would be fine. I'm not rich. Would a crack house be out of the question?"

"Yes," I say. "A crack house would be out of the question."

Lila says, "I can't believe my talk of naked women isn't tempting you guys."

"Actually," I say. "James finds the vagina deeply troubling, especially when it's opened."

James says, "I find the vagina a beautiful thing."

"In the dark," I say.

"In the dark, of course," James says. "What if pussy tasted like Mike's Hard?"

"Lots of under-aged boys would be drunk?" Lila says. "Under-aged girls maybe. Housewives. Who drinks this stuff?"

"I wish I was better at sex," James says. "I like thinking about it more than doing it."

"Remember that time I sat on your face?" I say.

"Stop," James says. "She's going to think we're serious."

Lila says, "I take nothing you two say seriously." She finishes her Mike's Hard in a sip. She disappears from the rearview mirror to get another bottle. She says, "But seriously, let's go to a strip club."

"They really are expensive," I say.

"Expensive?" Lila says. "You guys are like professors."

We go to The Cricket in North Oakland, a couple miles from the Pitt campus. I haven't been here in years, mainly because lots of the strippers are students or student-age. Once I started teaching, I didn't want to see students naked, not because my students weren't worth seeing naked but because I don't know, just because.

It's a five-dollar cover at the door. I'm first in so I pay for everyone. The drinks at Hemingway's Bar were free. James bought the sixer of Mike's Hard. Thanks to Kentucky Jim, I still have money. I still have two one-hundred-dollar bills. James grabs my shoulders, a hug, and gives me a shake. I know we'll drink this night out, the whole way.

The bouncer says, "Nothing smaller?"

I say, "Sorry." I say, "It's the first hundred I've had since ever."

James says, "Mr. Moneybucks."

The bouncer says, "Eighty-five dollars back at you. You can get singles at the bar." He's my height, maybe my age, but covered in tattoos. He's mellow for a bouncer which means he's a badass. The big badass bouncers are always nothing. He says, "Have a good time, gentlemen and lady," and nods as we pass through.

Lila says, "Did you just pay for me? Thanks Professor Charles."

I say, "Let's go with Dan tonight. Professor Charles sounds a little weird."

Lila says, "I was being funny."

James says, "Let's hope so." Then, "This is nice."

Lila says, "I've never been here. The strip clubs in West Virginia are not like this."

Either my memory is off or the place has been remodeled. The Cricket used to be a dump, dusty and dull with old paint peeling off the walls, all the charm in the dirt and the coked-up girls dancing to hip hop and hair metal. This new room is neon and brass, a new stripper pole up on a new stage with new cushioned chairs lining the catwalk. There's wallpaper. There's a sofa and a screened-off area for lap dances. It's like a movie, a TV show from HBO. I've seen this strip club a million times even though I've never been in this version of this strip club. All that personality, all those years of boot scuffs on the tile floor and warped boards on the stage, has been replaced with props and red track lights and a DJ with his baseball hat on sideways.

Lila says, "I don't know. This looks boring."

I say, "Really. It's like fucking *Showgirls* or something."

James says, "I like it. I remember coming here back in the day and wondering if I was going to get shot. This has a nice safe vibe to it." He says, "Who wants what? I'm going to the bar to get the booze."

"Beer," I say.

"Absolut and tonic with a lime," Lila says.

James heads for the drinks. The bar in the corner glows with tiny bulbs and shiny leather and wine glasses hanging upside-down from a ceiling-mounted rack.

Lila takes my arm and says, "Is he okay?"

"Not really," I say. "But he will be once we get him through this night."

"You'll explain later?"

"Sure," I say. "You want to sit by the stage?"

"I think we have to."

Lila's right. The room is empty. No old men lusting for hornier days with a couple quiet drinks. No frat guys on an afternoon bender. Even the construction workers and road crews are still on the clock, building and paving. So we move to the stage and take a couple seats.

Almost instantly, music starts to play. It's Frank Sinatra. It's deadening. If I never hear "My Way" again, it won't be a mistake.

"If she comes out in a Fedora, we should leave," I say.

Lila says, "I stripped once."

"In West Virginia?"

"At a truckstop," she says. "That's gross, huh?"

"That's hilarious," I say. "I used to live at truckstop strip clubs."

"When?"

"When I was a trucker."

"That's worse than stripping," Lila says and laughs. "I knew you were cool."

"Tell me about your stripping adventure," I say.

"It was a contest thing. My sister and a bunch of her friends were going out for somebody's twenty-first birthday and I tagged along. I had a fake ID and we bar hopped all night. I got smashed on Long Island Iced Teas."

Lila adjusts her top. She's either sticking out her breasts or hiding them. It's awkward and sort of sexy and sort of not.

I say, "I remember Long Island Iced Teas."

"Weren't they awful? But they worked. I was trashed. My big sister or someone knew this other girl who was stripping at the truckstop. They all hated this girl for some reason. She'd fucked one of their boyfriends or something. So they decided we would go to this strip club which was having a Best Chest in the West"—and she holds up a finger, "wait for it…Best Chest in the West…Virginia Area contest and, ta da, they thought I could win. Like I said I was seventeen. I'd had sex with one guy and he seemed to like my boobs so I said sure. Anything to get attention, to piss off my aunt and uncle."

James walks up and distributes our drinks. He hands me two Coors Light bottles, both dripping wet like they've been in ice. Lila takes her vodka tonic.

James says, "Frank Sinatra, nice. Where's the dancer?"

"She's yet to appear," Lila says.

"Lila used to strip," I say.

"One time," Lila says. "It was a contest."

"Did you win?" James says.

"Yeah," I say. "Did you win?"

James leans over and puts his face on the catwalk. I think he might throw up or pass out. He closes his eyes. I nod at Lila and she touches James gently on the shoulder.

James says, "Fine. Just breathing. I'm almost ready for a comeback."

Lila says, "Are you sure? We could go."

James opens his eyes and says, "But did you win?"

"I got second place," Lila says. "Which was better than the girl who I was supposed to beat. I don't think she even placed."

"Did they douse you in water?" James says.

"It wasn't a wet t-shirt contest," Lila says.

"I didn't know there was a difference," James says.

"You never went back?" I say.

"Not to strip," she says.

James says, "We need ones."

"You're right," I say and go for my wallet.

Lila pulls out a twenty and says, "Here, you guys have been paying for everything."

James sits up. He says, "That was the best thirty-second nap I've ever taken." He takes her twenty and goes back to the bar for a stack of singles.

Lila pulls her hair back and lets it fall. She says, "Is he okay?"

I say, "I believe so, yes."

I do a little drum roll on the catwalk with my knuckles. The catwalk is so tight, the wood so perfect, it barely makes a sound. I do it again with my palms and it's louder, like a slap.

Lila says, "So tell me about this truck driving thing."

"It was my safety net," I say. "Once I got a master's in poetry, I knew I'd fucked up and that I wouldn't find a job and that I'd just wasted a bunch of money. So I got a CDL license."

"That's hilarious," Lila says.

"It is now," I say. "But you might want to reconsider stripping if you're seriously going to get a degree in writing."

"I could get a degree in stripping," she says.

"With a minor in writing," I say.

I look across the room at James. He's being charming with the bartender, a young woman in her mid-twenties with a buzz cut and lots of piercings. Even from here, I can see she's beautiful. Even from here, I can see she needs to take some of that metal from her face. James says something and lifts his leg up on the bar like it's a beam for a ballerina. He tries to put his forehead to his knee and comes close. The bartender laughs and claps. She gets the manager, another sexy woman, but older, dressed down. I think James is auditioning.

"Did you see that?" Lila says.

"I did," I say.

"Is he always this funny?"

"I think so," I say. "Until this month, he hadn't had a drink in eleven years."

"Is this brewing to be a disaster?" she says.

"Let's hope not."

"Do you guys hate Kentucky Jim?"

"What makes you think that?"

"James called him a fuckhead then threatened to take a dump in front of his door."

"I didn't hear that," I say. "Did James really say that?"

"Stop," she says and touches my leg. "I won't tell. Do you guys hate him?"

"Not really," I say. "Do you hate him?"

"He tried to fuck me," Lila says. "Not in a bad way or anything."

"As long as it wasn't in a bad way," I say.

"You know what I mean."

"I do," I say. "Old Kentucky Jim is pretty harmless."

"He invited me back to his house. We were supposed to go over my story. We actually did go over my story, but his comments didn't make any sense. I think he was stoned when I got there. He was watching a black-and-white train movie, a hobo movie. We had a couple drinks and he asked to kiss me. I said probably not. Then he asked if I was interested in watching some movie about bluegrass music or clog dancing or something up in his bedroom. Naked. I said probably not. I wasn't in the habit of watching movies in the buff with my professors."

"The old bluegrass movie usually works on undergraduate chicks."

"He was nice after that," Lila says. "He didn't try to touch me or anything. It was just weird. Then it wasn't. He's been as nice or nicer ever since."

I say, "I just think—" and I stop. "I don't know what I think. He's Kentucky Jim. He feels like he has to get drunk and try to get laid. He hasn't written a book in thirty-some years. If he didn't get drunk and try to get some pussy, he wouldn't even count as a writer."

"Why doesn't he write anymore?"

"I don't know. He doesn't know. I asked him that question myself."

"Did you read his book?"

"I did."

"Well?" she says and laughs.

"He's my boss. It's the best book ever."

"Yeah," she says. "I couldn't get through it either." She says,

"Isn't it okay if writers drink and get laid? I thought that's what they did."

I say, "Well."

There is a disco ball above the stage but it's shaped like a diamond and it's hanging from a chain made of glittery rocks.

I say, "Writers probably never really got that drunk. A few did. Then people quit reading and buying books so writers had to become teachers. A couple kept having fun. Then teaching jobs became scarce and now everyone is broke and no one has time to get drunk."

"But Kentucky Jim?" Lila says.

"But Kentucky Jim, exactly."

"And you and James?"

"Well," I say. "I don't have an answer for that."

Lila says, "I bet you do."

She's right, I do. But I don't explain. Drinking was there before I read and wrote. Writers didn't exist. There was no Hemingway or Gerald Locklin or Richard Brautigan. It was all school work. It was exams. It was part-time jobs and born-again Christian parents. So I drank in fields. I drank in cars. I drank with old men at the Irwin Hotel and any other bar that would serve me and everyone knew my name. I drank for fun. I kept drinking for fun. I got drunk and punched the fun right out of it. I drank myself right into violence and stupidity and fights and young women I couldn't stand. When I started reading and writing, the drinking became something else, a celebration, a reward. It's what I like to do when I get away from work or when I've done good work or read well or taught well or my kids are jumping on my head and I need to be happy and not angry, then I drink. I drink so I can talk to my wife and hear her voice and not the world. If I was a plumber with six kids, I'd explode with booze, but I'm not, so I don't. I read and write and stay happy. Afterwards, there's a nice beer or ten.

Lila says, "Everyone in West Virginia drinks."

"And does crystal meth," I say.

"That's only a few people, but they're the loudest."

Lila looks at James and the bartender, still chatting, still laughing. James does a pirouette. Lila looks down at her hands and adjusts her rings. She's thinking. I don't want to know what.

I look at the stage. There's still no dancer. There's a swing, like a porch swing, but it's empty, steady. Another Frank Sinatra song comes on. My mouth is dry. My head is not. I'm thinking I'd like to get arrested tonight. I'm thinking getting arrested is better than teaching. I'm thinking I should go home. I should call home. I think I've been getting drunk a lot lately because of other people when I'd rather get drunk because of myself.

"Lila," I say. "Do you think you can keep up with James for a couple more hours?" and I mean without me, I mean by herself.

Lila says, "Do you think I'm pretty?"

"What?"

She says, "Do you think I'm pretty?"

Of course she's pretty. She's twenty-five years old.

"Sure," I say, even though I'd rather not.

Lila says, "Really pretty?"

I never flirt with students. I think it's okay for professors and students to flirt and date and have sex and do whatever comes natural. But I never do. Even single I wouldn't. Once my girl-students start talking, they sound so young and sweet and innocent and uninteresting, I can't imagine them as sexual beings. Like I know Lila has big firm tits, but now, after she says, "Do you think I'm pretty?" those big firm tits don't even count. Her green eyes, her reddish-brown hair, nothing. She's just another girl, another student, a fine young writer.

She looks like she wants advice and a grade and possibly written comments and encouragement.

If I wanted to talk to someone and get laid, I'd go home, I'd do it with my wife, I do it with my wife every chance I get. If I need something else, something without the talk, then it's not Lila, it's not anything like that. I'd be in this strip club alone, trying to arrange something in a backroom or my car or late-night in a motel that charges by the hour. I've done it. I'll do it again. It's better than being an explosion, an emotional traitor.

I say, "You're very pretty."

Lila says, "Thanks," and looks down at her tits, but not seductively, just shy.

I say, "And your stories are amazing. Really. The way you write about poor people and drug addicts in West Virginia is amazing."

It hurts my brain to be this thoughtful when I'm drunk.

She says, "Really?" She says, "Thanks." She says, "I really loved your class. I was probably too shy to say anything when I had you, but it was amazing." She says, "I don't know if I should say this, but I thought your book was amazing. Also amazing. I'm not kissing ass."

"Thanks," I say. "Here comes James."

James has a drink. He's dancing. He's strutting and twirling.

"Is he doing the Cha Cha Cha?" Lila says.

"Oh yes I am," James says. Then, in a Mexican accent, "Cha cha cha," and a hip thrust. He says, "But the dancers won't be on for fifteen more minutes. They are, according to my new friend Gina, the manager of this place, limbering up backstage and getting into their costumes."

"Another round?" Lila says and shakes the rocks in her glass.

The first stripper comes out in a fedora, in a cabaret-style outfit but sleazier. She's middle-aged but in good shape with the long legs of a dancer. Her hair is jet black, probably a wig. The Frank Sinatra is on a loop. We're back to "My Way" but it's louder now.

Lila says, "I told you."

I say, "I thought I told you."

James says, "It's like *Dream Girls*. Did you guys see that?"

"No," I say. "I hate musicals."

I excuse myself and go for the bar but before I get there I see a payphone. I haven't seen a payphone in years. It's a black metal box slammed into the wall by a money machine. I dig out some change. It's not enough. I don't know what enough is anymore. I get five bucks in quarters from Gina, the bartender.

She says, "You're not tipping with these, are you?" and laughs.

"I can't resist a payphone," I say.

I drop some change in the machine. I dial my home number.

After two rings, Townes answers.

He says, "Hey Dad, I thought you were Terrance. Terrance was supposed to call. We're supposed to talk about Club Penguin."

Club Penguin is some kind of computer game where the kids are penguins and they build igloos and they invite other penguins, other kids online, over to hang out. It's moronic.

"Great," I say. "How was school?"

"Terrance is going to be calling in like ten seconds."

"Great," I say. "How's Abby?"

Townes says, "She's good. She got her report card. It was all pluses and stuff. She doesn't get real grades yet."

"Pluses are good," I say. "They're like As."

"Why's there music playing in the background?" he says. "Are you at work?"

"Go get your mother for me," I say.

"Mom wants us to move to Alaska or something. I told her that's way too cold."

I have no idea what the hell he's talking about. Probably penguins.

I say, "I'll be late tonight. Can you get mommy for me? I love you."

"Okay, but Terrance is calling."

"I got that. I won't be long."

"I love you," Townes says.

"I love you, too," I say.

Then he screams his mother's name into the house and into the phone at the same time. It's like getting hit in the ear with a wrecking ball, which feels right.

Lori gets on the phone and says, "Hey, did he tell you?"

"Yeah, Terrance is calling. We need to get off the phone."

"Not that," Lori says. "The University of Alaska called and they want me to come out for an interview. Can you believe that?"

"That's great," I say, because I know Lori hates her job teaching at a small conservative branch campus and waiting tables on the side, but I also think: Alaska? I can't remember when Lori applied, though she's always checking job listings, always looking for something better.

Lori says, "I know, Alaska, right."

"It's not Greenland," I say. "That's good."

She says, "Where are you? Are you listening to Frank Sinatra?"

I say, "I'm in a strip club."

She says, "That's not exactly Alaska. Is there a story behind it?"

"Yes," I say. "James saw Carrie Polinski and he's still wigged out about being a character in her memoir. Then Richard got beat up by a student. Then we all started drinking. Then we tried to find Kentucky Jim so he could see that James was drunk and behaving like a real writer and hire him but Kentucky Jim is either home sobering up or getting eye surgery. So somehow we ended up at a strip club."

Lori says, "I thought you were supposed to take James to AA?"

"Yeah, that's probably out," I say. "Tell me about Alaska."

I look out over the club. A man and a woman have taken seats opposite James and Lila. They are maybe thirty and good looking. He has on a blazer and his hair is styled. She has on a different blazer and her hair is wild and long and free. They look nervous and sexy.

Lori says, "It's Alaska so there's that."

I try to imagine Alaska. Mostly I see ice. I see ice and snow. I see seals and polar bears and penguins, things that live on or near or under ice and snow. Alaska is almost Russia, I think. What I need is a map. I know Alaska is up there, but not really up there. It's up there and over. It's as far away as I can imagine. Caribou.

Lori says, "The director of the Writing Program called and we really hit it off. She was just easy to chat with so we chatted. That was this morning. We talked for almost an hour. She wanted to do a more formal phone interview with some other university people on the line. I thought that would be next week or something, but she just called back an hour or so ago. The head of the English Department was on. A couple professors. They were all really nice. The job is a two-two teaching load which is half the work I'm doing now."

"What'd they say about pay?"

"They didn't," she says.

"I'm sure it pays great," I say. "It's Alaska."

"It's crazy, isn't it? Am I stupid to consider this?" She stops. "We, I mean. Are we stupid to consider this?" but her voice is happy, excited.

I turn and face the stage. James and Lila are close. I wonder if she's asking him if he thinks she's pretty. The dancer is down to stockings and lace-up boots and her hat. The guy has taken off his blazer. His girl has kept her blazer on. I turn back to the payphone, the black metal box. If I could, I would plant myself in this room, in this wall, in this city. You can be anything in Pittsburgh, a stripper, a writer, a student, a bartender, or something else, or everything else, all of it at once, and no one cares, or if they care, they mean it, it's love. For one hundred years, men walked into fire and made steel. In Pittsburgh, you are tough or you are not. You write or you don't write. You start hearts or allow hearts to wind down like old clocks. I almost never think about what Pittsburgh means because I know it. I have known it my whole life. There were men and women, and they worked. What we have now is made from that.

I try and think about Alaska, that fucking block of ice.

"It sounds great," I say. "A two-two teaching load is awesome."

"Do you think so?" Lori say, even more excited. "Can you come home?"

"I don't know," I say. "I'm afraid to leave James alone," which is true and not true.

The lights near the stage are dim, colored. Over by the payphone, it's bright, white. I'm not sweating but close. I try to feel cold but I can't. I close my eyes. I try to feel colder than I've ever been in my whole life.

'm off the phone. At the bar, I get a Long Island Iced Tea, vodka for tequila.

Gina says, "Any good news on that payphone?"

I think Gina might be fifty, but she looks twenty except for the deep lines around her eyes and smile. Maybe she's thirty-five and sexy. It's hard not to love a woman bartender in a strip club even if she's dressed conservatively in jeans and a button-up white shirt. She shakes my drink in a silver cup shaped like a rocket.

I say, "I don't know. Is Alaska good news?"

"Maybe," Gina says. "Do you fish for salmon?"

'm back at my chair by the stage. The Long Island Iced Tea has gone down easy so I get another. The stripper is grinding. It's mechanical. It's like she's been studying hip-hop videos but missed the fun. James touches the stripper's ass with his pointer finger, right on her left cheek. The stripper turns and shakes her head, no no no, but in a sexy way so James is confused.

The stripper has stripped for the couple dressed in blazers and for us and the couple dressed in blazers again and now she is mostly naked, except for pasties and a g-string that she keeps pulling aside so we can see her pussy. She's on her hands and knees, doing a butt-dance close to James' face. James is not interested in a butt-dance. He likes the Frank Sinatra songs and the burgundy curtain leading backstage. The boobs were okay but not an ass in his face. He sticks a small pile of singles between the stripper's legs. The tip makes the stripper think she's doing great. James thinks he's paying her to go away.

I'm thinking: Alaska.

Lila says, "I'm getting drunk."

I look at her. She looks drunk. Her smile is ridiculous.

She says, "Are you drunk?"

I say, "I've been there for a while."

The spinning diamond above the stage shines tiny light-diamonds on the walls and floor and the stripper's ass that James has again politely pushed away.

The stripper says, "Remember, we don't touch here. No hands."

James, very drunk, against the music, either hears or doesn't hear. He hands her two more ones. He smiles and waves.

Lila says, "You're great," to the stripper.

The stripper says, "What?"

I had no idea Frank Sinatra could be so loud. Then I realize this is a remix. This is Frank with a beat and booming bass underneath. It's worse than before, and before was bad.

Lila says, "You're great. I love your style."

The stripper says, "Thank you." She says, "I dance."

Their voices are like megaphones. They're talking through strung-up cans.

Lila says, "Cool."

"Not right now," the stripper says. "But I used to. I hope to again."

Lila says, "Where did you dance?"

The stripper says, "Like, everywhere."

She's still on her hands and knees, ass in James' face, though she's turned her neck to face Lila and talk. The stripper is bored. The worst ones always are. She has forgotten her body and moved on from her act even though her ass is still out there, and her pussy too, the tiny black bush barely visible from behind. Her clothes are everywhere on the stage. Some tips are too, scattered like patches of weeds.

Lila says, "Well, you're really beautiful."

I can't tell if Lila is turned on by this. It could be the recklessness.

The room smells like cinnamon. Someone in here has lit a candle or burned some incense. It's nice. I breathe in the cinnamon. If the stripper brought her ass over here, I would give her two dollars and at least pay attention. I would say, "You smell like cinnamon."

James taps the stripper on the ass with both hands, not hard, supposedly comical but probably not, and says, "Okay, move that caboose."

The stripper, surprised, falls forward, but she does it dramatically.

Lila laughs then says, "Oh god, I'm sorry. Are you okay?"

The stripper says, "Watch your boyfriend. He's an asshole," and she grabs for her nearest piece of clothes, a black vest, and covers her tits.

It's the sexiest thing all night, not because it's violent (and it's not violent), but because it's not choreographed. The way her tits moved when she went for her vest was great.

Lila says, "He's not my boyfriend."

I say, "He's her professor."

James says, "The train has left the station," and he makes a train whistle sound.

don't see the bouncer leave the door and make it across the room. Later, James will say, "That guy was like a ninja or something." Probably, we were all too smashed.

The stripper is standing now, more clothes, more bills, clutched to her body. The bouncer has James by the back of the neck. James won't stand though. Lila has scooted back in her chair. The bouncer could use two hands and get James up, but he's only using one, like it's a rule, a test. James pulls forward. He moves to the side, trying to get free.

James says, "Get off me, you fucking goon."

"We don't touch the ladies," the bouncer says.

"Don't touch me," James says. "You fuckhead."

"I want him out," the stripper says, mean, in charge. She motions towards the door.

Lila says, "This is all a misunderstanding."

The bouncer says, "It's time to go, sir."

James says, "It's time to stay," and latches onto the catwalk so he can't be pulled.

I take a sip of my Long Island Iced Tea. It was eleven dollars, plus a four-dollar tip. The diamonds keep spinning from the diamond ball. The swing on the stage sways a little like it's been bumped by all this commotion.

The bouncer says, "Don't make me use my other hand."

James says, "Use it, you fucking Judas. I dare you."

The bouncer is tougher than me but smaller and he's focused on James. I haven't sucker-punched anyone ever, but I could. I could hit him in the ear and knock him out. My car is outside. I could back away with the lights off, the license plate hidden until we're far enough gone. I try to decide. Lila looks at me like: help. I'm still thinking. Gina comes from around the bar. She moves slowly. She appears calm. At the bottom of her jeans are high heels I hadn't noticed before. She is confident in her walk. She, too, could be a ninja. I stand up. I finish my Long Island Iced Tea and am prepared to get beat up if necessary.

Gina says, "Okay, okay, everything is fine."

I say, "I agree." I say, "We were just about to leave."

Gina touches the bouncer on the shoulders with both her

hands, gently, and he instantly lets go of James' neck. James turns and pops up like he's about to fight but everyone, especially the bouncer, knows he's not.

Gina says, "This is all just a misunderstanding. Everyone breathe," and she breathes deep to show us how.

I breathe deep. Lila breathes deep. James and the bouncer do not breathe deep. They are rigid as stripper poles, only inches apart.

James says, "Back up, you fucker." He says, "I write books."

"Yeah," the bouncer says. "I live in a trailer."

Outside, I drive away backwards with my lights off even though no one has followed us out and it appears we are not being prosecuted and Gina, the bartender, had said, "Sorry about everything. It was just a misunderstanding," as we moved across the strip club to the door.

In the car no one says anything. I can hear James breathe.

A block away, at a stop light, Lila says to James, "I didn't know you had a book."

James says, "I don't. I said I wrote books. I didn't say any of them were published."

James has never actually finished writing a book, but it's a good idea.

I say, "James is a better writer than a drinker."

James says, "I feel bad that guy lives in a trailer."

"Yeah," I say. "But what a grip."

The light changes to green. I touch the gas. I hope this is the end of the night, even if the night is barely evening. I look in the rearview mirror. Lila has taken James in her arms. She's touching his hair, nurturing every strand.

James says, "That feels good."

Lila says, "What made you so mad at that stripper's ass?"

I look back again and James is kissing Lila or Lila is kissing James and James is allowing it. The kisses are tender, one small peck then a deeper peck then a small peck. I think they could be lovers. James could use a lover. James could use a woman who won't put him in her self-help memoir and call him The Punter. Lila could use something here, too.

"Hey," I say. "Where can I drop you guys off?"

"A hospital," James says.

"Are we really done?" Lila says.

"I am," I say.

"Party-pooper," Lila says and laughs.

I'm alone in the car with my one thought: Alaska. If I have another thought, it's this: Pittsburgh. James and Lila are at James' dumpy house in Squirrel Hill. They are probably making love or not. I drive around Squirrel Hill. On the Sabbath, Hasidic Jews with their identical black suits and black dresses and white shirts and yarmulkes and funny hats, looking like something from another century, politely walk to and from temple. Now it's students and shoppers, an older woman in a green velour sweat-suit weeding the flowerbed in her front yard.

I hang a right. I hang a left. Lots of money still left here, but the huge houses are a hundred years old or more. For every three or four renovated mansions, there's a duplex with living room furniture on the front porch and a kids bicycle chained to the railing.

I think about James and Lila making love then I imagine James throwing up over the edge of the bed or rubbing the back of his sore neck and Lila writing notes on scratch paper or thinking, "Professors, ha!" and I promise myself I won't think about James and Lila anymore.

I'll think about Pittsburgh and I'll think about Alaska and I won't go home until I have something to tell my wife about both.

On the corner, you can get a good Italian ice but I don't stop.

I don't stop at the Squirrel Cage for a beer, either.

I leave Squirrel Hill and drive to Shadyside but I hate Shadyside. Shadyside is all fancy bars and stores that sell make-up and purses to rich women. I go back to Squirrel Hill.

I could drive like this around Pittsburgh all night, neighborhood to neighborhood. I've done it for years, South Side to Downtown, Downtown to North Side, bar to baseball game to a bookstore or something to eat. The streets aren't straight, they end without warning, nothing is like a grid, but you can feel your way forward and back.

By the time I was twenty-seven years old, I'd written five terrible unpublished novels set in and around Pittsburgh and some two hundred poems, some good, many awful, about rolling through these very streets, looking for drugs and music and food and the chance to get laid, all those wonderful things about Pittsburgh that never appear in books. Pittsburgh seldom appears in books. The writers that live here teach and they tend to think of language in the abstract, where meaning is constantly debated and the desire to communicate directly ignored, and I think of language in terms of my children's names and neighborhoods where I've lived and what it feels like to jump from the second-story window of a row house during a party just to impress a beautiful woman. I want something great for Pittsburgh so I write about it, knowing also that my only chance for greatness is if Pittsburgh says it's so. I don't want to leave, ever.

But then I have a beautiful wife who hates her job, who is forty-six years old and still waits tables for tips and slings drinks and has to decide if she feels like wearing her tight skirt or just being friendly or maybe smiling a lot.

But then I have beautiful children who need food and clothes and heat and electric.

But then I have beautiful children.

But then sooner or later, my teaching job is going to be gone because that's the kind of teaching job it is, that's the kind of university I work for, and I'm middle-aged and don't want to be a truck driver again or manage a store and review other poor middle-aged employees on their customer service skills and work sixty hours a week and miss my family.

I keep driving.

I hang a right past the movie theater where I once saw *Slingblade*, what a beautiful and terrible movie that was, all those years ago when BillyBob Thorton could act and write and he created Karl Childers, a simple man with a voice like dirt under a car tire.

I drive past the tailor who wanted a week to hem a pair of pants when I had a job interview the next day and he said, "You know nothing about the stitch, you asshole," when I told him that was too long.

I hang a left past the schools and the churches.

I drive up a hill.

I drive down a hill.

I drive up a hill.

This church looks like Russia. This church looks like Serbia. This church is an afterhours club for Irish people who have never been to Ireland, who drink because they believe it's in their blood. Here's a temple. Here's an old warehouse, abandoned, cleaned up, turned into another temple for people who believe but not quite, for people who need the spirit but not all the rules. Here are the Jews and the Catholics and the Protestants and the rest of us, believing in something. Drive to the North Side and there's a church with murals of poor people singing with angels, poor people kneeling with their children, god everywhere, Mary in a gas mask, a mother holding her dead son, all of it painted against the war, back when workers could paint. Here's a building from two years ago looking bland, looking lost without any history. Here's chain restaurant. Here's another chain restaurant pretending to be local. Here's a Starbucks some kid has tagged and sprayed "Starbucks sucks" on the side of the wall, a guy in a hardhat stomping the Starbucks logo. Here's a bar. Here's a better bar. I drank there. I drink there still.

I drive.

Evening is a good time to be alone. I like the sunset even if I can't find the sun over the brick buildings and the tall trees. The metal fences don't keep anyone out. The metal fences aren't supposed to keep anyone out.

I turn right and hit a street paved in brick. I slow down to ten miles per hour and it's still like riding in a covered wagon, the bricks bouncing the wheels, the wheels bouncing the driver.

Gerald Stern, the great poet, grew up here. I don't know where exactly. I think everywhere. His father was either a dry cleaner or a dry-goods salesman. His mother was a nut who would weep to keep her son home. Her son didn't want to be home. He wanted to be a poet. I have read every poem Gerald Stern has ever written ten times. I forgive him for going to Paris. I forgive him his years of teaching in Iowa and his lust for fame. The poems of Gerald Stern have walked so many streets in Pittsburgh and fought with so many beautiful women in this city that he can grow old in Lambertville, New Jersey with his millionaire poetess wife and still be something like a saint, the little red coal of poetry still burning in him, and all that matters is he loved Pittsburgh enough to write it down.

I f ever there was a place not to leave, it's here.

T essaro's is packed. The waitress takes my name and gets me a Coors Light bottle. The whole room, the whole restaurant, the whole street if you're outside, and maybe all of Bloomfield, smells like hardwood smoke and charred beef. The Coors Light is cold in my mouth. I keep my eye on the bar. If a seat comes open, I'll go there.

Across the street is Paul's CDs. Richard could be in there, working his other job, recovering from the pen-whacks he took from a student.

A hipster guy in a funky hat and shades says, "You here alone?"

I say, "Yeah."

"Waiting for a bar seat?"

"Hoping," I say.

He touches my shoulder and laughs and says, "Me, too. I say I'm going to get the fish but I'm not going to get the fish."

"It's always the burger."

"I get the red-skinned potatoes, too."

"I know it's sacrilegious to say so but I wish they had French fries here."

He leans close so the brim of his hat bumps my head and says, "Me too, friend, me too."

I finish my beer and go to the bar for another. It takes a minute but the bartender sees me and I order with a nod. We exchange bottle and money over other customers' shoulders.

The inside of Tessaro's is dark and woody, like a place that serves beef should be. The ceiling is embossed metal. The owner is around somewhere, being friendly, shaking hands. The owner looks like he played linebacker in college—broad shoulders, needs a shave, huge hands when he touches your shoulder to lead you to a table. His mother is here too, ancient, kind, checking on customers like they're her children. She's a stoop of a woman in an apron and a peasant dress. The walls are covered with murals she painted, mostly of her family, doing work, being together.

A woman in a business suit points to something on the wall, some detail, and a hunched old man in a suit, probably her father, puts on his glasses and looks.

I know there are places in Alaska to get a good burger.

But the burgers in Tessaro's are mine. I've eaten a dozen or more a year for two decades. The butcher in the basement is a fireman, and I once got drunk at the bar with an old man who insisted his brother got knocked out by Mohamed Ali at a gym in Harlem when Ali was still Cassius Clay, before he'd even fought at the Olympics and won gold.

The bartender says, "Seat. You want it?"

"I want it," I say.

"Menu?" he says.

I say, "Bacon burger with American cheese, barbecue sauce on the side. No lettuce or tomato. Hash browns. Double order." I think that I am placing my last order at Tessaro's in Pittsburgh, in Bloomfield, the Italian neighborhood with the Polish bar on the corner and the best music store in the country beside that. I think I am going to leave this place forever so I need to eat and drink it now.

The bartender says, "Double hash browns?"

I say, "Double hashbrowns. Two burgers. Both medium."

"Let me get you another beer," the bartender says.

When I get home, I am very tired and still drunk and very full. Lori is in bed with her computer, reading about Alaska. She is in red pajamas with reindeer on the pants. She is beautiful without make-up. Every year she is more gorgeous and I am more fat and worried and less handsome. I stand in the doorway and have to lean I am so tired.

She says, "Are you okay?"

"I am so stuffed," I say.

"From the strip club?" she says and closes her computer.

"From Tessaro's. I ate two burgers."

"With James?"

"By myself."

I start to undress. I get my button-up shirt off and my shoes. Then my belt. I fall on the bed and stay there. The ceiling is yellow. We paint all the ceilings in all the rooms in the house because we like it. My pants are tight. I know I should piss and brush my teeth but I can't move.

I say, "Are the kids okay?" and stuff a couple pillows under my head.

"The kids are fine," Lori says. "They have burgers in Alaska."

"I know they have burgers in Alaska," I say. "They're made of elk."

V

Townes says, "I don't want to go to school today."

I've put out two pieces of toast he's not going to eat. I've poured orange juice he's not going to drink. He knows his mom is in Alaska but he doesn't know he could live there.

I say, "Why don't you want to go to school this morning?"

"I miss mom," he says and stares down, sad.

When Townes was two I caught him in the bathroom, standing on the vanity, making faces in the mirror, learning the look for sad, learning angry. The next day he wanted a toy. I said no. It was like watching an actor wipe his face with make-up and tears before a scene. I said, "You're kidding me?" and then he got pissed but not just on the face, his little fists going tight.

I say, "You saw mom last night. You can't miss her yet."

"I worry about her flying," he says.

"She's fine," I say.

I move to the hall where I can see Townes but Townes can't see me. He goes back to playing with his little guys, smiling, making smashing sounds as the Lego characters go after each other with battle-axes and swords.

"Where's mommy?" Abby says. "Is she in Alaska yet?"

It's eight in the morning. Abby has preschool at nine. She's still in bed, sleepy. Townes' bus comes at eight-thirty. Today there's more overlap than usual. It takes me forever to do Abby's hair, to get a ponytail that's straight and stays. Lori can do braids in seconds.

Abby says, "I bet Alaska is so cold."

I say, "I think it's getting a little bit warm."

Abby says, "Right, it's Spring."

"Exactly," I say.

She stretches and kicks off her blanket like she's running in place.

Abby says, "Mommy will probably see a moose."

I say, "Maybe."

I undo Abby's braid, the one that keeps her blond hair from knotting. She shakes it out. I shake my short hair back. My goatee is out front so she tugs it, two times, like a train whistle. I love having the kids by myself, on my own clock and track. I set the speed. The speed is perfect for getting things done and playing, naps when we need naps, reading by ourselves and together, picking up the mess because the mess needs to be picked up, but no boring moments. No standing by the door, waiting for mommy to put on her make-up or shout at her computer or wonder how things became so hectic and a wreck. Lori is gone today and home late tomorrow. It could be three or four days, all weekend, and we'd be fine. We'd miss her but still be happy.

I have been teaching and sober and thoughtful for a week, getting ready to be a single parent. Tomorrow I have to teach but I've told the students it's off, no surprises. Class canceled, family issue, my wife in Alaska.

James is gone. One of the secretaries asked if he was going to be okay. I said, "Sure," but it sounded like, "Sure?" I hoped she wasn't talking alcoholism or some sort of destruction. I said, "It's tough, but I think he'll be alright," and smiled and looked concerned but not overly, just thoughtful. Later, James left a message on our office phone saying he'd gone to West Virginia with Lila. He said, "If anyone asks, I fell and fractured my skull." He said, "Lila's great."

Now Abby says, "What's Mommy doing in Alaska? Writing books?"

"Talking about books," I say. "She loves to talk about books."

"Oh," Abby says. "Alaska's great. They have permafrost."

Abby's five and she can read and operate a computer. All week she's been on the Discovery page, playing kids games that relate to Alaska, reading the entries in the kids encyclopedia about the Great North. She's obsessed with Eskimos and whale blubber.

"Go see your brother before he leaves for school," I say. "Cheer him up."

"Townes is going to be so happy to see me," she says.

She says this every morning.

Townes is not always happy to see her.

Townes hates school. We, his parents, pretend he doesn't but he does. He's not allowed to say he hates school and he's not allowed to complain about school and I make sure all his grades are 90 or better but I know he's bored.

He's in third grade and they read books like *Sheila Plants a Flower* and *Jimmy Fell From His Horse* and *Where Did Hurricane Rita Come From, Anyway?*

At home, we read S.E. Hinton, especially *The Outsiders*, a book with action and tough kids, a book that moves through a recognizable world. Townes is nine but he knows people get damaged. He knows some kids have parents who don't care and other kids, like Johnny, our second favorite outsider, have parents that are vicious and violent, and some kids, like

Ponyboy, our favorite outsider, don't have parents, they get raised by family. Books help Townes deal with his own small world, his parents who need to make more money, his friend Marco who is living with his grandma because his mom's in jail for running numbers and his dad is gone. When Johnny stabs that rich kid to save his best friend's life, Townes knows it's bad and he knows Johhny didn't want to hurt anybody but it was Ponyboy those rich kids were drowning, Ponyboy, the most sensitive and fastest and coolest friend a guy could ever have, and those rich kids were going to put him under for good if Johnny didn't act, so he did, he used his knife and saved Ponyboy's life. For months, after we finished *The Outsiders*, Townes and I walked around the house, saying, "Stay Golden," to each other and I'd say, "Just like the poem," and he'd say, "Just like the book," and I'd say, "Just like the book," and he'd say, "Just like the movie," which we had finally watched and Townes didn't turn away once, even when there was a little blood.

I hear Abby say, "Good morning, Townes," like it's a song.

Townes says, "Why are you up?"

From the bedroom where I'm matching tights and shoes and a sweater and a skirt, I raise my voice and say, "Hey Townes, stop it."

When I come down the hall, Abby's wide awake, playing her maracas.

Abby says, "Mom's in Alaska."

Townes says, "Mom's in a plane. That's dangerous."

Abby says, "Alaska has permafrost. Their dirt is ice."

Townes says, "Who cares? Why aren't you worried about Mom?"

Townes is an emotional sham. He knows sadness is a good con. Right now, it's his mom. Other times, it's his stomach. He would break his own toe to skip school for a week.

Abby says, "I'm hungry." Then, "Please."

I go to the kitchen to get Abby a breakfast bar and some dried fruit. There are notes on the refrigerator, things I'm supposed to remember that I know already. Lori was up at three in the morning, just as I was falling asleep, doing her hair, packing an extra outfit, writing notes and sticking them on the refrigerator with magnets shaped like flowers and letters. There were oral instructions too, things said in the dim light that I am supposed to do with the kids but I am with the kids every day so I didn't listen. I said, "Yes," and, "Okay," and, "Call," and, "Good luck," and, "I love you," while Lori packed a winter hat that wouldn't mess her hair.

Back in the living room, I say, "Who doesn't want to go to school today?"

Townes' whole body goes rigid with excitement and he says, "Oh my god, yes!" then, because he's not allowed to say, "Oh my god," lowers his arms like flags comings down poles and says, "I mean, oh my gosh, yes."

Abby says, "I like school."

Townes' eye puff like they are trying to explode and he says, "Stop Abby," and he moves over her like a blanket to block out her voice.

I say, "School or movie? You guys decide."

"Oh," Abby says. "I love popcorn."

Townes, releasing Abby's head, says, "Oh my goodness, exactly."

The movie theater by our house is old and junky and the old ladies who work there are mean and the bathrooms smell like piss. The best theater for kids is on the South Side. It's new and has an escalator and the popcorn is fresh.

Everyone is dressed and ready. I have money and my keys.

Townes says, "Can we take our video games?"

Abby says, "No!" and slaps Townes in the back, a solid shot.

Townes says, "Abby!" Then, remembering, "I forgot."

We've already gone over the rules today. Be nice to each other. Lots of love and hugging. No video games. No computers. TV only in the evening. Townes knows. He doesn't like it. But home without technology is still better than school. A movie in the city is the best.

Townes says, "Are there going to be drunks on the South Side?"

Sometimes I can't even imagine.

Townes says, "The South Side is probably packed with drunks."

I say, "It's nine in the morning. The movie theater isn't even open. There are no drunks out at nine in the morning. Why do you want to see a drunk? We need to get some breakfast to kill time until the movie theater opens up for business."

Abby says, "Eggs!"

Townes says, "Bacon."

At Tom's Diner, I get an omelet with ham and cheese. Townes gets the special which is almost everything on the breakfast menu. Abby gets scrambled eggs and toast. I order extra toast because she always wants it and the waitress isn't always near. The toast takes forever to cover with grape jelly. I use the back of a spoon. My omelet gets cold. I'm barely hungry. The kids eat and talk. They pass the salt shaker and try to sneak handfuls of salt from their palms to their mouths and politely blow pepper at each others' noses.

The waitress asks if everything is okay. I take a bite of my omelet and say fine, thanks. She's maybe twenty-one, very skinny, very white, very hungover, very much in need of a cigarette, but still nice. The tattoo on her forearm is a pink-and-purple lion.

Everyone else in Tom's Diner looks young and hungover or old and homeless. Three guys with three teeth sit at the counter on silver stools with red vinyl tops. I once saw Plaxico Burress in here, stretched out in a booth, right before the Steelers traded him to the New York Giants and he went to a club with a gun down his pants and shot himself in the thigh. He was pouring something from a flask into orange juice. He was with three very beautiful women. It was three a.m., and he announced he wouldn't be signing autographs.

Townes says, "Didn't you used to live here with Mom?"

He knows we used to live here but he likes to hear it. He was born in the women's hospital and brought home to our apartment on Carson Street, the main drag. Carson Street is so filled with bars it smells like a stadium, all spilled beer and sweaty people. Townes can't imagine kids here. All his other friends were born away from this and stay in their own backyards. Their parents think Pittsburgh is a ghetto or, at fourteen miles, just too far. The city somehow makes Townes famous, experienced. I used to take him on the roof of our broke-down apartment and rock him in the evening sun when he was five-months old and couldn't sleep. The delivery trucks leaving and the drunks arriving lulled him back to his crib.

I say, "We used to live near the Tenth Street Bridge, that-away," and I point.

He says, "Didn't we live above a bar or something?"

"Dee's Bar," I say.

"That's pretty gross," he says. "You could get arrested for that."

"Not really," I say.

I'm not even sure if the food at Tom's Diner is good but I used to come here with Lori after we stayed up all night fucking and drinking wine and we were too tired to sleep and we didn't have kids or those responsibilities. Lori always had the cinnamon French toast. I got the fish sandwich, fries with gravy. I am always so happy when I think of then and I am always so happy when I think of now but it was so much easier to think back then. No one ever played drums on her water glass like Abby is doing or grilled me on why someone would want to smoke like Townes is doing as he stares at a No Smoking sign.

Abby says, "More eggs please."

Townes says, "So why'd you let me stay home from school?"

I say, "So why'd you ask to stay home from school, tough guy?" Then, before he can answer, I say, "Isn't that really the question?"

N ear the green dumpster out back, it smells like a garbage strike, but away from the alley, the air is better, not fresh but not hard. We get back on Carson Street, our bellies full.

Most of the businesses are still closed. The bars and restaurants look abandoned, dark lights behind glass. A cleaning crew, three women in white uniforms with rags and brooms, is inside Fatheads, but no one else.

The cigar shop is just open. The owner, very old and wrinkled in his crooked baseball cap and windbreaker, sets a chipped wooden Indian near the front door. The Indian is missing a feather from his headdress. Most of his color has gone pale. The old man has a cigar in his mouth but it's not lit. He coughs a bomb, spits, excuses himself.

He says, "Can they have a loli?" but quiet like the kids can't hear.

"Sure," I say.

He steps inside and comes back with a basket of lollipops.

Abby screeches with joy. Even Townes is happy. He gets a rootbeer. Abby gets a grape. The old man pulls a couple extra and puts them in my hand.

Abby says, "Thank you, old man!"

Townes says, "Abby!" then everyone laughs.

The old man smiles and lights his cigar with a wooden match.

Abby and Townes both say thank you. I take their wrappers and we head out, sucking and twirling our lollipops, jumping on the sewer grates just to hear them rattle. We cross the street to see some posters advertising rock shows in a window, then cross back just to cross. Abby points to the ice cream place, all the pictures of sundaes in the window and specials on homemade fudge. Townes sees a kid on a skateboard and wants to be him.

This is why we come to the city when we should be at school.

A mailman steps from the Post Office, still stuffing his bag.

A guy with a dolly rolls up and into the back of the truck.

The flower guys are on the corner, stuffing their flowers

into buckets, picking the dead petals from the roses, getting ready to sell to cars on the fly.

Everything is so compressed it's like a poem compared to the wide spaces and open lines of our neighborhood. We'll see a movie but we don't have to. We could watch the lady opening the jewelry store, how she's already covered in necklaces and bracelets that sparkle with gems and turquoise. Her face is as brown and wrinkled as a leather purse. Abby does a dance. Townes holds her hand at the crosswalk and I didn't even tell him.

Now an old woman, very fat and sweaty, in gray sweatpants and a gray sweatshirt, steps from a stairwell that leads to a gym or some fitness club.

Townes touches the storefront to a bar that advertises a midget on premises. That's too confusing to even ask about. Abby presses her face to the front door and rattles the handle.

The alcoholics wait outside the basement door to the Presbyterian Church so they can go inside and eat donuts and tell stories and save each other.

Townes reads the word Alcoholic on a wooden sign.

He says, "Isn't James an alcoholic?"

"Sure," I say.

"So he can't drink? Not even like one beer or whatever?"

"Nothing."

"That's just weird," he says.

It's weirder that James is in West Virginia with a student but I don't say that.

Abby says, "Where is Cookie Crumbles?"

I say, "Somewhere."

She says, "He's the best guy to ever buy me a puzzle."

Townes says, "He really is a good guy, even if he can't drink."

Alice in Wonderland is worse than I expected and my expectations were low. It's very loud and bright with lots of screaming and no likable characters. Tim Burton, the director, is emotionally retarded. He sees the world in colors, not people. Nothing here has any feeling. Alice is cold and too white. The rabbit appears overly confused. Johnny Depp is awful as the Mad Hatter. He wears lots of make-up so you can't see his expressions and he talks in a funny voice that may or may not be an English accent.

Abby hoards the popcorn.

I sip relentlessly on my forty-four ounce diet Coke then get a refill. I'm sure the kids would be fine if I loitered by the concession stand but I don't. I come back in as Cheshire the Cat smokes something and magically disappears. Neither of my kids mentions marijuana.

Townes eats his Sourpatch Kids and messes with his 3-D glasses.

The theater is completely empty.

Townes says, "This is really loud."

Abby says, "Shh!"

I say, "There's no one else in the theater."

Abby says, "Shh!"

Her 3-D glasses are too big for her head. I've got them threaded through her hair. She hovers over the popcorn like she's guarding the entrance to the bucket, shoveling fistfuls between 3-D objects jumping off the screen.

Townes says, "Why is Johnny Depp acting like he did in *Charlie and the Chocolate Factory*? That guy is so creepy. Is he like a pedophile or something?"

Abby says, "It is! It's Johnny Depp!"

It's impossible to be five and a girl and not love Johnny Depp, even when he's purposefully destroying children's literature and selling out for millions of dollars.

Abby says, "Oh Johnny Depp," like she's about to swoon.

Townes says, "At least the drinks have a lot of ice in them."

"Exactly," I say, as the Queen of Hearts with her digitally-enlarged head screams with so much force her breath comes off the screen and it startles my ear drums and I start hoping this movie loses lots and lots of money.

Townes, sitting on a park bench like an old man, both of his arms riding the top of the green wood, says, "I really like the park when no other kids are here."

Abby, on the swings, says, "Where are all the other kids?"

For an early dinner, we have ice cream. Not until later, when Townes is bolting around the house, does it occur to me that coffee ice cream is probably loaded with caffeine.

I'm having a sandwich at the dining room table, reading through Ben Lerner's new book of poems, feeling as I almost always do with poetry that plays with language like a puzzle that can never be put together properly: bored. The language in the poems says he is making fun of people who died in the 9/11 tower crashes but of course that can't be true because it's poetry and he's a professor with a degree from Brown. I close the book.

Townes says, "Where next?"

I have him on errands, trying to kill the caffeine.

I say, "Try downstairs, next to the washing machine."

He says, "What are you reading?"

"Nothing," I say and mean it.

"Okay, downstairs," he says and bolts, his back and neck wet with sweat.

Abby is already asleep on the couch, dirty hands and dirty face, her teeth not brushed, but everything else okay, ten fingers, ten toes.

Townes comes back and says, "Not there."

I say, "Try my office."

He says, "Can I stay home from school tomorrow?"

I say, "Absolutely."

He says, "Yes!" and throws himself backwards into a wall then thrusts his hands into the air like he's done the three-minute mile and not escaped reading class and Chapter 9, *Heather Has A Hole In Her Bucket.*

Ten minutes later, he's asleep on the floor.

Ten minutes after that, Lori calls from Fairbanks, very happy and very appreciated by the faculty who have just thrown a potluck dinner in her honor.

VI

It's almost one in the morning when Lori comes home. The kids are asleep and have been for hours. Today was a repeat of yesterday with a trip through the museum instead of a movie. None of us are interested in movies after *Alice In Wonderland*. Townes and I no longer like Johnny Depp. If Johnny Depp were to come to our house, we would kick him in the balls and make him apologize. Townes said, "It's like he's sick or something." Abby said, "Weird." Townes saw a homeless man throw up in an alley then take a swig of grape Mad Dog, rinse, and spit. The next sip he swallowed. Townes was very impressed. Abby said, "Gross."

I'm on the couch in cut-off sweatpants, shirtless, flipping through channels. TV is outside of my interests completely. Flipping through channels is great. Watching this stuff is absurd. If I could afford HBO or something where they didn't bleep out the best parts, maybe.

Lori opens the door, bags hooked over both arms.

"You're home!" I say and jump up to help.

I am always happy to see Lori, always. Always, within seconds, I know if she is happy to see me or if she is happy to have someone to bitch at and vent to because the world is a dark and brooding place, especially for Lori. Now, she is tired and still smiling, all of her leaning my way.

"I'll get everything," she says. "It's late. You're not dressed. I love you."

I kiss her before she can set anything down. It's slow but not like a romantic comedy. We use our noses and foreheads and eyes as much as our mouths. The going-away kisses bore me, but the coming-home kisses make themselves welcome. Lori sets down the bags and I take her by the head and do more.

She says, "Let me get the stuff."

"I love you," I say. "I could just crush your skull."

"I could crush your skull, too," she says and grabs my head back. "Let me get the stuff from the car or I'll have to gouge your eyes out."

"I could rip your ass off and eat it," I say, and I squeeze her ass and lift but it's solidly attached to her legs and back.

She kisses me and says, "Stuff. Now."

"I'll get it," I say and follow her to the car.

From behind, I grab her under her coat. I get her around the waist. We walk like we're connected. If I could get my dick in her like this, I would.

She says, "You missed me!"

The whole neighborhood is dark, not even a porch lamp but our own. In this light, it looks like we belong, like we're a normal family. The books inside the house don't show. Our crazy kids are under blankets. The rust around the wheels of the car is invisible under the gray sky. Lori leans back and takes my whole head like she is going to flip me like a pro wrestler then touches her mouth to my cheek. Then my ear. I pop open the trunk. The trunk is loaded with bags. Lori's luggage has multiplied.

I say, "You must be freezing. You've probably brought home terrible weather."

She says, "It wasn't even cold."

I grab a couple bags, stuff from the airport or a wilderness department store.

I say, "You smell like moose."

She says, "You're not going to believe it, but there was a moose loose in town. I turned on the local news in the morning and it was all the rage. I went out for a muffin and a coffee and I was actually afraid. Everyone carries guns in Alaska, even the liberals."

"I love liberals with guns," I say and close the trunk with my barefoot.

She says, "Are the kids sleeping?"

"They haven't been to school in two days."

"Good. I hope you took them to the city."

"Come to the bedroom," I say. "There's something I want to show you."

"Yes," she says. "Your cock. I've never heard that before."

We throw the bags on the couch and on the living room floor. Most of the gifts are for the children. I get socks that say Alaska and a floppy hat from an adventure movie.

Lori says, "I need a quick bath."

"Me, too," I say and follow her into the bathroom.

Alaska was great. Lori says so in the hall. She says so going down the stairs. We are out of the bathtub, finished in the bedroom, and now heading for the shower. It's almost three in the morning. I can't stand sleeping when I have sex oil all over my balls. In the downstairs bathroom, I turn on the warm water. Lori likes it hot. I'm covered in sweat. One bead rolls past my eyelid and closes my right eye with a sting.

Lori says, "Everyone was just so nice."

"Even the head of the department?" I say.

"Especially him. He was eighty-years old, like a grandpa. He said, 'You're a nice normal size for catalog shopping.' I wanted to hug his wrinkled head."

The water is too hot. I turn the cold knob. Lori turns it back.

I go down to her tit and take a suck, a kiss.

Lori says, "That felt nice," and touches me. She says, "But I am so tired."

I say, "Seriously." I say, "You were on vacation." I say, "They had a potluck dinner in your honor. I was home with your rotten children."

She says, "They're your rotten children, too."

I say, "Townes faked missing you then he forgot you existed when I told him he could stay home from school."

"He's a class act," she says. "I bet Abby missed me."

"She gave it some lip service, but mostly she was interested in Johnny Depp."

"How was the movie?"

"Awful."

"It looked awful," Lori says. "I actually brought home two Alaska newspapers. I just wanted to read and check things. I wanted to see if they get first-run movies and concerts."

I say, "You could probably find that on a computer."

"I like newspapers," she says.

We step into the water. It's still too hot but I'm okay.

I say, "What about money?"

"I told them you teach and I made your job sound better than it was."

"Maybe they'll hire you and you're so great they'll hire me, that type of thing."

"Maybe," she says and puts her hair back in the water.

"That's sort of gross," I say.

"People do it all the time."

"Yeah, but those people are gross."

Lori says, "Can you hand me the shampoo?"

I hand her the shampoo. We're so seldom in the shower together, so seldom get to be naked and relaxed like this for long, that I'm starting to get hard again. Lori reaches down and squeezes my cock. She finishes her hair and we kiss.

Lori says, "Turn around. I'll do your back."

She takes down some sort of scrub.

She says, "We'll talk more about Alaska tomorrow."

Then, when I turn around, without warning, she tries to stick her finger up my butt.

As I squirm away, she laughs hysterically.

Early the next afternoon, when the phone rings, I know it's the University of Alaska. It's probably morning there. They are probably loving my beautiful wife, all her writing skills and academic prowess, discussing the brilliance of her interview and how funny she was at the potluck dinner. I'm at the dining room table, correcting papers. My kids are playing video games in the living room. Lori is in bed. I doubt she's still asleep but she could stay in bed for days mostly because she seldom has the chance to stay in bed. The kids don't even know she's home.

Abby grabs the phone and says, "Alaska."

"Don't answer that," I say.

Townes says, "Is it Terrance? We're supposed to meet on Club Penguin."

Townes is in boxer shorts, jelly from toast smeared across his face.

I get the phone from Abby. I check the caller ID. Our phone rings twenty times before the voicemail picks up. I don't know if I should answer. Lori might not be ready. She should have some sort of ballpark figure in mind and I don't know if she does. I should have some sort of ballpark figure. One million dollars, I think.

The distance between here and Alaska narrows.

I can measure it in rings.

Abby runs back to the video game.

Townes says, "Is it Terrance?"

I say, "Stop."

The phone rings.

Townes says, "Let me see," and tries to grab the phone.

"Back off, Townes."

"Just let me see it."

Another ring, then another.

I shove Townes by the head. He stumbles back. He looks stunned and hurt. Later, he will accuse me of choking him. I feel like choking him. Later, when he accuses me, I will say, "Do you want me to choke you? Because I will show you what it's like to be choked." He will weep.

I say, "Lori, it's Alaska," and she's instantly out of bed and in the hall.

She smiles and clears her throat.

I say, "What's your ballpark figure?"

"What?"

Townes starts to cry.

The phone stops ringing.

Lori says, "Why's he crying?"

"Because he's pissing me off."

Lori turns to Townes and says, "Honey, what's the matter?"

Abby appears again, a glob of jelly in her hair, her mouth full of breakfast crackers, and says, "Mommy! You're alive! I thought you were still in Alaska!"

The phone starts to ring again.

Lori says, "Hi honey," then, to me, "I have to take this."

"How much money?" I say. Then, "Townes and Abby, go downstairs. Get some toys out of the chest and play. Go now. Do not come up until I call you. Have fun. No crying. Don't come up until I call you. Then we'll all open presents from mommy."

I try to sound happy.

Abby says, "Why?" but she's moving towards the gameroom.

Townes says, "Because they hate us."

Lori says, "Townes," and, because she hasn't been with him for two days, looks sad.

I say, "Don't baby him."

The phone rings. I hand it to Lori.

Lori says, "Mommy has an important phone call. Just go downstairs for fifteen minutes."

Abby says, "Did you say presents?"

I say, "Go. Presents later."

The kids go. I feel like kicking Townes in the back, realizing his worst fears.

"Ballpark?" I say to Lori.

She says, "As much as our two salaries combined?"

"Good start," I say and don't know if it is.

Lori takes the phone into the bathroom, our one refuge. As a kid, I didn't understand why adults were always in the bathroom and for so long. But now I sometimes lock the bathroom door and sit in a dry bathtub with a book and say, "Daddy's not feeling well," when anyone knocks.

I go to the kitchen and make some iced tea. I drink that. There are Pop Tarts, two flavors, strawberry and brown sugar. I eat one of each. I drink more iced tea.

Outside the kitchen window, there are trees. My mother-in-law died in this house without ever living more than a few miles from where she was born. My father-in-law, who I never knew, lived and died the exact same way. Business and money have done everything possible to make America one long street that repeats itself endlessly, but geography still wins. There is no view anywhere like the one I see now out the window with the dogwood tree and my neighbor's redwood porch and their pool which is covered but still swimming in gunk and the yard where my kids have made millions of passes, chasing balls, dodging water from plastic guns.

Lori comes into the kitchen, smiles, and gives me the half-half sign with her hand. She says, "Well certainly, I don't want to be ridiculous," into the phone and walks off.

Lori hangs up and says, "They're fifteen grand lower than our combined salaries."

The kids are downstairs. I hear swords and laughter. She puts the phone back in the charger. I sit on the kitchen counter, eating pepperoni with cheese. Lori is still in her yellow Alaska pajamas, an igloo on her ass, salmon jumping on her thigh. She sits at the table by the phone. She taps her fingers, one rap for each thought.

She says, "Fifteen grand is a lot."

"Fifteen grand is a lot," I say.

She says, "God, shit."

I say, "Really."

But Alaska has more to offer.

They are negotiating.

I never knew how this worked.

There are phone calls to come.

Lori says, "Should I ask if they would consider giving you a job?"

Lori says, "Don't be insulted. It's not an insult."

Lori says, "This whole process is ridiculous, but they are so nice."

The pepperoni is gone, so I eat dry cereal with my hands.

The kids come to the top of the stairs to eavesdrop. Their whispers sound like giggles which feel like knives prickling the inside of my brain.

"Go back downstairs," I say, almost yelling. "Now."

Lori is off the phone. She says, "They're ten grand lower than our combined salaries. The teaching load is half of what I teach now. The classes are better. I'd be working with grad students. Their salary cap is eighty-thousand dollars higher than ours."

I say, "What's a salary cap?"

Lori says, "You know, a salary cap."

When I hear those words, I think of football teams paying their linemen less so they can pay their star quarterback more. When I played football, I was a lineman. When I write I am the same. As a professor, I'm barely on the squad.

Lori says, "You really don't know what a salary cap is?"

I say, "Lori, I work on a yearly contract. The only reason I'm employed next year is because the head of the department is an alcoholic."

She says, "You have more publications than anyone else in your department."

"No one cares about that stuff."

"They should."

"Stop it," I say. "This isn't about me."

We have talked so little about money over the years because money has so seldom seemed a real possibility. Our checkbook is never balanced. We have no retirement. Our financial life is a swindle. Trying to live a life like the life we were given by our working-class parents—our dads in factories, our moms at home—has left us broke and confused.

"Tell me how a salary cap works in the academy," I say.

She says, "Right now, I can never make more than seventy-seven thousand. Salaries have been frozen for three years so I haven't gotten a raise so I'm never going to get there anyway, but if they started giving raises again, the most I could ever make, after twenty more years of raises or whatever, is seventy-seven thousand."

"But at Alaska, you could make one hundred and fifty-seven thousand dollars?"

"Yes."

"Teaching half the classes?"

"Yes."

"When are they going to call back?"

"Soon. Ten minutes or so. Burns has to call one of the deans."

"One-hundred and fifty-seven thousand dollars," I say.

"After I cap out."

"How long does that take?"

"I don't know, but they're talking about waiving tenure. Just having me come in as a tenured professor."

"Wow," I say and feel stupid for the word but I mean it, too: wow.

She says, "Should I ask for anything else?"

I say, "A signing bonus?"

"Do they have those?"

"I think I was joking," I say.

The only thing left is a spousal hire, the University of Alaska calling back and saying, "We've found a position for your husband." Without Lori asking, they've already offered me part-time work at a pay-rate that would almost match my current salary. None of this, somehow, feels good. My brain is as nauseous as my stomach and my stomach could explode. The academy is awful because the people are awful, they take advantage—I don't want to be that.

I have been reading and writing seriously for almost twenty years, publishing for most of the time. I've won awards. I have a graduate degree that wasn't funded by the university I attended at a time when they funded almost everyone. My book was reviewed favorably in magazines, small but literary, and my blurbs, from writers I have never met, say I'm a fucking genius. Yet I am only employed at my current job because my alcoholic boss has no one to drink with and my other possibility for advancement is to accept a position from a university that wants to hire my wife.

Lori says, "The kids are being quiet down there."

I say, "They're probably smashing the place with swords."

Lori is so happy she looks drugged. All her years of writing and teaching and writing while teaching and writing while teaching and raising a family and working as a waitress are about to be rewarded. Everything she deserves and has deserved is coming across the line in little offers from a world of snow and ice three thousand miles from our home.

Lori says, "What do you think?"

I say, "Great." I say, "This is going to be fantastic."

L ori says, "I told them I'd call them by Monday at five o'clock."

"Really?" I say. "Do you need that long?"

VII

I am not at the University of Alaska. Monday came and Lori said, "Thank you so much," and The University of Alaska said, "But?" and she said, "But no thank you."

I said, "I would have gone." I said, "Happily."

She said, "I know." She said, "But Jesus, Alaska. Think about it."

"Oil spills," I said.

"Polar bears eating oil workers," she said. "They don't even put it on the news."

"It's that common," I said.

"Think about it," she said.

But we were done thinking about it.

All weekend, we'd thought about it at our dining room table, a bottle of vodka between us, limes and lemons in a bowl, tonic and soda on a tray. The kids came around when they were bored and hungry and we fed them and made up something funny or interesting or put on a movie or ordered them downstairs with weapons made of foam. Then we went back to thinking about it at the dining room table with our vodka drinks filled with citrus wedges.

Our lives, we decided, were this: each other, our children, our writing. We tried to think of other things but it was only the same things in the exact same order: love and family and art.

We both had friends we cared for, close friends, friends who were writers, and yet our friends didn't have children and most of them seldom wrote anymore. They were too tired to write, too distracted. They were overwhelmed by their writing so they didn't do it, they went to the market and bought fresh tomatoes and came home and made sauce and still didn't write. "It's distracting," they said. They didn't say exactly what it was that was distracting and Lori and I couldn't imagine their quiet, empty houses.

Years ago, all of us had shared stories and poems and said encouraging things, genuine and thoughtful things. We stayed up late, reading each others' narratives, marking them with comments, making suggestions for publication. Everyone believed in everyone else.

But eventually, the sharing stopped like a bottle had been emptied and everyone had swallowed enough. Everyone had been a little drunk on art then everyone was a little hungover on our lack of success. When we talked, it was about our jobs. Teaching and publishing became other, sometimes terrible, things. Writing was a distant dream, like we were all going to grow into it, though each of us was older now and should have been what we were going to be.

But Lori and I still write. We still read each other. Every year we write more and publish more and do it because we have to, because we love it. Between basketball practice and dance class and teaching and waiting tables and the laundry, we write. When we're done writing, we sit at our table and we talk about our work and write it again then send it out.

Our friends make plans to write. They have ideas for novels and long poems. They start projects but they don't finish projects. They blog. One guy I know posts stuff about wine and sells t-shirts on his site. He hopes his blog will help his writing career. Another friend blogs about dogs. One of Lori's friends, a woman with a book, blogs about being fifty and single because her agent said it would be good to blog, to have a presence, but the blog says things like, "Another date last night. Good wine but no spark," and the second novel doesn't get written.

None of our friends are getting married or having kids. They talk about their pets and the different ways to make coffee in the morning. They all live like Bohemians, like expatriates in Paris, but they've forgotten to write or maybe forgotten how or they just don't care and they realize what all writers realize: writing is as hard as making clouds and the sky is already filled.

Lori and I and the kids and our writing would have missed our old lovely friends, the writers who didn't write, but we could have gone to Alaska. Alaska had money. Money matters. Money always matters, and it matters most when you have children. Neither of us balked at Lori making six figures in the years to come. If I hated being a spousal hire, it wasn't death. The money and security and my kids' happiness would have floated my pride.

But then, all we had at home—each other, our kids, our writing—might somehow be damaged if we moved it to Alaska, a place neither of us wanted to live, when we were living in a place we loved. Lori was born in an orphanage on the East side of Pittsburgh. In that year, both my father and grandfather were working on the hospital downtown. If we left, our stories, and maybe our love, would have to be reset, rewritten, relearned.

After Lori turned down their final offer, I said, "What if they said a million dollars?"

"Yes," she said. "What if they said a million dollars."

Now I am at work in Pittsburgh, in the office by myself, happy, proud of my wife but disappointed for her. Those offers don't appear often. Money and time are hard finds, even when they're covered in snow and distance. The grace Alaska offered is gone forever.

All morning, I have been on the computer and the phone, looking for part-time work. Turning down a great job offer from a generous university had made us feel rich but we are not rich. We are broke. What I'm looking for is something labor-intensive on the midnight shift. I can work with my hands and back while Lori sleeps and the kids sleep and I can sleep some other time, maybe while I teach. One guy, the manager of a metal shop, said, "Come see me tonight." I said, "Great, thanks," but I don't even know what a metal shop is.

Someone knocks on the door. I hope it's not James. I hope it's not Richard. James is, I think, still in West Virginia with Lila, pretending to have a broken skull. Richard is teaching, maybe worried about being destroyed. I am very quiet. The knocking stops. It goes away, shuffling down the hall. It doesn't come back.

I look at my watch and pack my bag.

Richard should find another job. He should play rock 'n' roll and get rich or write something and sell it to the indie kids who almost loved his music. He should never let a student beat him down with a pen again.

I hope to never tell him this.

When James comes back, I can neither drink with him nor save him from his drinking. I cannot parade him drunk in front of Kentucky Jim or encourage him to write stories or read his stories because he suddenly finds inspiration. I will love him and tell him I love him and share an office with him and never tell him that I can't think of him anymore.

There is only Lori and our children and the books we've written and the books we will write here in Pittsburgh and not Alaska.

I have been distracted and now I'm not.

My classes are perfect. I lecture and don't look at the students. I don't ask questions. I say, "Write this down. It's important," but like it really is important and not like I just want them to write. In the hallway, I avoid other faculty. On the parkway, I avoid other drivers. At home, I kiss Lori before she goes off to wait tables. For dinner, I make bacon and eggs. The kids are in bed by nine-thirty. I don't know what to wear for an interview at a metal shop, but I think jeans and a polo shirt are probably fine.

Lori rushes home early and I kiss her and say, "I have to go."

The metal shop is Parson's Metal and Recycling. It's on the outskirts of Braddock so I have to pass through downtown on Braddock Avenue. Braddock used to be a thriving steel community but now it's dismal. A horror movie, set after some sort of apocalypse, was filmed here. The director wanted realism. In the trailer, I saw the butcher shop where my parents used to buy meat, the door boarded up, the hand-written signs advertising specials still hanging behind broken glass. There are more abandoned buildings in town than there are families. The remaining businesses are mostly bars. The pawnshop is still open. UPMC just closed the hospital. Large brick houses sell for three or four grand. No one buys them. The murder rate is down because there are fewer and fewer people to kill.

As I pass through Braddock, no one is out. Even the hookers and drug dealers are inside or have gone somewhere less demolished.

Past a grocery store that looks like it was raided with machine guns, I hang a right. The area immediately gets better. The street lights return. The crushed glass has been swept from the road. The potholes are filled. A convenience store is open, people pumping their own gas, not looking afraid. Another mile and it's fine. The houses aren't abandoned. The cars in the streets aren't up on blocks.

My directions are confusing but I find Parson's Metal and Recycling fifteen minutes before my interview is supposed to start. The outside of the building is cinder block and aluminum, a few windows up high near the flat roof. It looks new, solid. A guard sits at a desk behind the double-wide front doors. I chew a piece of gum and head inside.

The guard is old, possibly retired, working this job for extras. He yawns and apologizes. His uniform is standard. I look at his belt but there's no gun, just a stick and some pepper spray. He's black with pink spots around his nose and mouth like the skin has flaked away. Most of his short hair is gray. The thick lenses of his glasses make his brown eyes look enormous and kind.

He says, "My first day back is always my most sleepy."

I say, "Long weekend?"

He says, "Not really. My long weekends are probably behind me now."

He has me sign in. I can hear metal slamming into metal in the room behind the doors. I make sure I don't look tired. If they're going to hire me for midnights when I have a day job, they have to know I can stay awake.

The guard says, "Have a seat. The man should be out to see you in a flash."

He picks up a walkie-talkie and says something. The walkie-talkie says something back. I have a seat against the wall in a plastic chair. There are many plastic chairs lined up. The line is very straight. The unemployment office feels like this. Everything is neat, orderly, desperate. The guard pulls out a magazine, *Sports Illustrated*. He flips to the middle.

He says, "There's a water fountain and a restroom if you need it."

"Thanks," I say. "I'm good."

He goes back to his magazine. Ben Rothlisberger, the quarterback for the Steelers, is on the cover. The headline says: "The Hangover." Ben has just been accused of raping a twenty-year-old girl down in Georgia. Last year, he was accused of raping a waitress in Nevada. Around the city, he is known as a terrible tipper, a self-centered jerk. Waiters and waitresses pass stories about Ben's obnoxiousness around town like a gift no one wants. Bartenders wish he would get drunk in other bars. Ben avoids signing autographs. He ducks small children. He seldom talks to the local media. I try to imagine what an old black guy working as a security guard thinks about a young rich white guy who may or may not be a rapist, who is unquestionably an asshole.

I tap my foot but silently. The floors are not carpeted, just concrete, very scuffed.

The manager walks through the door leading from the shop. I see sparks behind him. The metal sounds get louder until the door falls shut. He looks like a linebacker. He has on coveralls but the sleeves are cut off and his arms are huge. The coveralls are gray, darker in the places that are soaked with sweat. His head is shaved. His goatee is not as long as mine but it's thick. He looks happy to see me, relieved that I have shown up, which means no one wants to work here, which means I am the only one who called about the job.

He says, "Dan Charles?" and comes at me with his extra-large hand for a shake.

"Terrance Murphy?" I say, standing up to meet him.

"Look at you, all awake at this hour," he says. "And a white man to boot."

"You don't want to hire this man," the security guard says and lifts the magazine so we can see Big Ben in a devil shirt and hat, looking drunk and violent.

"No," Terrance says. "We do not hire rapists or douchebags here."

"I don't care if he's a rapist," the security guard says. "He's an asshole. My wife works at a doctor's office over in Shady-side. The girls there have a story about Big Ben. Now I don't know if this is true, but I'm going to tell it."

"You tell it," Terrance says. "It's not like I'm trying to conduct an interview."

"Interview?" the security guard says and laughs.

I laugh but not too loud. Terrance nods like it's okay. I nod back.

The security guard says, "Now one of the women works with my wife has a daughter in her twenties. Maybe twenty-one. She's out one night with some girlfriends at a bar. Being young. Being drunk, I guess. As young girls get. I'm not judging either. But her and one of her girlfriends go home with Ben to his penthouse or whatever. They're having another drink, laughing. Neither girl likes him, he looks like a ogre, but they stay. It's not every day you get to have a drink with a Super Bowl MVP."

I say, "I had a drink with Santonio Holmes once."

"Really?" Terrance says.

"No, I'm lying," I say and everyone laughs. "But I was in a bar when he was there."

Longo says, "How was he?"

I say, "Rude."

The security guard says, "Drink? It'd probably be weed if you were with Santonio Holmes. That boy is brain dead from smoking blunts." He puts down the cover and goes back to his story. He says, "These nice young girls are having a drink with Big Ben and suddenly he disappears, goes to get another bottle from the refrigerator or something. To the bathroom. Only he comes back buck-naked. All his clothes gone, ugly white balls dangling. Gray dick. That's what the girls said, too—gray dick. He sits down like nothing's up. Has himself another drink. The girls both start laughing. They can't stop. Laughing and laughing. Ben gets pissed off. He says some rude comments. Finally, he shakes his balls at the girls. He has some more rude comments to make and he disappears to wherever his clothes were and the girls make their escape. A ghost-dick motherfucker, that's what I think."

I say, "Were they scared?"

"Not in the version I heard," he says. "They thought he was ridiculous."

"He is ridiculous," Terrance says. "He's a ridiculous rapist."

"Not convicted of nothing," the security guard says.

"Still an asshole," Terrance says and laughs and puts his huge arm around me so I can feel his bicep on my shoulder, talking as he leads me back to the shop-room floor and the sounds and the sparks of whatever they're making.

Those weren't sparks. They're having a problem with the electrical system. The lights dim and flash for no reason. The electric company comes out and fixes it and the power works for a day then fizzles again. It's like a lightening storm in here.

"Fucks up my TV reception," Terrance says.

"Your TV reception?"

"Yeah, we don't have cable."

I can barely hear him. I nod.

He says, "You get used to it." Then, "That old guy out there is my great uncle."

"He seems like a good guy."

We're practically shouting at each other. The machines are small and large, grouped together by size. Some of them are presses. I don't know what the other ones do. There's a forklift in the corner. I could drive that. I know how. The sound is like a rock concert where all the instruments are hammers. The guys at the machines have earplugs and safety glasses. They're all black. I look for a white guy but there are none.

Terrance says, "What's your take on Rothlisberger?"

"I hate him," I say.

"Good answer," he says. "Vote Republican?"

"Never."

Terrance explains how to make a hubcap. We walk towards some sort of staging area. There are pallets and more forklifts. The sound lessens but not much. A machine in the corner unwinds plastic for packing like a giant roll of Glad Wrap.

Terrance says, "The only place in America that makes hubcaps is right here. Can you believe that shit? Every rim on every other car comes from fucking Taiwan or China or wherever the fuck. Made by little tiny Taiwanese fingers on those little Taiwanese children that should be in school learning about Taiwan."

"I think I have some shirts those kids made," I say. "Not good."

He says, "We make the discs. Basically, we take a big square of sheet metal and cut it down into lots of little squares of metal. Then we cut those into circles. No design or nothing. Just a disc. We load the discs on pallets. Trucks pick up the pallets and they go to another company that stamps the discs."

"Then to an auto factory?"

"Exactly."

"Ford?" I say.

My dad works for Ford and I could talk about it. But this probably isn't the kind of interview where it matters what you say.

"Naw," he says. "Fucking Kia."

"Your American-made hubcaps go to Kia in South Korea?"

"Naw," he says, touching my shoulder again, laughing again. "Kia down in fucking Georgia or South Carolina or somewhere. Those fat redneck fingers putting our American hubcaps on those little fucking Korean cars. It's a mixed up world, Dan Charles. A very fucked-up place." He takes a second and says, "But I have a job and you need a job—correct?"

"Correct," I say.

"Okay," he says. "Come on in my office. It's quiet and I need to eat my bologna sandwich before it gets hot and spoils. The heat in this place will spoil a man's meat."

The next night I'm scheduled to work at the metal shop. Teaching is fine. Lori has dinner ready when I get home. I eat pasta and hot sausage until I'm stuffed.

Lori says, "I don't work tonight so just relax." She says, "Are you sure you're going to be okay?" She says, "Maybe I can free-lance, make some money that way."

She wants to feel bad that I'm working midnights. I won't let her.

The kids are mellow. Townes watches a movie and rewinds the action parts. I fall asleep on the couch, Abby snuggled into my side.

When it's time to go to work, I am wide awake.

The security guard is still reading the same *Sports Illustrated*, his thick lenses still magnifying his brown eyes. He puts down the magazine and has me fill out some paperwork.

He says, "You can take the tax stuff home if you need to."

"I'm fine," I say.

I've marked up so many tax forms at so many bad jobs over the years. I check the boxes. I shuffle the pages underneath the stack. I do another form. I take the clipboard and sit on a blue plastic chair. The room feels better today. The building holds less bottom-end. The sounds of metal on metal from the shop floor are the sounds of things working, not the sounds of my life failing. Another signature on another line. Another page. I look for a form that tells me what I'm getting paid. I can't find the number. I think about asking but don't.

When I finish the pile, I say, "Should I go see Terrance in the back?"

"Get you a badge first," the security guard says.

"What's your name?" I say.

"Anton," he says. "It's French."

"Anton is a nice French name," I say.

He looks at my paperwork and says, "You're Daniel."

"Dan."

"Dan is not a French name," he says and smiles.

He moves from his desk to a small counter with some sort of digital camera mounted on a stand with wires running back to a computer. There are so few people here, and only one security guard, I'm surprised badges are necessary.

The guard says, "Okay, back up until your feet are on the tape lines."

I move then find a pose. I find another pose. I've always hated pictures.

He says, "You don't have to smile."

I say, "Say something funny."

He says, "You're getting very sleepy," in a hypnotist's voice.

I smile, genuine. The flash is small. I blink.

He says, "The badge'll be ready when you leave."

"Should I see Terrance now?"

He says, "You really a professor?"

"I teach at Pitt. I'm what they call a lecturer."

"What the hell are you doing here at 11:15 at night?"

"Yeah," I say. "It doesn't pay what you think."

Terrance is on a press, his huge bicep pumped from working the handle. He wears safety glasses and the noise is like an army of trash cans being held off by an army of wrenches. I stand to the side and hope he sees me. I don't look at anyone else. Terrance moves a square of metal into place. He slams the press and a circle of metal goes down the line.

It feels good to be in jeans and a t-shirt, ready to work instead of think. I remember my earplugs and reach in my pocket and stuff them in my ears. The sounds become distant. I hope I wasn't supposed to bring my own safety glasses.

The press looks easy to use but then I think of my arm going numb and look for other, easier jobs. I can't tell what's what. Two guys feed the belt. A couple other guys stack the pallets. Terrance slams another piece of metal. He turns around and raises his safety glasses in a friendly way. He hits a button and the line stops. A buzzer blasts three times and everyone moves away from their machines, happy for the break.

Terrance says, "I thought that was you back there."

"Where do you want me?" I say.

"You got it," and he points at the press. "Squares into circles."

He shows me what to do with a couple quick gestures. I take the press and pull. Terrance makes a motion, easy. It's like his big arm is a dancer. I do a square. I do another, more graceful.

"What else?" I say.

Terrance says, "If you miss a square, set it aside and come back to it later."

"Sounds good," I say.

He says, "Your quota is sixty an hour."

"Is that a lot?" I say.

"Not unless you're some kind of college professor," he says and laughs and drops one of his large arms across my shoulders. His arm feels like an Easter ham.

"Sixty pieces an hour," I say. "I think I need some safety glasses."

"Uncle Anton is slipping," he says and hands me the glasses off his face.

lose track of my number and make eighty circles my first hour. My shoulder is numb. I am more proud than I should be. Large ceiling fans fill the shop with a breeze circulating air that must be ninety degrees. Tomorrow, I'll remember a rag, a headband, something for my face.

Terrance says, "Eighty circles? No." He says, "You can't maintain that."

He takes an earplug from my ear.

I say, "I hear you."

He says, "Keep it simple, stupid," and does a hubcap, slowly, a batter warming up in the box, not swinging for the fence.

I take a swing, slower, steady.

"You're not pulling your pud," he says.

"I'm not pulling my pud," I say.

I do another.

He says, "Better."

I say, "Okay," and nod, no problem.

He says, "If you need a break, look for me, I'll be there."

"I'm fine," I say. "Thanks."

He says, "You're sweating like a motherfucker."

I look at Terrance. He's soaked and he's supervising, watching TV in his office.

"Nice and slow," I say.

"Nice and normal," he says.

He shows me how to flip the handle so I can pull with my other arm. He shows me how to flip it back and lock the bar.

He says, "Only switch it when the line is stopped." Then, "You're doing good."

No one, in all my years of teaching, has ever told me I'm doing good.

"Thanks," I say and wipe my face with my shirt.

The warning blows and the line starts. I pull another

hubcap. My left arm is strong. The line stops every hour for a five-minute break. Lunch is at 3:30 in the morning and the whole plant shuts down. I make fifty-five circles my second hour. Terrance nods. My third hour I make exactly sixty. The pace is reasonable. My arm aches at the end of each hour but I'm never tired, never sleepy. I like the sweat, the heat.

Terrance says, "Lunch is coming, hang on," and pats my back.

I don't look up from my machine. The buzzer sounds.

He says, "Reasonable," and motions with his clipboard, calm.

I am not tired but I feel the work like I've been doing it for years. Then I look at the people who have been doing it for years. One has a do-rag and a tattoo on his face. Another guy is bald on top; a gray sweatshirt three sizes too big and full of holes hangs down to his knees. Terrance should be playing professional football somewhere, smashing quarterbacks for millions of dollars. Of all the things I imagined for my life, the simplicity of a machine press, the mathematics and power, was not an image. If I thought of forty at all, being middle-aged, it wasn't as a man who builds hubcaps.

But I like to build hubcaps.

Love it.

Terrance says, "Don't think too much."

"I'm not thinking," I say.

"You're not thinking about quitting?" he says.

"Never."

"You're sure."

"I'm sure."

Soon, I am unbelievably thirsty. I haven't been thirsty in years. In my office at school, I keep diet Coke and water and sometimes Gatorade. At the next five-minute break, I find a water fountain. The line is short. I drink, take a breath, drink again. No one is behind me. Most of the guys carry sports drinks in large plastic jugs. I walk back to the line. No one says hi. No one says anything, not to me, not to each other. The distance between stations and the noise make conversation almost impossible.

If I had to talk, I'd find a new job.

The buzzer sounds and I slam down another disc.

Then it's our lunch break. Men start moving slowly, locking down their machines then walking away. Things relax. I pocket my ear plugs. Music comes on over the speakers. The music is hiphop, something I haven't listened to since I was a teenager. Everyone here is black, but they're all old, old-ish. I assumed hiphop was something you outgrew like getting laid in your parents' basement or smoking weed in a bong made from an apple. Either my ears are punched out or the speakers are quiet because all I can hear is a beat and a deep talking voice. Maybe it's just the radio. Maybe it's my imagination. If they play "Fuck the Police," I'll dance.

I look for a cafeteria. I look for a snack machine. The only doors are an exit and Terrance's office. I look for a place to buy a Coke. Everything here eats metal. Nothing gives food. Guys walk around and talk or lie down by their machines, using rags as pillows. Most head for the parking lot. I go to my car and grab my meal and some extra clothes. Some people eat outside, leaning on their rides, talking in the cool night air. Nobody drives a nice car. The parking lot is filled with junkers, one car held together with tape and twine and plastic sheeting.

A few guys stretch out on a small square of grass that lines the side of the factory. The grass is mostly brown. I go there. I drink my Gatorade. I change shirts from wet to dry. Lori packed me a turkey sandwich so I take a bite but I'm not hungry.

One guy says, "You new?"

"First night," I say.

I'm sitting. He's standing. He extends his hand for a shake. I give him my professional, business clasp and he works it through a couple more variations.

"I'm Ronald," he says.

"Dan," I say.

He looks young, maybe twenty-five. He's dressed in expensive boots, the laces untied, his jeans tucked in. He wears a jersey, the Timberwolves. I can't remember if the Timberwolves are a basketball or hockey team. Ronald is not sweating.

He says, "You on a press?"

"So far," I say.

"How's your shoulder holding up?"

"Not too bad."

He touches his own shoulder.

"Bad shit that first day," he says and laughs. "I couldn't hoop, throw a ball, nothing when I started here." He says, "You gonna get pneumonia out here, sweating in the cool air."

"It feels good," I say. "I'm not used to the heat."

"You need anything, holler," he says.

"Thanks," I say and go back to my turkey sandwich.

He walks away, the number 69 on his back.

get home before eight in the morning. Lori's asleep. Abby's asleep. Townes is on the couch, watching cartoons, eating dry cereal from a bowl.

Townes says, "You go to the gym?"

"Sort of," I say.

I don't know what Lori told Townes last night. He's old

enough to know about money so we keep things from him. My second job would destroy his nights.

I say, "You want a juice? Anything?"

"Grape, please" he says.

I get him a juice then I get his clothes. He's big into jeans and plain long sleeve t-shirts. Anything with stripes embarrasses him. Leather shoes embarrass him. I set his socks and tennis shoes by the door. In the bathroom, I piss. I wash my face. I brush the metal from my mouth. I put toothpaste on Townes' brush and spill some kids fluoride rinse into a plastic cup. In the kitchen, I drink three glasses of ice water straight down.

Townes says, "Are you going to walk me to the bus? You don't have to walk me to the bus. You're very sweaty."

"Up to you," I say.

"Maybe you can walk me tomorrow," he says.

Back in the bedroom, I gently touch Lori on the leg. She moves like I've reached down her throat for her breath.

She says, "Jesus! Oh my god, I slept in! Where's Townes? Is Abby sleeping? Shit shit shit," and she stumbles out of bed, dragging the covers behind her like a train on a dress.

I say, "Everything is fine. Townes is getting dressed. Abby doesn't have to be up for half an hour. Sit down, relax."

"Oh my god," Lori says. "I completely forgot to set the alarm." She falls back on the bed and grabs an armful of pillows and blanket. She says, "You're home. How are you? Are you okay? Was it awful? You can quit if it's awful. I'll do something. Thank you for doing that." Her eyes are closed and her face is a blur of tenderness.

If I had a wish, it would be money. My next wish would be for Lori to sleep.

I say, "Everything is fine," and it is. Today, I have papers to correct and an old lesson plan to look over. But tomorrow I will come home from work, kiss everyone, awake and asleep, shower, and drive back to work, teaching, the job I like less.

I sleep until noon and feel wide awake. My arms and chest are sore like I've worked out and I remember the feeling, when there was time for exercise, and I love it. I stand in front of the bathroom mirror and flex both biceps, a toothbrush hanging from my mouth. I brush some more and flex again. It all looks the same, middle-aged, solid in a few places, fat in others, but I feel the strength in me somewhere. Torn fibers are being repaired.

I drink some juice. I drink some water. I need a shower but I haven't figured out when to shower when I work nights and sleep days.

I dig out the papers I need to correct from my leather bag. I sit at the dining room table. My favorite pen is missing, probably with Lori at work. The papers are for my fiction class.

I read a few random lines and go back to bed.

The phone rings. It may have been ringing. I am as panicked as Lori was this morning, the phone's electronic bell going through me like a jolt. Outside the light is too bright for me to be waking up. This is why people don't work midnight, why people beg for 9-5. I don't know what time it is and I'm scared of the phone.

I run down the hall. I stumble. The fibers that had been repairing themselves have not been fully repaired. My legs ache. My feet are swollen. The phone rings again. I think terrible thoughts. I'm sure the caller is Townes' school and something tragic has happened to my son. They've been trying to reach me but I've been in a coma. I stand there. I breathe.

Before I answer the phone, I am overcome with shame.

I say, "Hello?"

James says, "What time is it there?"

He's drunk and happy. I feel neither. I look at the kitchen clock. It's almost two. I look outside to make sure it's afternoon.

I say, "You're fucking kidding me."

He says, "I'm just joking. I'm still in West Virginia."

"Where else would you be?"

"I don't know. It's a time zone joke."

"How drunk are you?"

James says, "You really cut to the chase on that one."

I say, "Sorry."

James says, "I have a story for you."

"Good," I say and I say it so I mean it because I don't. I mean the opposite. "No thanks," I want to say. Or, "I could have slept another hour."

James says, "I'm either a genius or a fool."

"Let's go with genius," I say.

I walk the kitchen. An empty juice container sits on the counter. The dishes need to be done. Our table is tiny, ancient, metal and pressed-wood, a leftover from my wife's parents. My father-in-law sat here and ate a loaf of Wonder Bread every night with dinner. Outside, on the back porch, he smoked two cigarettes. He quit drinking when he was twenty-six and paid for this house by his forty-third birthday. I pull out the toaster. I pull out the white bread. The credit I have is no good. The house I moved into, this house, my in-law's house, was paid for and now is mortgaged beyond its worth.

James says, "Lila is so great."

I say, "I know Lila's great. I've had her in class. I was with you guys."

"No, she's great," he says. "I love her."

"Good," I say. "Love is good."

"Love is good," he says.

I drop two pieces of bread into the toaster.

James wants me to teach his classes. Or not teach his classes. He's talking a lot, excitedly, not slurring but not making complete sense either. Maybe he just wants me to collect work from his students. Maybe nothing. But James is not teaching his classes. He has contacted the university to explain this. Lila has contacted all her professors and explained her illness. James doesn't say what Lila's illness is. I'm assuming James' illness is still a head injury, a concussion, possibly worse. Maybe a broken neck. Maybe he was life-flighted into West Virginia.

Lila's uncle is a doctor. He's vouching for all of this. Lila's uncle has excuses, letterhead, a phone number, an email, a secretary he's been fucking on the sly for twenty years. Lila's uncle is an old drunk. "Like ninety," James says. "But super fun."

James really loves Lila. No, he really really loves Lila, like love-love, and they are drinking in a cabin in West Virginia, and he can't come back. "It's not really a cabin," he says. Then, whispering, "It's like a house, like a little mansion." Then, even quieter, as if Lila has her head in his lap, "Lila is fucking rich. I mean super rich."

James says, "Lila. Lila? Lila, baby, I'm going outside with the phone." I hear a door open and close then, I swear, birdsong. Little tweets fill the line like static. James says to me, "I think Lila is passed out."

"At two in the afternoon?" I say.

"We've been on it," he says.

Then he says he's only drinking beer. His head is clear and his shirts are clean and unless he ends up on whiskey, which he isn't planning on, his goal is to maintain.

"Clean shirts are important," he says.

"Why not come back and teach?" I say.

I sit down and look at my fiction students' papers. The stack is thick. They are mostly terrible writers and average students and, away from the university, probably nice kids. I shuffle the stack. I look at the first line: K-Rod was dead, a fucking bullet in his head. I put the story face down in another pile.

James says, "What?"

I say, "Just come back and teach."

"Why come back and teach?" he says, almost-mean. He says, "I fucking love Lila."

"I know," I say. "I was with you guys. She's great. She's funny and she likes strip clubs and Flannery O'Connor. That's the best."

"We want to be together," he says. "We're going to be writers together."

"I'm happy," I say.

"Thanks," he says, his voice shifting to a better mood.

I know now to listen and agree. If we were in the same room, I would nod. Yes, yes, you are right, stick with beer, trust the alcoholic doctor, avoid all brown liquors, it's better for your bruised skull and newfound heart, Lila is great, be writers together, get a doctor's excuse.

James keeps talking. It's like the birdsong in the background, little tweets I don't understand. I okay it all. If he needs it, I have it, I will get it done.

I eat my toast. I eat more toast with extra butter. It helps steady my stomach, anchor my nerves. Townes will be home from school in ninety minutes. I haven't looked at my papers or my lesson or thought about what to make for dinner or cleaned the kitchen.

James says, "I'm drinking a beer called Duck's Ass. It's an ale or something. While I was sober, there was a microbrew revolution."

"It's true," I say. "There was a microbrew revolution."

I want to talk about microbrews less than I want to talk about Lila and teaching.

It's 2:15.

It's 2:30.

It's 2:45.

I wait for James to ask me something, about my kids, about Lori and Alaska, about why I'm asleep at two in the afternoon, about hubcaps and driving to work through a city that looks like a bomb exploded on the sidewalk. He could even ask about teaching and writing, things we share, things directly related to James, but he never does.

James says, "I think there's another beer called Swan Song. That's a great name for a beer. Lila says I should put that beer in a story."

"Definitely," I say. "You should."

VIII

Kentucky Jim, the head of the writing department, died yesterday. Early this morning the secretaries sent around an email and now a bunch of us stand around the copy machine, acting sad. Maybe there are ten of us. I don't know everyone. Three or four are young enough to be grad students. The rest are faculty.

The email said Jim died at Shadyside Hospital. He went in for eye surgery, something minor, and collapsed in the waiting room before they could even check his blood pressure. Attempts to revive him were futile. The email called it a catastrophic stroke.

One of the grad students says, "It's just so sudden."

I say, "Not really," then stop.

I don't say Kentucky Jim has been dying for years with his vodka and weed and buckets of fried chicken and the diabetes he ignores.

"I saw him last week," another grad student says. "It's a shock."

"What about you?" another grad student says. She's in a professional outfit, a skirt and a blazer, surely a literature person, possibly philosophy. She smiles sadly and touches my arm. "Really," she says. "What about you?"

"Well," I say, but I don't know.

I think she means I had some sort of connection to Kentucky Jim, that we were pals or drinking buddies or writers of the same stripe, but I never liked the man. I thought he was a fraud and a moderate backstabber and an artist of very little talent, save his lust for booze and fortified wine and undergraduate pussy.

Nikki Grant, a tenured writing professor, a black woman, very famous in the black community for her own writing but also for helping other black writers, someone who, at best, tolerated Jim and all his manly Southern ways, walks by and says, "So sad," and shakes her head and touches my shoulder, one hard clutch, but she doesn't stop.

"She's so right," the first grad student says.

Casual deaths are the worst in public. The rest of us stand and stare, our eyes and hands and shoulders repeating the same sad gestures. There are so many wrong things to say, so many fake and disingenuous thoughts between us, that we don't want to speak, and those of us who do speak sound idiotic.

Finally I say, "I wonder if anyone's called the newspaper?"

Everyone gestures and mumbles and nods. A few people shake their heads and move on past the copy machines and mailboxes to what's left of the department without Jim.

A middle-aged couple, Jane and Laurence, married, both scruffy, who teach part-time composition, clutch hands. They are very poor and dress in baggy clothes that are threadbare. Laurence's shoes are pulling away from their soles.

Donald Whit, a dumpy 44-year-old gay man with black-rimmed glasses, keeps pushing his bangs from his face and sighing. Donald is always sad because he hasn't had a boyfriend since grad school and now he feels too fat to even date and sometimes he says, "I hate being fat," and pinches his own gut with both hands like he could pull it away from his body and put it in a box. If there's a new sadness about him, I can't find it on the face of his old sadness. He is still overweight and needs a shave.

One lady, an Indian woman who teaches Indian Literature, dressed in traditional garb, who always hated Kentucky Jim, who thought he was a pig, who argued with all his decisions and hires and constantly implied he was a racist, is crying. Her tears appear to be genuine. I think her name is D.O. Narayan. I don't know what the D.O. stands for and I'm afraid to mispronounce Narayan. When I see her around the department, I smile and say, "Good to see you!" and hope she doesn't attack me for being a racist.

D.O. Narayan says, "You knew him best. What should we do? Is there something we should be doing now or in the next few days?"

She sounds sincere but this could be an accusation. Academics are always trying to trick other academics into statements that can be framed and used against them in an academic setting. She touches me like I need to be touched, like my emotions need to be sturdied.

Donald Whit says, "Did he say anything...before? Was there a hint? Did he realize he was so close to death? I hope I'm not being insensitive. I'm so curious. It's so sad. What did you hear? You had to hear something."

The other people look at me. I look back. They are all colors and genders and nationalities and have many different sexual orientations and some are white and men and straight and yet, somehow, maybe because I watch football and write about work and don't weep in meetings, I am the straight white male, like Kentucky Jim was a straight white male. They shuffle from foot to foot and want to know what straight white males need and do under these horrible conditions.

It takes more time than it should to understand that something is required of me, that I am expected to be a spokesperson for this community of straight white males that is so vast as to not be a community. Kentucky Jim was older than my dad. He'd written one book. He'd never held a real job or maintained a marriage or fathered any children. I'm the opposite of that. But no one in this circle knows anything beyond what they want to know.

So what this straight white male does is pick up his copies from the copy machine and act sad and put the copies in my bag like the copies are too young to deal with death.

D.O. Narayan says, "Are there customs?"

"I don't know," I say. "He grew up in Kentucky."

She says, "Are his people in Kentucky?"

"I don't know his people," I say.

"I believe he returned there often," she says.

Donald Whit says, "Death is just so sad."

Jane says, "It is sad," like she'd been feeling something else but now she knows exactly what to feel: sad.

Laurence says, "It's a mystery, really, if you think about it."

"Please," D.O. Narayan says and closes in on my space. "Anything."

"I just knew him a little," I say.

"I thought you two were pals," Laurence says.

Jane says, "He blurbed your book."

"He did not blurb my book," I say, which is true.

I politely asked Kentucky Jim to teach my book when it was first published and he said, "Are you fucking kidding me?" and made me do a shot with him at the bar. He said, "That tome of yours would get me arrested." He said, "You, sir, are a pornographer," and slapped my back and bought the next round which I somehow took to be an affirmation, but he never taught my book or mentioned my book again, not even in my yearly review.

D.O. Narayan says, "Did you know his wife?"

"Only a little," I say, meaning: which one? Kentucky Jim had three wives, none current.

Jane says, "I think he's divorced."

Laurence says, "Jane and I could collect for flowers. We could send something from the whole department."

Jane says, "Maybe five dollars a person?"

One of the grad students says, "That would be sweet," and goes off to teach without giving anyone five dollars.

A few other people shuffle off. The group of mourners starts to diminish. I pull out my wallet. I flip through the bills. I have a twenty and two tens. I hand Laurence the ten.

Laurence says, "Do you need change?"

"Just put it towards the flowers," I say.

"That's very generous," Jane says. "Laurence and I are really struggling right now."

"It's not a good time to be an academic," Laurence says.

I nod. It's like they're the same person, one with a beard, one with small breasts. Their movements are slow and deliberate, so sincere as to not be sincere or maybe extra sincere.

Donald Whit says, "I guess I should teach or something," and leaves, probably to eat a sandwich, without making a donation.

D.O. Narayan says, "I should like to give twenty dollars," and she pulls some bills from her beige canvas purse. The bills are mostly singles, a crumpled clump.

Jane says, "That's very generous."

D.O. Narayan turns to me and says, "Call if there's anything I can do. I could not always agree with a man who called himself Kentucky Jim but I know his heart was true."

"He was a good guy," I say.

D.O. Narayan says, "I fear sometimes I errored in my judgments."

"Jim was an easy guy to misunderstand," I say.

She says, "I am sometimes hard to understand myself."

She takes a wad of tissue from her purse and blows her beautiful brown nose. Her hair is like fine thread flowing to her shoulders.

Laurence says, "I should start collecting money."

Jane says, "We should make a can. People are more comfortable with cans than they are with other people," and she takes Laurence by the arm and they head off together, two poor academics in charge of money and flowers.

D.O. Narayan says, "I suppose we could stand here all day."

"That wouldn't do any good," I say.

"I suppose many students from the past will appear for the funeral."

"I guess so. I hadn't thought of it."

D.O. Narayan takes my hands, both of them, and says, "I am deeply sorry for your loss."

"But it's all our loss," I say, matching her cliché.

"Yes," she says. "All our loss."

Though, of course, it's not our loss at all.

It's something else all together.

This is a university and everyone here is a thinker and they have thought themselves into Kentucky Jim's life, a life they didn't believe in until it was gone, a life they would have exiled from the university if there would have been a vote.

D.O. Narayan and Donald Whit and the married twins, Laurence and Jane, and all the graduate students and everyone else who hated Jim have confused death with business, love with money, mourning with their careers in the academy.

But I haven't and I'm tired.

I've worked all night and I have to teach all day then work all night again, and who's going to run this program now, and did Kentucky Jim, that old dead pussy hound and alcoholic, that weed-addicted shitbrain of a writer, file the paperwork for my reappointment next year or am I standing here, all alone, completely fucking fucked?

In my office, between classes, I call Lori. She's not there so I leave a message, saying some practical things and, "Kentucky Jim died yesterday." Lori liked Kentucky Jim. Kentucky Jim liked Lori. He liked her book. He taught her book. Lori knows Jim was a small confused asshole but she will be saddened by his death or worried about what his death means.

The office is dark. The room is roasting so I turn on the air conditioning to fight the radiator. The sound of the fan blocks out the sound of the university. I know students are coming but I'm too tired to see them. They can knock and wait.

Last night at the metal shop was fine, my pieces were perfect, one square into one circle after another, but now I can barely stay awake.

I know I need to call James but I don't have his number and he's probably too drunk to care about Kentucky Jim dying anyway.

I call Lori again.

When she doesn't answer, I stack two books on the floor as pillows and I sleep.

sleep through my next class. When I wake up, I'm confused and the phone sounds like a train. I'm soaked in sweat. Getting up is difficult. When I stand, the air conditioner slaps my face and hair. My back aches from crashing on the tile floor. My arms ache from slamming a press in a metal shop. It's ten minutes until my third and final class. I pick up the phone and hope it's somebody who doesn't want anything.

Lori says, "Kentucky Jim is dead, that's so sad."

"Sort of," I say.

"It really is sad," she says. "I know he was a borderline creep, but he had good qualities too. He helped a lot of young writers."

"I guess," I say.

"He taught my book. He helped Sharon Engels."

Sharon Engels wrote a historical novel about strip-mining in Kentucky while she was still in grad school. Sharon Engels was ambitious, a recovered drug addict whose new vice was writing. Jim introduced her to one of his famous writer buddies, who she then sucked off in the bathroom at a party. The famous writer buddy fell in love with Sharon Engels who was twenty years his junior. He read her manuscript. He let her use his agent. Sharon Engels got a book deal and told the famous writer buddy to fuck off. Her book got published. Her book tanked. She came back to Pittsburgh, broke and embarrassed, and blew Kentucky Jim for a three-year lectureship. During her three-year lectureship, she did a bunch of blow and died.

I say, "Sharon Engels was pretty much an asshole."

Lori says, "But she wrote that great book about Kentucky and moonshine."

"It was about strip-mining for coal."

"Really?"

"Really," I say.

"It's still sad," Lori says.

I clear my throat. I find a napkin and wipe my face.

"How are you holding up?" she says.

"I didn't really like him. You know that. I've made that clear."

"No, with work and missing sleep and everything."

"I think I just slept through my class," I say.

"Good. They didn't deserve you."

"I wish I would have made an appearance."

"Why?"

"To avoid the hassle."

"Can you cancel your last one?" she says.

"I hadn't thought of it," I say. "But yes."

IX

I open the front door and James says, "Surprise!"

Lila says, "I hope this is okay."

"Of course it's okay," I say, repeating mantra, but it's not. I taught yesterday and didn't sleep through my classes. I worked last night making hubcaps. I'm drinking an energy drink which tastes like cough syrup and looks like slime and it's not acting like fuel.

James says, "Miss us?" He looks happy and has a nice glow.

I say, "How could I not?" and chug from my Red Bull.

Today is Saturday, Kentucky Jim's funeral. I missed the viewing. I was working and teaching and taking care of my kids. The viewing was, supposedly, packed with famous writers and hillbillies and famous hillbilly writers. One of my students, Vessa, sent me an email saying it was a good time and she got stoned behind the funeral home with a bunch of people. I looked for a write-up in the book section of the newspaper but there was nothing, not even an obituary.

I'm not dressed yet. My kids are on the couch, in their jammies. It's barely eleven, and the funeral isn't until one. Lori isn't dressed. She hasn't showered. Last night, she waited tables until three in the morning. We paid a sitter last night so we could work our second jobs. A different sitter is coming this afternoon. She isn't here. If this keeps up, my kids will be someone else's kids, the sitter's kids, whichever one is available.

The house is covered with toys, Legos and Barbies and bouncy balls and half-made puzzles. I still have to make lunch and bug the kids to pick up and everything else that comes with being a parent who is about to leave his children.

Two days ago I left a message about Kentucky Jim on a number that I hoped was Lila's cell phone. No one called back. I assumed James and Lila were drunk and dangerous, nursing their imagined illnesses in their mountain cabin.

I finish off my energy drink in a chug.

James says, "You okay? You're hammering that Red Bull."

"I'm fine," I say. "Just getting ready."

"Invite us in," he says. "We're not that drunk."

"We're just residual drunk from last night," Lila says. "Like my hair?"

"It's very shiny," I say.

James and Lila are dressed in fancy clothes. James has on a black blazer and a white shirt and a black tie and dress jeans. Lila has on a short cream dress, very shiny, sort of a gown but not a gown, too tight for a gown, but nice. The front is low-cut and her tits bubble out. She looks older, not like a student, more like a bridesmaid. Her hair is done in an up-do and held in place by a small tiara. James has a small black silk handkerchief in his breast pocket. They stink of booze and possibly sweat and maybe sex. They step inside my very messy home.

Townes doesn't look up from the videogame he's playing but still says, "Hey Cookie Crumbles," to James. Then, "Who's your lady friend?" in a hubba-hubba voice.

James introduces Lila.

Townes says, "Lila," in a sexy voice, long and drawn out.

I give Townes a look: it's not funny, it's obnoxious.

He goes back to his video game.

Lila waves. She looks embarrassed, suddenly young again, her shoulders drooping. I stop to imagine a calendar. Lila is closer in age to Townes than she is to James. By seven years.

Abby, finally paying attention, says, "Your hair is beautiful! It's a crown!"

Lila says, "Thank you, sweetie."

Abby says, "Wait one second!" and runs for her room to get something.

Lori comes up the stairs and into the living room, dressed in a towel.

"Sorry," I say. "I didn't know you were in the shower."

She stands there, dripping wet, her hair plastered to her head with hair goop.

She says, "I thought the voices were video games," and smiles.

Lila says, "I'm Lila. I just read your book. I love it."

"Thank you," Lori says and puts her hand on the knot of the towel and cinches it tight. A small trickle of blood slides down her leg where she shaved.

James says, "Hey Lori. Good to see you," and he looks embarrassed to be a happy mess, like Lori is somehow different than the rest of us, more respectable.

"Well okay," I say.

But before I tell everyone to sit, before I offer the drunks drinks and tell Townes not to speak in a hubba-hubba voice anymore and before Lori escapes to our room, Abby runs back down the hall, dressed in her own gown, a Cinderella thing from Halloween, a shiny plastic tiara lopsided on her head.

"Ta da!" Abby says, hitting a pose like a model. "What do you think?"

James says, "So you probably guessed we're getting married."

"I hadn't guessed that at all," I say.

He says, "You're kidding?"

"It's great news," I say. "I just hadn't guessed."

I'm showered but I'm in a robe. I'm standing between the kitchen and dining room, a spatula in one hand, an empty skillet in the other. I make a congratulations gesture with the utensils. I sort of bow. A wedding is no more shocking than a death at this moment, though the wedding is not particularly practical. I know my job is to talk James out of this, marrying a student half his age, but I quit that job. If I have to work here, I want to DJ or be the bartender.

James says, "It is great news, isn't it?"

"It is," I say. "It's good to be in love."

James and Lila sit at the dining room table in front of a bowl of barbecue chips and two vodkas I poured from an old bottle stored in the garage for emergencies. Lori is dressed, hiding in the bathroom, blow drying her hair. The kids are back on the couch, eating scrambled eggs, finally clothed, their hair combed out, toothbrushes waiting.

Lila says, "Do you have any tomato juice? Even a V8?"

James says, "What do you mean you hadn't guessed we were getting married? Why the hell else would I be dressed like this?" and he touches the lapel on his blazer.

"Kentucky Jim is dead," I say. "I left a message. Today is his funeral."

Lila says, "I lost that phone. I have another," and she holds up her new phone, some sort of expensive video thing with a screen and keys, and demonstrates.

James says, "Kentucky Jim is dead?"

"Stroke," I say. "Or heart attack, I forget which."

"How?" Lila says. "Where?"

"He went in for eye surgery and dropped dead," I say.

Lila says, "I told you guys he was going to get eye surgery."

James says, "I never liked the guy."

Lila says, "James," incredulous.

James bends down and picks up a foam sword. He touches the blade. He holds the handle. He says, "Kentucky Jim always made me feel like a fucking servant." He bends again and picks up a couple Lego blocks. He pieces them together and sets them in front of Lila.

Lila says, "James, be respectful."

James says, "He tried to screw you."

Lila says, "Only once."

James says, "He was always pissed at me because I didn't drink, like I couldn't write because I wasn't a drunk. Tell her, Dan."

"It's true," I say.

"We should still be respectful," Lila says.

James says, "Fuck him," and grinds his pointer finger into the palm of his other hand.

Lila says, "I don't know," and she sounds naive, innocent, like she's turning to James, her spiritual advisor, for guidance.

James says, "I do know," and sips from his vodka.

"He's dead now," I say.

The blow dryer stops and Lori comes from the bathroom. She looks stunning—black dress, white tights, white fake pearls, black heels but not too high. Her prescription sunglasses sit on her head like jewelry. She touches them to make sure they're there.

Lori says, "Are you guys talking about Kentucky Jim? It's really sad."

I say, "James and Lila are getting married."

Lori says, "That's wonderful. When?"

"We were thinking today," James says.

"I was hoping you'd give me away," Lila says. "I really loved your book."

"I would absolutely love to," Lori says, and she comes and hugs Lila—Lori the pro, Lori the natural, probably genuinely happy for these two alcoholics, twenty years apart, hammered, sitting at our table, oblivious to laws and marriage licenses and the courthouse which is most definitely closed on Saturday.

I have a phone in one hand, my other hand tapping keys on the computer. No one believes me about the courthouse and Saturday weddings and laws. James and Lila stand behind me, stunned.

"Look," I say, pointing at the screen. "You have to have a marriage license three days before the wedding."

James says, "You said a blood test."

"I thought there was a blood test, too," I say. "I just knew you couldn't walk in and get married like that. Pennsylvania is not Las Vegas."

James says, "This day is going to shit." He rubs his face with both hands, one move, straight up, like he's trying to push off his nose.

Lila says, "It will work out," and pulls herself close to James and hugs him tight.

Lori says, "It'll work out." Then, "Who needs a drink? You guys?" She heads for the kitchen before anyone can answer.

James says, "I was supposed to get my car back today too. I'm sure that asshole mechanic hasn't fixed it right or at all. It's only been since fucking forever."

Lila says, "We'll use my car."

James says, "Of course, we'll use your car." He says, "Lila drives a brand spanking new Cadillac X 360 L 9 million billion or something. What the hell is it called, Lila?"

"Something like that," Lila says and forces a smile.

If the alcohol has hit her, it's nothing like the punch James is taking.

James is on the verge. His face, radiant with love and marriage plans an hour ago, is a red blotchy mess with angry lines and shined-up eyes. The booze, the three small glasses he's consumed, has attached itself to all the other booze he hammered last night and the day before and the night before that and back to the moment he started drinking in our office for the first time in eleven years because he was broke and couldn't afford to fix his car. All the goodness in him is going under now and the pain is rising up and it makes him mean and the meanness makes him guilty and the guilt makes him destructive.

James says, "This is turning into a real shit day," and he leans down, his hands on the back of a chair like he wants to choke the wood.

"Calm down," I say. "Things will work out."

James says, "But will they?"

Lila says, "Let's all be happy. Still. Everyone here is in love."

"Exactly," I say. "And we still have Kentucky Jim's funeral. That'll be fun."

James steps towards the kitchen, maybe to fix a drink or rush Lori along, but stops to kick the wall, the baseboard, hard. The sound is low, complete but not hollow, like he hit a stud. James grimaces and stumbles but doesn't scream. He stops to collect himself, his face puffier and lit by a deeper flame. He lifts his foot and shakes it. He sets it down and tries to walk.

My kids both appear from the other room, ready for a joke or a sword fight or something. Townes looks at James. Abby goes to Lila and touches her tiara.

Townes says, "Why's James all red?"

"He bumped his foot," I say.

Abby says, "Oh Cookie Crumbles."

"Thanks," James says, trying to be sweet. "I'm fine."

"You guys go in the other room. We'll be there in a couple minutes," I say.

The kids rush off.

"Sorry," James says, directed at me I think, but maybe to my kids or even Lila.

He leans on the wall, face first, calming, like he wants to kiss the plaster, like he wants to fall into whatever holds the house together and stay there.

"Everyone okay?" Lori says, coming from the kitchen, a tray of drinks balanced perfectly on one hand. Then, seeing James, she says, "Oh, obviously not."

Outside, in the sun, calmed again, James says, "We'll follow you guys."

"Just ride with us," I say.

He says, "I want to stop for a beer or get a six-pack, something booze related."

I say, "Do you know where the funeral home is?"

"More or less," he says. "It's Wilmerding."

"We'll meet you in the parking lot," Lori says.

"Thanks for everything," Lila says.

Lila looks at Lori like Lori is Ernest Hemingway.

James and Lila climb in Lila's Cadillac. Lori and I get in

our minivan. Our minivan is more trashed than usual. Popcorn covers all the seats.

Lori says, "Where did that girl get a Cadillac? She's like a kid."

"Her parents are rich," I say.

"I wish your parents were rich," Lori says.

The funeral is at LePont Funeral Home in Wilmerding, an old mill town a dozen miles east of Pittsburgh. Kentucky Jim had no religion, therefore no church. I don't know who organized this, if it was his family from Kentucky or someone in the department or if Jim had a twenty-year-old girlfriend he kept hidden with specific instructions regarding his death and burial.

Wilmerding is a weird town, maybe two thousand people, equal parts black and white, most of them old, many poor. The houses and the YMCA sit on a hill that slopes down to the town and its one fancy restaurant and one pizza shop and one barber shop. The railroad still runs, though I don't know what the cars carry.

Westinghouse Airbrake, a huge mill that made parts for locomotives and used to employ some three thousand people, is here but empty. The eastern wing is rusting aluminum and busted glass but on the west side, near the hill, the brown bricks look solid and clean and modern, like the factory still served a purpose.

George Westinghouse had a castle built here and stayed in one of the towers occasionally. The castle is still there, run down but huge, the dirty gray stones like something from an old horror film, something from Transylvania. Most of the rooms are blocked off. A couple rooms are open and they call it a museum. A room air-conditioner hangs from a window on the top floor, sealed in by an old piece of plywood.

Lori and I pull into the parking lot of the funeral home. The parking lot is sloped asphalt, cracked but covered in tar. It's not empty but it's not close to full. I have no idea what the funeral inside will be like, who will attend, if it will be outrageous or subdued or if there will be flowers or whiskey bottles stuffed with candles.

Lori says, "Shouldn't there be more cars here?"

"There were supposed to be all kinds of writers and Kentucky people here last night."

"This looks deserted. Maybe they went home."

We sit and wait for James and Lila. They could be in a dive bar, lost. They could be smoking dope on a service road behind an abandoned factory. I close my eyes. I have been sleepy every single day since I've had children. There is nowhere I won't nap. A few minutes pass. I hear cars and car doors. I open my eyes and Lori is dozing too.

D.O. Narayan pulls up in a very small green car. She looks hunched over the steering wheel. When she climbs out, all the cloth from her sari follows behind. She's crying again, dabbing her face with a tissue. A few people, dressed in suits, not easily identifiable as academics or hillbillies, pull up and go inside.

Later, I see Nikki Grant, the African-American narrative poet who always scoffed at Kentucky Jim. When I was hired, Nikki Grant was on the committee. I'd been her student years before. She liked me but only in the way she liked white students—we were allowed to love her as a teacher and a poet but we were not to expect her to help us or defend us or guide us like she did the black students. People said, "Why'd she hire you?" meaning a white guy. I said, "I have no idea," and I didn't. But I was very happy to be hired and still am.

Lori opens her eyes and says, "Are you sleeping?"

"I was dozing."

"Are they here yet?"

"Not yet. Nikki Grant just walked in and this other woman who teaches Indian Literature. No one else from the department that I know."

Lori says, "We should go in, but I'm so tired," and she closes her eyes. Almost asleep, she says, "Nikki Grant likes you."

I say, "She probably does."

"Did she ever say why?"

"Not really."

"You're white," Lori says.

"I know."

"And a guy."

"Yes."

"And straight."

"That's three strikes," I say. "But she hired me."

Lori says, "Weird. But thank god."

Carrie Polinski shows up. She looks mean and manly, her loose slacks flowing around her thunder-thighs. Across her shoulders, a black shawl. She moves like a fullback, up the stairs and into the funeral home like it's an end zone and she's paid to score. Maybe this will end up in her new memoir. Maybe she will parallel Kentucky Jim's life and death with some local sports great then add some love advice. Maybe she'll write, "What we've learned from the life of Kentucky Jim is that writing is a sport that anyone can play as long as they get drunk enough, and I really need a boyfriend to watch Tom Cruise movies with. Help."

James is drunk somewhere. James, the Punter, the star of Carrie Polinski's memoir, has never been drunk around Carrie Polinski. Many things could happen. None good.

Lori pulls down her sunglasses to cover her closed eyes.

An old car, a yellow Cutlass from the early 70s, huge and rusted, pulls in and parks. A man in poorly-fitting suit and a short stubby tie climbs out from the driver's side. He goes around the car and gets a six pack from the backseat. His hair is short on the sides and longer in the back, not quite a mullet but close. He pulls shades from his suit-jacket pocket, puts them on his head, and cracks a can of Bud. He chugs the can, all of it, and tosses it through an open window into his car. He cracks another can and tries to chug it down but stops when the foam froths up. With the can stretched away from his body like a smoke bomb, he bends and spits away from his shoes. He's a big guy, close to three-hundred pounds. He goes back to the beer and finishes it.

"Lori, look," I say.

Lori opens her eyes and says "Is that Jim's brother?"

"Illegitimate son?"

"Cousin?"

"Oh shit, that's his weed dealer," I say and I'm not joking. I remember the guy at one of Kentucky Jim's parties, set up in a side office, rolling joints and selling them to undergrads. Jim walked in, stoned and drunk, put his hand on this man's shoulder and said, "This man right here is the only artist in the goddamn room."

Lori says, "We should go in."

"Look," I say and there's James getting out of Lila's Cadillac, a huge homemade bandage wrapped around his head, lopsided, possibly covered in fake blood.

"What are you doing?" I say.

James adjusts his bandage. Lila touches it to make sure the gauze is tucked. Lori stands there, smiling, confused. The man chugging beers is still chugging beers.

James says, "How's it look?"

"It actually looks pretty good," I say. "But why?"

"My head injury," he says. "Remember? I haven't taught in a while. I called in with a severe concussion and some other complications I found on the internet."

"But a bandage around the head?" I say.

"You're making me self-conscious," he says.

"It looks fine," Lori says.

"I did the wrapping," Lila says. "Most of it. My uncle is a doctor."

"You guys want a beer?" James says.

"Sure," I say.

Lori says, "I'll probably have a glass of wine afterwards."

James hands me a can. I hate cans. It's Budwesier. I hate Budwesier.

I say, "Bud cans, really?"

He says, "It was a bad bar. They didn't have bottles."

I hand back the Bud and start for the funeral home.

The man chugging beers stops chugging beers and says, "Did someone say Bud cans?" and laughs and raises his brew in a toast.

There are signs inside the funeral home directing viewers to different rooms. The funeral home is very old. The carpet is worn in places, coming up or slightly shredded. The drapes are lime-green. The wood work is an ugly blonde, over-polished with varnish. The water fountain by the rest-room has a rusted mouth to drink from. A small child walks from a playroom, pushing a lawnmower toy that pops balls. Other people stand around the lobby and whisper politely.

Lila says, "This place is old."

James says, "Which way?"

I look at his head, the slant of the bandage. It's like a war there, made for TV. I should limp or be on crutches. Being near James makes me feel damaged. Being near James makes me feel drunk. I should be drunk. I've been drunk for less before, many times.

Lori has found a bulletin or some paper.

She says, "Jim's funeral is at the end of the hall."

"Which way?" James says and points both ways.

Lila says, "We should have sent flowers."

We move through the different crowds, past the different rooms. I see a green casket in small auditorium. People kneel and pray and move on. There are pictures on corkboard on an easel. We pass another room and I don't look.

James says, "Funeral homes are creepy."

Lila says, "Not where I'm from."

James says, "Are West Virginia funeral homes that different?"

Lila says, "Everyone I know was laid-out at home."

James says, "Creepy," in a monster-movie voice.

Lila says, "It's actually very nice."

James says, "I love you."

Lila says, "I love you too, pook-ums."

Lori gives my hand a squeeze.

I say, "Pook-ums?"

James says, "It's love, man, love."

We stop by a sign that has Kentucky Jim's name in fancy

script. Organ music drizzles from the room like light rain. Nobody steps inside. The casket is open but too far away to see. I hope they didn't put Kentucky Jim in a suit. I hope his mustache is wild and untamed. There are seats but not many people, thirty bodies on one hundred or so folding chairs. D.O. Narayan turns and waves and I wave back. She motions we should sit with her. D.O. Narayan must be having some kind of breakdown and imagining Kentucky Jim's death as part of her own crisis. I nod that we'll be there. The music changes to something with voices. It's all pre-recorded, not live like I'd imagined when I heard the organ roll. Most people sit by themselves. The between-chairs look like tombstones, like wooden grave markers.

Lila says, "It's so empty."

"It looks like a baseball stadium in there," James says. "For a very bad team that no one gives two shits about."

Then Lila says, "Shh."

Everyone in our circle starts to whisper.

Lori says, "I thought there would be more people."

"Maybe that was last night," Lila says. "Weren't there a lot of writers or something?"

"I heard that," I say.

Lori says, "Maybe they had to be somewhere else today."

"A lot of his friends are dead," I say.

"That's fucking true," James says. "It's very sad that this whole rigamarole makes me want to have another drink. Can we bring beers in here?"

"Probably," I say, "Bud cans."

Lila says, "We cannot bring beers in here."

"Probably not," Lori says.

"Sorry about the Bud cans," James says. "I didn't mean it."

James leans in to the room, past the white wood double

doors on old tarnished hinges, and sniffs twice like he's smelling for something specific.

He says, "Weed."

"Anything's possible," I say.

"We should go in," Lori says.

"Is that Carrie Polinski?" James says. "She hated Kentucky Jim."

"Don't pay any attention to her," Lila says. "She's not worth it."

But she is worth it to James.

While Lori and I politely move towards D.O. Narayan and her elegant sari, James positions himself in the row behind Carrie Polinski. He taps her shoulder. She doesn't turn around. He taps her again. He flips the finger to her head.

Lila mouths, "James honey, don't."

James touches Carrie Polinski's head, politely angling it back to Lila.

When Carrie Polinski finally looks, James introduces her to Lila, Lila who Carrie Polinski already knows from class, Lila who is still a student, Lila who is beautiful and young and feminine and big-titted and everything Carrie Polinski is not, saying, "Carrie Polinski, I'd like you to meet my fiancé. She's beautiful and we're madly in love."

Then, before Carrie Polinski can respond, James says it again, "Madly."

D.O. Narayan stands and shakes Lori's hand.

I'm still afraid to mispronounce Narayan so I say, "This is my wife, Lori."

D.O. Narayan says, "I read about you in the paper two to

three years ago and purchased your book. It was a wonderful read. Our childhoods had so much in common."

Lori says, "Did you grow up in India?"

"In Detroit," D.O. Narayan says. "Right by the Rouge Factory that made steel for the cars, very much like where you father worked, yes?"

"For a while," Lori says. "He worked in a steel mill."

In Detroit? I think. D.O. Narayan?

I know people in Detroit. None speak like they grew up in Bombay.

D.O. Narayan says, "It's very sad about Jim."

"It is," Lori says.

"Did you know him well?"

"A little," Lori says. "He was always very kind to me."

"I did not get along with him but now I wish I did," D.O. Narayan says. "I was younger when we met, and he was a very different-type man. Now I think I will miss his honesty."

"He was very honest," Lori says and they both laugh.

D.O. Narayan says, "I see your husband around the department. He is very quiet, very kind." She smiles at me and says, "Are you holding up?"

"I am," I say. Then, maybe the first honest question I've asked, "How the hell did you end up in Detroit, Michigan?"

"We came when I was seventeen," she says. "So my father could get rich making suits."

"Did it work out?"

"No," she says. "Americans did not want his suits. He'd learned to make them from magazines that were many years old and his suits were outdated and silly. He went to work in a factory. I went to a school and didn't know a single word of English."

"That must have been very hard," Lori says.

"It was wonderful!" D.O. Narayan says. "I didn't have to talk to anybody," and she laughs and has to stop herself from laughing. She whispers, "I should have never learned the language."

Lori says, "My grandmother only spoke Polish. She refused to learn English."

D.O. Narayan says, "I know. I read your book."

D.O. Narayan seems like such a kind and complex person, more than she allows herself at the academy, more than the academy allows. The academy only wants boxes, types. At work, she is the Indian lady who teaches Indian literature and dislikes V.S. Naipaul and wears saris. Here, she is that and everything else.

I look at James, three rows up. He's making gestures over Carrie Polinski's head, devil horns and the middle finger. Lila keeps moving his hands, making him stop.

I say, "I wonder who's running this?"

"Maybe the funeral director?" D.O. Narayan says. "I smell marijuana."

"You're not the first person to say that," I say.

Lori says, "I smell whiskey."

"I like whiskey," D.O. Narayan says.

An old man in a nice suit with short cropped gray hair turns around and extends a small silver flask. His glasses are as thick as the basement windows in church.

He says, "I wiped it off with my hanky."

D.O. Narayan says, "Yes." She takes the bottle but she doesn't look like she wants to drink it. She raises it to her lips and stops and says, "To Kentucky Jim." She takes a swig like she's doing a shot. She finishes that shot and does another.

"Burns, don't it?" the man says, taking back the flask.

"Yes," D.O. Narayan says. "But in a good way."

The man chugging beers in the parking lot carries a guitar down the aisle and sits in the front row, guitar case in his lap, his fingers tapping the plastic like a drum. A brown paper bag, filled with cans of Bud, rests on the next chair over.

He turns to the rest of us and sort of waves.

He says, "I'm William, everyone. I met some of you last night."

The man with the whiskey flask says, "Hello William."

William waves then turns back to face the casket.

Lori leans into me and says, "Is he going to play that?"

"I guess so," I say. Then I lean close and whisper, "Don't let me fall asleep."

Lori says, "We'll keep each other awake."

Since I have started at the metal shop, all I think is: don't let me fall asleep. My days are dizzy and disorientated. Nights, while I work the press, I can feel my heart pounding in unusual places, like my feet and my ears. I am almost mad at Kentucky Jim for having a funeral when I need to nap and he's costing me eight-an-hour for a babysitter.

I say to Lori, "We made the right decision about Alaska, right?"

"Of course we did," she says and puts her hand on my leg.

All I've wanted to do all week is write and read. For years, after the kids were in bed and safely asleep, I've written. The writing energized me, so I read to calm and focus. From ten in the evening to two in the morning, when I should have been in bed, I managed an intellectual life, a spiritual life, something to sustain me against the university and being broke. Now I make hubcaps. I drink Gatorade and think: sixty pieces. I don't mind the work. I like the work. But I need to find a place in this for what's left of my brain, and by brain I mean soul.

Lori says, "We should have brought something to read, a verse or a poem."

D.O. Narayan says, "I have memorized many Dylan Thomas poems."

Lori says, "You may need them."

Nothing else in the funeral home appears to have anything to do with a funeral. No one holds a Bible. No candles burn. No preacher, of course. No people talking, remembering.

D.O. Narayan points to William, the man with the guitar, and says, "That man must be the featured music performer."

"Kentucky Jim liked an acoustic guitar," I say.

"Everyone does," D.O. Narayan says.

Up ahead, James and Lila are kissing. It's not making-out, but close.

Carrie Polinski makes repeated nervous gestures with her hair and necklace and watch. She turns and sees James and Lila and their affection and she immediately turns back. She adjusts her floral blouse. She itches her shoulder. Women like Carrie Polinski, twitchers and lonely souls, need men. They need boyfriends and husbands to calm them, to make them feel comfortable. But they never get boyfriends and husbands because they are always nervous, always twitching and in the wrong place. They say mean things. They forever mistake any kind gesture for love.

Lori says, "Carrie Polinski is really tweaking up there. Why would she come? She hated Jim. She told me he was a male-chauvinist. She always talks like it's 1967, like she's just discovered Gloria Steinman or some feminist."

"She does that because she's a douchebag," I say.

"Who?" D.O. Narayan says. "Carrie Polinski? I heard from my students that Carrie Polinski's memoir contained a narrative of love relating to one of her former students. I couldn't read the book, though. I do not like football. Football will always be soccer."

"Football will never be soccer," I say.

"This is Pittsburgh, true," D.O. Narayan says. "You are from here and you should always love football. Football is good for you. My football is good for me."

"I'm not much for sports," Lori says.

A man in a suit lingers near an old wooden podium. The podium is slanted, like the wood was smashed and nailed together with the wrong tools. William, the man chugging beers in the parking lot, adjusts his guitar case and moves it to another couple chairs. The chairs are old and wooden. William pulls a beer from his sack. The man in the suit moves in and says something into his ear. William nods the wrong way and cracks the can in a defiant way. The man in the suit, fat and bald, moves away, scared.

I politely crane my neck to see the casket. The casket is redwood, the inside a burgundy silk. I can't see Kentucky Jim. Nobody has viewed the body. Maybe we are supposed to view the body but don't know it. There are two wreaths of flowers. Laurence and Jane, the poor couple from the English department, picked out a tiny wreath; a sash across red roses and white carnations says, "You will be missed." The other wreath is better sized but there are too many colors and the colors, especially the peach and yellow roses, are too feminine and bright. Laurence and Jane are not here to see how their wreath has failed.

Lori says, "Is one of us supposed to speak?"

"I could speak," D.O. Narayan says. "I think I could be genuine. There are many Dylan Thomas poems to choose from." But she doesn't move.

Nikki Grant, off to the side, but still in the front row,

stands. She's in a stunning black dress and black heels, all class and money. She's in her early sixties but looks forty. She peeks inside her purse. Her purse is a half-moon of leather. She pulls out her cell phone, checks something, puts it back. She checks her purse again. She looks confused. It's fake. I've done the bit myself. She will leave the room, looking for something, find her car and drive off. I give her ten seconds. She takes three and starts down the aisle. She sees me and waves. She mouths, "Hi!" and smiles. I smile and wave back.

Lori says, "See, I told you she likes you."

The man in the suit takes to the podium. There's isn't a microphone. The room isn't big enough for a microphone. I wonder if my life, someday, will be big enough for a microphone. The man in the suit coughs and clears his throat intentionally. He does it again, into his fist.

He says, "Welcome, everyone, welcome. My name is Wilson LePont. I'm the head funeral director here at LePont Funeral home. First, I want to thank all of you for coming. I'm sure Jim would have appreciated it. I recognize many faces from last night. Second," and he pauses, "I don't really have a second. Mr. Jim left a note, instructions of things he didn't want at his funeral. He was very specific. He didn't want a preacher. He didn't want flowers but obviously we've allowed two wreaths. He didn't want prerecorded music. No pictures."

He stops and adjusts his tie. He pulls a handkerchief from his back pocket and wipes the corners of his mouth. He touches his forehead and pats the sweat, not wiping.

I feel like we are about to be dismissed. I am a student in one of my own classes and the funeral director is the professor and he, like me, has no idea what to do. Class cancelled.

"One thing Jim did want," Wilson LePont says. "One thing he did want, one thing he made perfectly clear, is that he wanted his good friend William to play guitar. And I see William has his guitar and he looks like it's all tuned up."

William nods and extends his guitar, one arm out like he's giving it away.

Wilson LePont says, "I think we're ready then." He starts to leave the podium and stops. "After the song, feel free to view the body. No formal reception is planned. And of course Jim wanted to be cremated. Thank you all for coming. You're welcome to take the flowers."

Wilson LePont walks straight out of the room like it's not even his funeral home.

William straps on his guitar. He picks up a Bud can and approaches the podium. He turns and faces us. He sips his beer. He sips it again, wetting his throat.

William says, "I'm nervous."

The man with the pint of whiskey says, "Don't be."

"Thank you."

"You're welcome."

William says, "Mr. LePont was nice enough to inform me that drinking wasn't allowed on these premises. I was nice enough to inform him that Kentucky Jim wouldn't have wanted it that way. Jim would have wanted a party."

The man with the pint applauds so I clap a little. James, up ahead, claps. No one else does. Lori politely stops my hands. There are not enough of us here for the party Jim would have wanted. Jim would have wanted a party at his farm. He would have been in charge. We would have been required to attend. Those parties, like Jim, are a book no one will ever read again.

William raises his beer and says, "This song is for Jim. I

think I can say we all loved him. I'm not good with words like Jim was. I never wrote a book. But I did spend a lot of nights at Jim's house, being happy, drinking and other things. I know this was Jim's favorite song. I'm honored to play it for him tonight."

William drinks what I think is a toast. The man with a pint raises and drinks. I wish I had a beer, not to honor Jim but for something to do, to feel less uncomfortable.

Kentucky Jim's favorite song, according to Kentucky Jim when he was alive, was "If You Want to Get Laid, You Better Get Drunk," a country novelty song from the 70s made popular by Mitchum Price then a hit for David Allan Coe.

I hope William knows differently.

And he does.

He puts down his Bud on the podium then moves it to a sturdier spot. He pulls a pick from his pocket. He strums a chord. It's a sad opening, the first thing here that sounds like a funeral. He strums it again. He starts singing.

"In the great book of John," he sings, and I know the words and the melody but I can't remember the title. He keeps going, "You're warned of the day." He's picking and strumming, something intricate, so it sounds like more than one guitar, like a band, the kind of band Jim loved and drank with all night.

Lori leans in, "Do you know this?"

I nod that I do.

"The angel of death," William sings.

When the chorus hits, I remember it's Hank Williams, Sr. from one of his gospel albums. It's a gorgeous song, something from my own childhood and religious mother.

Williams' voice, the singer at the podium and not Hank, is deep and powerful, more like Tom Waits or Blind Willie. It's not reedy like Hank, Sr. but better, not as afraid. "The Angel of Death" is about being ready to meet your lord. William sings it for Kentucky Jim who had no god. Of course, then, he was ready. All those whiskey bottles and vodka bottles and joints and undergraduate women were what Kentucky Jim believed in and he met them and now he has gone to nowhere, where he wanted to be.

I look at Lori and she's trying not to cry.

Past Lori, D.O Narayan is in tears.

As we're going out the front door and down the steps, Erica Mun rushes from the parking lot. Erica Mun is another tenured fiction writer in the department. She is on campus so seldom and publishes so little, I forget she exists. She's written two novels—one from fifteen years ago, one from ten years ago when she was coming up for tenure. I haven't read either, except for the blurbs and the back covers in the campus bookstore. The novels are supposed to be about foreign lands and the immigrant experience. Years ago, I asked Kentucky Jim if Erica Mun was worth reading and he said, "If those novels were set in New Jersey, they wouldn't have even been published. I don't see how South Korea makes a book interesting."

Kentucky Jim hated Erica Mun.

Erica Mun hated Kentucky Jim.

Erica Mun jumps up the last two steps and turns. She is probably forty-five but looks thirty or younger. She points at me. She smiles. Her teeth are perfect. She is out of breath and her keys dangle from her pointer finger.

Lori hooks my arm. I lean in to her.

James and Lila are in the bathroom.

D.O. Narayan is still viewing the body.

Erica Mun says, "You."

I say, "Yes."

She says, "You," like maybe I killed Kentucky Jim, like maybe she is about to congratulate me on the murder.

I say, "Me?"

She says, "You work in the department."

I say, "I do."

Erica Mun says, "I thought so."

She doesn't ask my name. I don't offer it. We stand there and smile. Erica Mun has on a blue skirt and a white sleeveless blouse. Her arms are thin but muscular, veins rolling down both biceps. Her neck muscles look flexed. She is five feet tall, barely, but she is two steps above me, looking down. Her hair is short but styled. She could be an office manager or on Wall Street, rushing to make a sale, nothing academic about her, no glasses or frumpy clothes.

Erica Mun says, "You aren't going to the funeral?"

I say, "We were just at the funeral."

Lori says, "It's over."

Erica Mun says, "You're fucking kidding?"

She's not smiling now. Her arms drop to her side. Her keys jangle.

"It was a quick ceremony," I say.

Erica Mun says, "I just wanted to peek in from the back."

Lori says, "You can still view the body."

"Yeah," Erica Mun says. "I don't want to go that far."

Erica moves and looks down. A piece of the patio, the top step, is crumbling. With her foot, her high heel shoe, she pushes the tiny piece of rubble away.

I say, "You missed a great version of 'Angel of Death' on acoustic guitar."

Erica Mun says, "I have no idea what that means." She says, "I just wanted to make an appearance, a quick drop-in."

More people step through the front door and down the steps. Another funeral has let out. People linger or move towards the parking lot at a sad pace.

I say, "There was a wreath from the Writing Department."

Erica Mun says, "Really?" like she can't believe it. "Interesting."

A white man in a green leisure suit, something from the 70s, tries to excuse himself past Erica. He has on some sort of boots, flat-heeled with zippers. He needs a haircut and some exercise. He needs to learn how to tie a tie. When Erica doesn't exactly move, the man politely touches her shoulder and says, "Excuse me, coming through."

Erica says, "If you have to," and scrunches up her face.

The man smiles and shrugs and keeps going, politely.

Erica steps back and shakes her head like she can't believe the guy's outfit or she can't believe she's been touched by such a sad relic or she can't believe the funeral home with its ancient stained-glass windows and cracked concrete steps is all around her and underneath her or she can't believe she drove to Wilmerding to miss the funeral of the boss she hated who taught books by Harry Crews and Larry Brown and William Styron, all writers she despises.

Erica says, "I wish I had a cigarette."

I say, "I'm sure someone here smokes."

"I quit," she says. "I'm just wishing."

I say, "Oh."

Erica says, "You look like you smoke."

I say, "I don't."

"But you look it."

"But I still don't."

"Breathe deeply," she says. "So I can hear your lungs."

"Absolutely not," I say.

Breathing deeply is something I never do for strangers I can't stand.

Erica Mun, from various accounts, is obsessed with deep breathing.

One of my students, a young female writer with a lot of talent, loved Raymond Carver. She brought in a Carver story to present in Erica's class. The students read the story. They discussed. Everyone liked the story. It had popsicles and weed throughout. Kids love anything about marijuana. Erica Mun hated the story. She said, "Are they still selling you this white-guy crap?" Another student, a guy, either trying to make a joke or not, said, "I guess I shouldn't bring in a Hemingway story next week," and Erica said, "I guess not." Erica cancelled the rest of the presentations and made the students meditate during class-time. She wanted them to breathe deeply, to focus on the exhale. She encouraged them to be open to the creative process. She encouraged them to write in their heads instead of on the page.

Breathing deeply is not a literary technique that needs to be taught at the university level. Meditation is not a craft lecture. The papers students write in their heads are much easier to correct because none of us mind-read.

Then, during the last hiring process, when they were trying to find someone to teach poetry and fiction, the head of the entire English Department, a literature guy named Sam Norwood, had to twice stop the faculty discussion of the candidates and explain the university's policy on discrimination because Erica had said, "This woman is too old. I couldn't see myself as having a colleague that old," and before that, "Do we need any more white guys?" about a novelist from the South who loved William Faulkner.

Now Erica says, "I guess I don't need to be here."

I say, "I guess not," but she knew she didn't need to be here before she left her house.

"Well," she says. "Fuck it. I'm missing my yoga class."

"Nice to see you," I say.

"Right," she says. "I'll try to remember your face," and smiles.

I think she thinks I am a secretary.

I wish I were a secretary.

Erica Mun turns and walks through the crowd of poor people. Her high heels click so her beautiful calves pop and flex as she walks across the parking lot. I expect her to drive a Porsche or Jaguar, a car so fierce it eliminates traffic, but she gets in a Volkswagen, something new and sporty, and backs out without looking in our direction again.

Lori says, "What a bitch."

As we start down the steps, James and Lila appear at our side.

James says, "Is she gone?"

I say, "Who?"

He says, "Erica Mun."

Lori says, "She's worse than I'd heard."

Lila says, "I had her for class. All we did was breathing exercises. We wrote one story and breathed for a whole semester. It was ridiculous. Sometimes she taught in yoga pants."

James says, "I hope that," and he pauses and puts both hands to his bandaged head like he's making a joke or having a nervous breakdown. "I hope that," he says, "is not the new head of the writing department," and points at Erica Mun in her Volkswagen as she disappears past the Westinghouse Castle and the airbrake factory and the train cars that slowly roll towards what was once a mountain.

X

unch is late, four AM. Kias are selling and they need more hubcaps. Outside, I unpack my sandwich and my Gatorade. The weather is perfect, cool and dry. If I make it to summer, I will be down to one job that requires one motion: pull. The rest of the hours will be filled with Lori and the kids and reading and writing. Maybe the next book I make will be worth something, like a hubcap that goes on a foreign car. Maybe my next book will get legs and walk up to people who hate poetry and stories and novels and say, "Hello," and the people will say, "Hello," back and hand my book fifteen bucks. I bite down on my pepperoni and cheese sandwich and imagine a novel set in a hubcap factory. The bread is stale. My jaw is too tired to chew. I imagine someone from the hubcap factory reading my novel.

I drink from my Gatorade and cough into a napkin.

One guy, maybe fifty years old, gray-beard, no mustache, a black Abe Lincoln, sits down on the grass with me. I know his face. I know almost all the faces now. They know my face. We call each other, "Hey," and "Dude," and "What's up."

The old guy says, "Hey."

I say, "What's up?"

He says, "You got Steelers tickets?"

"Nope."

"You need Steelers tickets?"

"I can't afford them," I say.

"Really?" he says and laughs. "I heard you were a college professor."

"I am," I say. "It doesn't pay what people think."

"I'm Luther."

"I'm Dan."

Luther says, "College teaching doesn't pay—no shit? I'm glad I went to the army."

"The army was probably an excellent choice."

I set down my sandwich on my thigh so it doesn't get wet from the dew on the grass. I open a bag of pretzels. I'm down ten pounds since I started here. I don't feel any better.

Luther says, "I have two boys, one sixteen, one eighteen."

"Get them a trade," I say.

"Plumbers?" he says.

"There will always be toilets and drains."

"What do you teach?"

"Writing," I say.

"Like résumés?"

"Like stories and poems," I say.

"That," Luther says, "is why they don't pay you enough."

"I know."

"You should have got schooled in math and science."

"That's what my dad said."

"I was a postman for twenty-five years and got out before my legs quit. I walked thirty-eight miles a week, every week."

I say, "You ever read *Post Office* by Charles Bukowski?"

Postmen all know who Bukowski is.

He says, "I read it and saw the movie."

"What movie?"

"The movie about him, with Sean Penn and everyone talking."

"The documentary," I say.

"Where he kicks his wife off the couch," he says. "That one. With the Irish singer from the rock band his reading poems."

"That was a good movie," I say.

"Bukowski was a crazy old white guy," he says. "You got a book?"

"I do," I say.

"You don't make no money off your book either?"

"You're starting to make me feel really bad, Luther," I say and chug from my Gatorade.

We both have a laugh and Luther stands. I offer him a pretzel. He takes the bag and digs out a small handful, the pretzels hooked together like a chain.

Luther says, "You ain't gonna buy my Steelers tickets?"

"Next year," I say. "I'll probably be a millionaire by then."

Luther waves and walks off, saying, "Teaching poetry and fiction, fiction and poetry," like it's some kind of crazy new song.

Before I can finish my sandwich, Terrance comes outside with our paychecks. He looks like a jailer handing out mail. No one here has direct deposit. Last week, when I didn't get paid, when there was some mix up, I heard another new guy asking where he could cash his check and the security guard directed him to a bank downtown.

Terrance comes to me and says, "There you are, still relaxing in grass. You don't mind getting all wet and sloppy?"

"I'm already soaked in sweat," I say.

He looks through his stack of envelops and says, "Charles comma, Daniel comma, professor. There you are, sir," and he hands me my first paycheck.

"Thank you, sir," I say and salute him with my sandwich.

When he's gone, I crack the seal. I unfold the paper and tear off the check without looking. Then I look. Not minimum wage, I think, and it's not. It's ten dollars an hour, no taxes taken out. I fold up the check and clean up my lunch. I take everything to the car before we head back to our presses and our hubcaps.

I'd been hoping to make twelve dollars an hour.

I would have been happy with eight.

Always, I am at a job. The weekend is great but the weeks are endless. My kids miss me. When I get home from teaching, they say, "Daddy, don't go to sleep on the couch," and I take them in my arms and say, "I won't ever go to sleep on the couch again," then I go to sleep on the couch. When they wake me up to play, I say, "Daddy's sleeping."

Lori says, "We paid some down on the Mastercard."

I don't ask what some is. I don't mention our Visa.

She says, "We paid the electric in full and this month's gas bill in full and little of last month's gas bill that we hadn't paid."

I say, "Sounds great."

I haven't fucked or wrote or read in days or maybe weeks and I feel like I will never fuck or write or read again. Quiet moments, I think of having a drink but I tumble off before I can mix anything up. Some days I see Lori and I think, "I love her." Other days, I see her and do not think anything at all. The kids are on my nerves. They talk too much and want to be fed. I ignore my students or slather them with positivity so they go away happy. Almost everyone will get an A this semester. Total fuck-ups will get Bs.

Yesterday, in the car, I fell asleep at a stop sign, waiting for it to turn green.

Lori hasn't been working as much at the restaurant but she has to go in tonight. My responsibilities include dinner and baths and bedtimes. I do these tasks fast and without much emotion. I make eggs and bacon. The kids complain about eating eggs and bacon again. I mean to do the dishes but I don't. I make the kids shower. Abby says, "But I don't like showers, Daddy." Townes says, "Can I shower alone?" I make the water too hot on accident and they both scream. Abby gets shampoo in her eyes. At bedtime, they say, "Bedtime?" and moan.

At ten o'clock, I dress for work and brush my teeth then close my eyes on the couch, waiting for Lori to wake me up so I can drive to Braddock and the metal shop.

At 10:10, James calls. I am furious at the phone. I am furious at James.

James says, "You sleeping or something?"

I say, "I'm getting ready to go to work."

"Where?"

I can't remember if I told James I was working at the metal shop and he has drunkenly blacked it out or if I have been too tired to tell him anything at all.

James says, "Work? Down here? Correcting papers?"

I say, "No. I got a job working in a metal shop."

"Why?" he says, like he's coming off a swallow.

"Money. We're broke. I feel bad Lori passed up that job in Alaska."

James says, "What the hell does someone do in a metal shop?"

I say, "I make hubcaps."

"Jesus," he says. "I'm sorry. Can I help?"

"Of course you can't help," I say. "It's my job."

James says, "I'm serious, I'd be happy to help."

"I know," I say. "Thanks."

The word *help* is nice. I like to hear it even if it's useless.

James has been teaching again since Kentucky Jim died. He has been even-keeled, avoiding Carrie Polinski and charming students. No one in the department noticed he was gone or they didn't care or both. He wore the bandage for two days then stopped.

His wedding to Lila has been postponed until the summer because Lila thinks a summer wedding will be beautiful.

His car has been repaired.

James still drinks but only in the evening and only with Lila.

I know James shouldn't be drinking and he knows he shouldn't be drinking but Lila drinks, loves to drink, loves when James is drunk, and she pays for all their drinks, so I don't say anything and James acts like he's been drinking responsibly for years, like he never went to Alcoholics Anonymous and dried out for a decade.

But I think he is happy again.

But I think I don't know anything about anyone anymore.

I say, "So what's going on?"

James says, "I really am sorry you're working another job."

I say, "Thanks."

James says, "I hate to say this, but Erica Mun is the new head of the Writing Department. I didn't want to know it at the funeral but I knew it. I had a premonition. Then one of the secretaries told me this afternoon."

I say, "Are you positive?"

He says, "The secretaries know everything."

"It's true," I say. "They do know everything."

I try to think about Erica Mun. The kitchen light is too

bright. The linoleum is peeling by the door that opens to the garage. The door to the garage is chipped all around the frame. The chain lock is busted. I would like a new kitchen. When I'm conscious, I get greedy.

James says, "So?"

I say, "Yeah, give me a minute."

I think: Erica Mun.

I think: South Korea, Volkswagen, nice calves.

I should probably read her books.

Erica Mun, I think, and it sounds as distant as Kentucky Jim who, supposedly, went home on a freight train to be buried in Kentucky, not cremated as expected.

I say, "Erica Mun. That's good, right? She's lazy. She's never around. She doesn't write anymore. She doesn't care about anyone. She won't change anything. We'll keep our jobs. It'll be better than Kentucky Jim."

James says, "It's not good. It's terrible. She's going to fire all of the straight white guys and hire anyone else who is not white."

"We're the only white guys left," I say, meaning white guys aren't the problem.

But James says, "Exactly," and I hear him open another bottle of beer.

Lori says, "Let's just be positive."

We're in the driveway. The streetlights are on. My neighbor, two houses down, sets his garbage cans near the curb. The garbage cans make two solid thuds.

I'm going to work.

Lori's coming home.

She smells like fried fish and beer. I have my lunch bag in one hand, my Gatorade in the other. Inside my lunch bag, I have Poptarts. We are out of bread and everything that goes between two slices of bread to make a sandwich. I'm late. Lori needs to take the trash out.

I say, "I want to be positive. James says be negative."

Lori says, "Let James be negative. We'll be positive."

"I have to go to work," I say. "Can you take out the trash?"

"Absolutely," she says. "How did the kids go down?"

"They were pissed I wouldn't read them a bedtime story."

"Like anyone really cares about that," Lori says.

Most of the English Department is worried about getting reappointed for the following year. All of our applications have been submitted. Our CVs have been filed. Expectations are high then low then high again. People are worried about their race and gender and their field of expertise.

"Narrative is out, language is in," a black woman, a language poet, says.

"It's a good thing my narratives are made up of language," I say.

People frown and catch themselves frowning and smile.

I see Laurence and Jane by the copiers. They are as shabby as ever. If they were in a children's book, they'd be mice.

I say, "The wreath was wonderful at Kentucky Jim's funeral."

Laurence says, "It was all we could afford."

Jane whispers, "No one would give."

Laurence says, "We're going west to Portland. This place is crazy."

Jane says, "Erica Mun, are they kidding?"

Laurence says, "Jane, not so loud."

Jane says, "I'm just done with this," and adjusts the macramé bag on her shoulder.

"Good luck in Portland," I say.

Jane says, "Portland, shit."

I have started drinking coffee with my energy drinks and sodas. Any energy is the energy I need. When I get the time, I am going to see a doctor and get some Adderall.

I see Richard in the hall.

He says, "Have you heard anything?"

I say, "Nothing. How are your classes?"

"Awful," he says and looks at his loafers which are as worn as a football that's been tossed around in the streets. He adjusts his bowtie and says, "I know I'm a goner."

"Maybe not," I say. "I'm being positive."

Richard says, "If you hear anything."

"Exactly," I say. "If you hear anything."

Nobody hears anything.

We wait for letters or phone calls or emails.

They don't come.

Lori says, "Be patient."

James says, "I'm losing patience."

Lori says, "Ignore James."

James says, "Do you know how many dipshits teach here? And we're supposed to be worried about our jobs? My student evaluations are the highest in the fucking department."

Lori says, "You're more qualified than James. You have a book and ten times as many publications. You're just as good of a teacher, too."

I say, "Don't compare me to James. He's my best friend."

Lori says, "I love him, but he doesn't write."

I say, "He sort of writes."

Lori says, "I'm just worried."

I say, "Don't worry. Be positive."

James says, "I do everything around here, and for what?"

I say, "I wouldn't say you do everything."

James says, "Fucking please," and smokes.

Lila gives me some of her Adderall.

I say, "I didn't know you were on Adderall."

She says, "I'm not."

I go to work and come home and go to work.

I sleep and go to work and come home and go to work.

Lori says, "I have a good feeling. I'm being positive again."

James says, "We're fucked."

I say, "We're not fucked until we're fucked."

I stand in Pittsburgh at bus stops and walk on train tracks and sit on benches. I read signs. I read poetry. Gerald Locklin has a line, "there's a whole heap of fuckupedness going on." It's a great line I won't think about. I drink coffee and take Adderall. Students that know me say hi. I say hi back. Bartenders that know me say hi. I say hi back. Time is the thing. Still. Anything I need, time is the answer. If I can get one more year of teaching, two, maybe three, write one more book, two, maybe three. If I can get one night of sleep in my own bed.

Lori says, "You look worried."

I am standing outside by the mailbox, pretending the letters are not bills. My teeth ache from the Adderall. My jaw feels tight.

I say, "I'm not worried. I'm thinking."

"Think good thoughts," she says. "Be patient."

I am patient. I make hubcaps and teach and drink anything with coffee and sugar. I take more Adderall. I like Adderall. My kids like me on Adderall. When I say I'm not going to nap on the couch, they believe me. I don't know how much Adderall to take—three pills a day?

I make copies I don't need at the copy machine that barely works so I can eavesdrop on anyone who might know something.

One woman, who I think teaches creative nonfiction, says, "I can't teach. I can't focus. I have to know something."

Everyone wants to know something, some hint. The secretaries don't know anything. The secretaries have been grilled by the entire department, all of us who do not have tenure, which is almost all of us. Now the secretaries have a sign on the counter in the main office that says, "Sorry, we don't know anything," in red magic marker.

Part-timers don't want to be part-time anymore. They want health care and security. They are afraid to ask for health care and security. They say, "We love teaching!"

Graduate students are graduating and miserable with their prospects. They want jobs as Visiting Lecturers. They want to stay here and teach and make thirty-thousand dollars. Thirty-thousand dollars is a lot to a graduating student who doesn't realize the student loan company is waiting. I know the student loan company. I know thirty-thousand dollars.

I am asleep in the office when James walks in.

He says, "How are you holding up?"

"Too tired to think right now," I say, climbing off the desk, un-stacking the books I'd been using as pillows. "Does Lila have any more Adderall?"

James says, "We need to get you in front of Erica Mun."

"Why?" I say.

James appears to be sober and thoughtful. He is dressed in his best jeans and a blue blazer and his shirt is unbuttoned just enough to be sexy and professional. He smells like cologne.

My clothes are wrinkled. I smell like sweat.

He says, "Are you losing weight? You look good. Come with me for a cigarette."

The door outside our office leads to another door that leads to a ledge on the fifth floor of the Cathedral. The door is supposed to be bolted but the padlock has been snipped and smokers sneak out and look at the city while they talk about quitting cigarettes.

James says, "Here's the plan."

"I'm listening," I say.

"Erica Mun knows me. I had her for class. Before she had tenure, when she was still around, I was on a committee with her. I did all her work. When I see her around campus, which is almost never, she still smiles and says hi. She'll either hire me or she won't. I'm white so that's against me, but I'll do her work, so that's for me. But I have a chance."

"I think she knows who I am," I say.

"She doesn't," James says. "I saw her in the Crow Room yesterday and she was flipping through stacks of applications, a whole pile she'd just picked up from the secretaries, so I chatted with her for a while. Then I said, 'I need to get going. I'm supposed to meet with my officemate, Dan Charles'—and I really laid on your name, and she said, 'I don't think I know Dan Charles. Is he new?' and I said, "A little, but he's great.' So there, that's it."

"So there what?" I say.

"So there what what?" James says. "She doesn't know you. She needs to."

"Maybe she'll look at my credentials," I say. "There are only two lecturers with books and I'm one of them. I have good student evaluations. I publish like crazy."

James says, "Stop." He says, "Seriously." He says, "You're

being crazy. I know you write a lot and publish a lot and that's great, I'm happy for you, really, I'm happy for you, I'm not being sarcastic, but are you fucking serious? That doesn't matter here. Erica Mun is going to go through that pile and pick the people she knows and likes and give the rest of the jobs to gay folk from Cambodia. It's a fucking fact. She will not read a single application. Not one. It will all be people she knows. And the people she gets rid of will be people she knows who don't look like her or act like her or read like her. The other people, the people she doesn't know, the people like you, dipshit, will be gone in a second, without a fucking thought. Fact fact fact."

"I know it's a fact," I say, but I don't.

But I don't know anything else either.

The sun is miserable and it's not summer yet. The city is one thing at night, but during the day the cars and smoke and noise make it unbearable. A bus locks its brakes to avoid a student on a bicycle. A young guy, shirtless, throws a full drink, 32 ounces of soda, on another kid's back and the cup explodes. The soaked kid tackles his friend. Across Fifth Avenue, one of the ticket-takers from the parking garage rushes out with a sandwich board that says the parking garage is full. A car backs out of the garage and into traffic. Horns come and go and I imagine middle fingers, as many middle fingers as hands.

I say, "I'll go see Erica Mun, I guess."

"Tomorrow," James says. "It'll be fine."

He finishes his cigarette and lets it fall from his mouth and over the ledge. The cigarette is bright for a second then gone.

He says, "You should start smoking."

"Crack," I say.

Erica Mun, Nikki Grant, and Lois Smith are reading in the Laughlin Room at eleven. It's 10:50 in the morning. I finish teaching and swing by the office. James is already at the reading, getting us seats. I find a note by my desk, "I hope you have on a tie." I don't have on a tie. James is crazy. A tie doesn't matter. I have a book. I don't need to wear it around my neck.

The reading is somehow related to recruitment—the undergraduates that the department wants to come here or stay here are supposed to be charmed and impressed by their future professors and the way they read their own work.

I trudge up the stairs and try to look happy, to look literary and smart.

The room is half-full, maybe thirty people. Seats are available. The lighting is natural, the shades of the big glass windows pulled up to show off the city. My throat is dry. I haven't taken my Adderall yet, but since I've been taking Adderall, I need to drink all the time.

Lydia Wade, a part-timer, seventy years old, retired from forty years at a gas company, a woman who teaches because she wants to, comes close to my ear and says, "Awful, isn't it?"

I whisper back, "I'm pretending it isn't."

"Keep trying," she says and laughs.

There are more faculty here than students. Donuts and bagels are spread out on a table. Three rows of chairs line the back wall. An oversized desk and a podium line the front. People mingle. They snack. They touch shoulders and nod agreeably.

I see Erica Mun. I smile but she doesn't look. She's talking to a student, a white girl, long blond hair, impeccably dressed. I think: the white girl must be gay. Gay is more academic than female. I think gay is less academic than Korean but that could change. The white girl walks to the table and gets a bagel and a packet of cream cheese. She delivers it to Erica Mun. I wait for the student to prepare the bagel but Erica Mun does it herself. They each take half.

James is on the opposite side of the room by the other exit. He has on his tie and grad school glasses. He moves his hands when he speaks. He could be gay. He could be trying to look gay. He's talking to another white woman I know isn't gay.

Two seats over, a young black guy eats a cracker with hummus. He's a student. He doesn't look gay. Next year, he will come here on a full minority scholarship and the white kids who pay tuition with loans will worship him in the classroom then talk shit behind his back.

There is Jennifer Chin, my student. She's a great writer, a great reader. She borrows books from my office every week. Her parents are from China, students who escaped the Cultural Revolution and came to America; years later, they work bad jobs cutting hair and managing a fast food restaurant and don't understand their American daughter. They dream of going home. Jen thinks her parents are crazy and her dad smells like soy sauce. Her mom has carpal tunnel syndrome from using scissors, from all the snips.

Jen wanted to read about Asian-Americans. "But not Amy Tan," she said. So I gave her books: Bei Dao, Sigrid Nunez, Wang Ping. Jen said, "Is it weird that I only want to read Asians?" I said, "It's important to see yourself in books when you're young and then you'll start seeing other people as you read more and get older." Jen said, "What's it like being a white guy?" I said, "Exactly like it appears to be," which was not an answer. She said, "Hmm."

I see Jen now, my student, this young person who loves to read and write, and she looks Asian and female, nothing else. She looks like my boss.

Everyone here looks like something, a category, a genre

to be studied or written about. Everyone is female or gay or Asian or black or transgendered or some perfect combination thereof. They are all feminists. I hate thinking like this. I have pretended for years that no one thinks like this while my colleagues ask me white-guy questions and assume I don't have bills.

James waves me over. The room is cool but I feel like I'm about to sweat. A drop forms on my forehead. I wipe it away. I get a plate and a bagel and cream cheese and a plastic knife. I pour a glass of water and drink and chew up some ice. I am cooler but no less a bigot. There's a black girl. There's a kid who might be Taiwanese. I take my bagel and move towards James.

James says, "Hey. You remember Maggie."

I say, "Hey Maggie, how are you?"

Maggie is a literature person. She teaches Twentieth Century Literature. She likes Hemingway and Fitzgerald, Zelda and Scott, Gertrude Stein and nothing else.

Maggie says, "Hey Dan, how are your classes?"

I say, "Good."

Maggie says, "Is that a bagel? When did they put out the bagels?"

James says, "It was donuts a couple minutes ago."

"It's bagels now," I say.

The first reader is Nikki Grant. She's dressed casual in jeans and a black v-neck blouse but it looks expensive. Everything about her looks expensive. White pearls around her neck and wrist. Black heels, not too high. Her hair is down, done in tiny braids, and pulled back. Outside, I know, she has a BMW parked in her own space in the faculty lot.

"Thank you for coming," she says. "All of you."

She smiles and puts on her glasses. The glasses might be bifocals. They rest on the tip of her nose and make her look older or more sophisticated.

Nikki Grant says, "I thought I would be funny today." A couple people clap and Nikki laughs and says, "I haven't even started yet."

I like Nikki Grant's poems a lot. I teach her books. They are about being black in America, especially during the late Fifties and early Sixties, and the struggles southern families faced when they moved to the industrialized north. They are narrative and lyrical and bitter when they need to be bitter, loving when they need to be loving. But none of them are funny.

Nikki says, "Maybe I won't be funny."

"No, be funny," a student says.

Nikki is playing with the audience. She does this. I've seen readings where she doesn't read, just talks, just asks people questions.

James leans into me. He nods in a direction I've already seen.

Erica Mun is in the front row. She's eating a donut. After the reading, I will eat a donut on a plate of two donuts and offer Erica one and tell her how much I enjoyed her reading.

James writes a note that says, "Say something thoughtful."

I take his pen and write, "No shit, stupid."

Maggie, next to us, finishes smearing cream cheese on her bagel.

Nikki Grant takes off her glasses and says, "I don't feel like reading. The other readers can read. This is supposed to be for incoming students so I'll answer questions."

A student says, "No poems?" and sounds disappointed.

Nikki says, "I'll give you a copy of my book."

The student, a big white girl in a hoodie sweatshirt, says, "I have it."

"This is a new one," Nikki says and holds it up. She walks over to the snack table and picks up a bagel and holds it by the book like she's on the shopping network. She says, "My new book comes with bagels and donuts. It's a limited time offer."

Everyone laughs and settles in, more relaxed than if Nikki were reading. We all look around then a student asks a question then another and it keeps going, different students and different questions.

One student says, "How do you publish a book?"

Nikki says, "Work."

Another student says, "How do you write your poems?"

Nikki says, "Work."

The students are charmed.

Nikki is charming.

She answers, "Work," and later, "More work," and, finally, "Keep working."

The students clap and bounce in their seats. Nikki Grant has drawn their maps to success. There is work and, as implied, work brings rewards. Students will work and they will get books and money and cushy teaching jobs with their own students who will be charmed by one word answers. Everyone who is here and comes here will be successful.

Unless you end up like James or me or anyone else sitting in this room who is not Lois Smith or Erica Mun or Nikki Grant.

Up front, Nikki Grant says, "Thank you, everyone. I hope this was helpful. Come to school here. Learn to write." She looks at her watch and says, "I think my time is up," and she leaves the room, politely but like a star, not sticking around to hear her colleagues read or for me to kiss her ass in case she has something even remotely to do with hiring.

James passes me a note. The note says, "Bullshit."

I crumble the note, written on a scrap of napkin, into a small ball and eat it.

Lois Smith, the other reader, another poet, isn't here yet. We wait. We fidget. A couple people get donuts. I chew all my ice. James talks to Maggie. I stand up to get more ice.

Erica Mun moves to the podium and says, "Lois is still in class. She should be here in a minute. Let's everyone stay seated."

I sit back down.

Lois walks in the room. She's holding her new book and, in her other hand, what appears to be a dog mask. It's a tiny white thing with a snout and black spots, possibly a Dalmatian.

Lois Smith did not always write poems in the voices of dogs. Years ago, she wrote about the death of her alcoholic mother in a nursing home in Kansas. She used images and insights, narrative, lots of narrative. Occasionally, there were sonnets and easy end-rhyme, but so what. I connected to the material. Good material sometimes forgives bad writing.

Later, Lois Smith focused her poems on literary characters, mostly from previous centuries. The lines were about the act of creation and how Lois related to other great writers and how they created. There were references to French writers and philosophers and German theorists. She had a poem called "Simone Weil In My Typewriter" in which she imagined Simone Weil working inside a typewriter like a factory, helping Lois make her poems. The poem was better than I make it sound but the rest of the book wasn't. Without complete concentration, I floated in and out of boredom. I respected the work, I guess, but I was unmoved.

Lois Smith's new book is called *Dog Talk*.

Dog Talk is an extended narrative written in the voice of a dog who speaks like he grew up in a ghetto just outside of Atlanta. The main character's name is Dawg. His girlfriend is Dawglicious. Dawg goes looking for Dawglicious on a night when Dawglicious is out, possibly cheating on Dawg with another puppy. Dawg wanders the ghetto—not called a ghetto but the place is terribly run down and "firez burnz in barrelz." Dawg watches a pack of mutz rob a convenience store. Dawg watches a pug shoot his pistol in the parking lot of a Walmart. Dawg thinks thoughts like, "Da world is goin to da dawgz," and, "Dawgshit, y'all, dawgshit."

You can read the whole book in an hour, so I did that four or five times.

I gave the book to Lori and said, "Read this."

I might have implied I liked the book to throw her off.

She read *Dog Talk* in the bathtub and stepped out, naked and furious and without a towel, and said, "That's the worst piece of shit I've read in my whole life."

I said, "It is, right?"

She said, "Dawgz? Are you fucking kidding me?"

I said, "Is it racist?"

Lori said, "Of course it's racist." She went for a towel and threw the book like a stone and it landed in the tub and sunk. She said, "That ruined my bath."

I said, "I know Lois isn't racist. I don't mean racist."

The last thing I wanted to do was accuse someone of being racist.

Lori said, "It is racist. She's using the language of poor black people and putting it in the voices of dogs which she calls dawgz."

"But it's not racist," I said. I was struggling for language to describe something so bad. I said, "It's just stupid, I think, and we're not used to reading things that stupid."

Lori said, "But it's trying to be smart."

I said, "She wrote a long poem in the voice of a dog in hip-hop language."

Lori went into the kitchen and banged some food around. She went to the big freezer in the garage. She said, "Where's the ice cream?"

I said, "Do you think Lois even knows there's a rapper named Snoop Dogg?"

Lori, in a towel, holding a spoon, eating from a pint of chocolate ice cream, said, in a mock voice, "Lois Smith is in the motherfucking house."

I said, "I don't know anything about books anymore."

"No one does," Lori said. "That's the problem."

"How do you review a book like that?" I said.

"You kill it," Lori said. "But this chocolate peanut butter ice cream is delicious. It's the cheap stuff but it tastes better that the expensive stuff."

If a student brought a poem to class and it was in the voice of a dog, a hiphop dog, and that dog talked in clichés, I would write a short note at the end of the poem that says, "Some great stuff in here. Try writing about people."

People—characters, whatever you want to call them—should still matter in literature.

They don't.

Now we have dawgz.

One of the dawgz in Lois Smith's *Dog Talk* says, "I spitz

shit, it don't mean shit, you gotz to figure my shit out."

If I were to read the poem as a metaphor or even a nar-rative with a hint of depth, which Lois obviously wants the reader to do, and if the poem weren't so fucking stupid, I could look at that line and know that Lois is defining language for herself and maybe for writers everywhere. It's the same line she wrote twenty years ago in a poem about Derrida, when she said, "Language is the mask we all wear / the mask doesn't mat-ter / only who wears the mask."

Language is now used to build a body of language that is meant to represent language and language's lack of precision. The struggle is there is no struggle. The war with words is un-winnable. But Lois Smith keeps writing about language and its lack of meaning, only now in the voices of dogs. It's like writing poems about the futility of war and giving the reader a gun and saying, "Blow your brains out," on the last page and meaning it.

Lori said, "This has to ruin Lois Smith's career."

"Hopefully," I said.

Lori wanted to check the reviews so we went to the com-puter in the basement. My bookshelves were down there, all my books of poetry, hundreds. Lori got online. A newspaper in Dallas called the book, "Difficult but brilliant." A couple others said basically the same. Lori went to a local paper. She skimmed the review and got mad. She skimmed it again then read it completely with a spoon in her mouth.

I said, "Don't tell me."

She said, "I have to."

I said, "Don't."

"Scarily sober and wickedly funny."

"No."

"Yes."

"I don't believe you."

Lori said, "I won't quote anything else but she's comparing it to Kafka and—wait for it—Samuel fucking Beckett."

I said, "There's an epigraph from Beckett."

Lori said, "Of course there is an epigraph from Beckett. Lois wants people to think she's smart so she uses a smart epigraph. That doesn't change the fact that she's writing in the voice of a hiphop dawg named Dawg and his girlfriend Dawglicious."

I said, "I had a student write a story in the voice of Mario."

Lori said, "But that's a kid. That's video games."

"Let's not talk about it anymore," I said.

"Never again," Lori said.

"I'm serious," I said. "That's it."

But now Lois Smith is on stage, introducing her new poems. I assumed she would read from her new book. The new book holds many fine poems and many poems I don't like but would go over great with a bunch of students who want to study with Lois Smith.

Lois Smith is not going to read those poems.

Lois is going to read from the middle section, the poems in the voice of a dawg.

"For dramatic effect," Lois says and she puts on the dog mask and starts to read many many words that end in the letter Z.

Erica Mun doesn't feel like reading.

She pulls a Nikki Grant and says, "Why don't we just talk?"

But she is less charming than Nikki Grant so the questions don't come. Students fidget. Faculty sit like furniture. Lois

Smith is in the front row, drinking water, her dog mask in her lap. James is so shocked by the dawg poems, he hasn't handed me a note or gestured or anything. I am afraid to look around and find out that everyone loved Lois Smith reading her dawg poems. I stare at Erica Mun then past Erica and out the window then back.

So much of Pittsburgh, a city I love, has been reflected through the university which I want to love but can't because I am under its foot or, more honestly, I hate the university and its stupidity but want to stay in Pittsburgh and I need the work and doing this kind of work, begging, makes it hard to love anything.

Erica Mun says, "If we're all talked out, that's even better."

Erica Mun looks like she has another yoga class. She looks like so many bosses I've had, smiling but unconcerned. She touches her necklace and adjusts the gold chain. She hasn't published a novel in ten years. She may never publish a novel again. Teacher—being a professor—has somehow become more than writer. Tenure has replaced publication. Power and security have replaced art.

I know now my career here is over.

I should have known it years ago.

But I am middle-aged, and this is all I know how to do.

Erica Mun says, "Let's wrap it up then. All of us, I think, are pretty busy today," and before I can stand and pour another glass of water, she snags a bagel and a plastic knife and a packet of cream cheese then she is past me and through the door.

James says, "Your teaching career is not over."

I say, "It is over."

He says, "Because Lois read that awful fucking dog poem? No."

We're in our office. It is as dirty and yellow and gray as ever. The walls are still empty. The computer is still slow as an old train.

James says, "How is your teaching career over?"

"It just is," I say.

"It's not."

"You're fine," I say. "I saw Erica Mun smile at you."

James says, "Fuck," and opens a bag of pretzels that have been in the office for at least two years, maybe more. He bites a pretzel and says, "Sawdust." He says, "You're done? That's it? You're not even going to talk to Erica Mun?"

I shake my head: I'm not.

Because I know.

Just like I know James will leave here and love Lila and, in a few months, marry her. Lila's money, along with James' teaching, will make them feel rich. James will start to write again or he won't or he will write then stop writing then start again. He will keep drinking or he will slow down or he will stop. He will publish his first novel or he won't or it will be stories or a novel-in-stories or a novella or nothing. He will wear blazers and teach classes and do great or not do great on purpose. Lila will follow James and stay with him as long as he stays James and he will because James is many wonderful things, sometimes separately, sometimes all at once.

James says, "You can still get to Erica Mun."

"Nope," I say. "I can't."

I stand up and push my chair as far under the desk as it will go. I grab a jacket off the coat rack in the corner and ball it up into a pillow. I get on the floor and, with the jacket under my head, I close my eyes.

James says, "You're going to sleep?"

"I am going to sleep," I say.

"Don't," he says. "I need you."

"I know you do," I say.

Before we get to the letter that says my contract will not be renewed, before we get to my termination, which I know is inevitable, which I know as clear and true as the language so many people around the department want to deny holds any concrete meaning, I see Lois Smith in the stairwell by my office as I'm leaving for home.

Lois Smith would never help me.

Lois Smith, if she were to help someone, would help someone who writes and teaches and looks like Lois Smith.

But I say to Lois Smith, who I know is from Topeka, Kansas, who I know tells people she's from New York, who I once saw, years ago, weep outside a bookstore after a reading where no one showed up, I say, "Lois, I really loved your book," and I am sincere.

I am sincere about loving Lois' book, even though I hate Lois' book. It's easy the way words mean one thing and nothing at all and something else completely.

"Thank you," Lois says and stops on the stairs. She is a good-looking woman approaching retirement. Her hair is dyed brown with auburn streaks. She takes off her glasses and looks at me and says, "That really means a lot."

Lois doesn't know I'm speaking like she writes, that everything I say means something else or nothing at all, and maybe

I don't even know it or I do or I don't care or I do care or all of it at once. I think, in this moment, I like Lois Smith's book, how awful it is, or I like Lois Smith and I want her to know I feel bad for her, that all those years in Topeka, Kansas are gone and New York never existed and Pittsburgh where she teaches is not here.

Lois, I want to say, it's no good to write about dawgs and I forgive you and I know you don't want forgiven at all.

I want to be your friend, Lois Smith, so you can explain all those things you find unexplainable in words we both understand like thank you and love.

"Good luck with everything," I say.

"You, too," she says and blows me a kiss off her wrinkly hand.

XI

Today I see a Kia on the parkway, heading east into Pittsburgh. I'm with Lori and the kids. It's summer. Lori is working one job. The kids are out of school.

Fourteen miles west, where we started, our house is up for sale in the neighborhood we never wanted to live in, the neighborhood where we would never have the right kitchen cabinets or dining room chairs. My poetry books are all packed, even if we don't have anywhere to live. The dishes are wrapped in old newspapers and stuffed inside cardboard boxes.

Lori says, "Go to the North Side."

The North Side is lovely, brownstones with flowers hanging from every window. We have a newspaper with us, the pages opened to houses for sale and rent, and the kids don't care, they love the city and the bridges and the huge Cathedral where I used to teach but don't anymore. They love the water and how the rivers keep the neighborhoods separate and special.

"See that car," I say to the kids and point to the Kia, just up ahead, disappearing into the tunnel. "I made the hupcabs on the wheels to that car."

"Really?" Abby says. "That's great!"

"Pretty cool, Dad," Townes says without looking up. "Pretty cool."

Lori leans into me and kisses my face and says, "Let's write big beautiful novels."

"About Pittsburgh," I say. "And poems, too."

I change lanes and we get closer to the Kia.

"Are those the hubcaps, Daddy?" Abby says. "You made those?"

"I made those," I say. "Those are my hubcaps."

Acknowledgements

Thanks to Gerry Locklin, Alex Thiltges, Eric Miles William-
son, and, of course, Al Watt.

Made in the USA
Middletown, DE
04 August 2020

14398478R00189